Top 500 Gold & Silver Mining Stocks:
Metalproofing Your Portfolio from the Coming Inflation Shock

FRED MARION

PUBLISHED BY OCEANIC MEDIA, LLC
P.O. Box 750562
Dayton, Ohio 45475

Copyright © 2012 Fred Marion

ISBN:
ISBN-13: 978-1469976877
ISBN-10: 1469976870

CONTENTS

ACKNOWLEDGMENTS

This book would not have been possible without the support of my remarkable wife, book-publishing research by my friend William Sullivan, photography by Weebrian (online at www. sxc.hu/profile/weebrian), and that immortal phrase from Nike, which forever echoes in the back of my mind: "Just Do It."

CHAPTER 1
HOW TO USE THIS BOOK

I've spent the past six months immersed in thousands of NI 43-101 Technical Reports, press releases and corporate fact sheets. I had two goals: one was to uncover junior gold and silver mining companies that have metals in the ground, or – at the very least – promising pockets of land near productive mines or on the grounds of historic mines.

My second goal was to get background information and "hard numbers" on each of the 500 largest gold and silver mining stocks on the exchanges as ranked by market capitalization. After all, a gold or silver mining company is only as good as the amount of metal it controls. I present my findings in Chapter 3 with a detailed paragraph on each of the companies. Keep an eye out for my Top 100 favorites scattered throughout the list (highlighted by the "editor's pick" notation).

Chapters 4 and beyond of the book are where things get really interesting. It's chock full of tables that point to last year's biggest winners, companies sitting on top of large gold deposits, gold and silver stocks by market cap, volume leaders, dividend payers and more.

This book was written primarily with an American audience in mind. All the companies featured have shares that trade on exchanges available to American investors without having to deal with the tax complexities that come with investing in foreign securities. The vast majority of companies also have shares available on Canadian exchanges as well.

Before you dive in, though, I will give you this advice: do your own due diligence before investing in any company – particularly in the shares of so-called penny stocks (companies trading at $5 per share or less). Knowing why you're investing in a particular company will help you weather the sometimes stomach-churning gyrations in the precious metals market.

FOUND A MISTAKE?

We've made every effort possible to ensure that the data in this book is accurate. However, errors could have crept into the pages that follow. To address those, we've created an erratum online where we'll list corrections found in this book after publication. You can find our erratum page here: http://www.tradingstocks.me/erratum.

Of course, if you notice any errors or omissions on these pages, we'd love to hear from you. Please contact us at info@tradingstocks.me. Beyond that, we hope that the black and white comparisons between junior mining companies in this book will help you separate the wheat from the chaff.

CHAPTER 2
INTRODUCTION

2011 was not a banner year for gold and silver stocks. Of the 500 stocks analyzed in this book, only 81 managed to eke out positive gains for the year. Even over the past five years, the majority of gold and silver stocks have underperformed (with just 156 staying in the green).

Rather than taking that as a sign to get out of the gold and silver markets, I prefer to look at it as a remarkable buying opportunity. You'd be rich if you would have shorted real estate and financial stocks in 2007. Gold and silver stocks appear to be at a similar tipping point (this time, though, it's on the buy side).

My guess is, that in a few years from now, our peers will be looking back and saying "I should have bought gold and silver stocks in 2012."

To think that a well-run gold or silver mining company with actual metal in the ground should be worth less than it was five years ago (in 2007) defies logic. Not only have we faced inflation nearing double-digits over the past five years (per ShadowStats.org), the price of gold has risen 156% and the price of silver has risen 130%.

Companies with gold and silver resources should reflect gains in the price of gold and silver. They should reflect a dollar with less purchasing power than it had five years ago, and they should reflect the new gold and silver discoveries junior mining companies have made in the past five years. Instead, gold and silver stock prices have fallen precipitously while investors focus on debt in Europe, a dysfunctional Congress in Washington, and a dollar that's propped up by virtue of the fact that there's nothing else to take its place.

My contention in this book, though, is that sentiment will eventually shift back to gold and silver stocks. When it does, it will happen quickly, and I believe that 2012 just might be the year that shift occurs.

WHAT'S BEAT DOWN GOLD AND SILVER MINING STOCKS?

Several factors have colluded to drive down the price of gold and silver mining stocks over the past five years. Here's my list of the Top 5:

1) The emergence of gold and silver ETFs that allow investors to profit off the metals themselves.

2) Investors who are unwilling or unable to accept that higher gold and silver prices are here to stay.

3) Extreme volatility in the gold and silver mining sector.

4) High levels of risk when investing in specific gold and silver mining stocks.

5) The relative strength of the dollar (as Europe's debt woes overshadow America's).

Investor sentiment affects all of the factors above. That means they could easily reverse themselves. ETFs, however, pose a bigger hurdle to a strong rally in individual gold and silver mining stocks. But I don't think they have the ability to depress the entire sector. Here's why:

• There are ETFs specifically aimed at junior mining stocks (including the Market Vectors Junior Gold Miners ETF), which funnel cash into specific gold and silver stocks.

• Some gold and silver mining stocks pay dividends and more will likely do so soon. That's something that the SPDR Gold Trust ETF just can't do.

• Returns on winning gold and silver mining stocks will dwarf the performance of even leveraged ETFs.

WHY IS 2012 DIFFERENT?

Assuming that the European Union finds a way to stamp down debt fears across the pond, investors should start seeing the dollar for what it is: a poor store of value. Throw your capital into a money market account, and you'll be lucky to earn 1% in interest. Even then, you'll be losing purchasing power as the official inflation rate stands at 3.39% (ShadowStats.org calculates the inflation rate at an eye-popping 7% at the time of this writing).

Gold and silver mining stocks give investors an opportunity not only to protect their purchasing power, but to hopefully profit in the process. As the price of gold and silver rise, the value of a junior mining company grows at a compound rate. Why's that?

Here's an example: Let's say a gold mining company has claims on 1 million ounces of gold in the ground. If the price of gold goes up 10 percent from $1,000 to $1,100, that gold mining company is instantly worth $100,000,000 more ($100 x 1,000,000 ounces)! On top of that, a company's cash costs to extract gold typically go DOWN over time (with much of the cost of mining required up front).

It's a bold prediction, but I believe 2012 could be the year that Americans and investors abroad begin to lose faith in paper currencies. The United States government's debt obligations leave the country few options outside of printing money. And printing money ultimately leads to inflation. Sooner or later, we'll see that inflation and we'll be forced to seek out alternative ways to protect our capital. That's where gold and silver mining stocks come into play.

HOW TO IDENTIFY A WINNING MINING COMPANY

It's impossible for any one investor to always pick winning junior mining stocks. There are just too many risk factors involved. There are, however, factors that winning mining companies have to have in order to succeed. Focus on these factors, and you'll probably outperform your peers:

1) *Winning management.* Look for companies with board members who have spent decades learning the ropes at a Newmont or Agnico-Eagle. If a small exploratory miner can entice a high-level exec away from a cushy job with a major, there's a reason why.

2) *Gold and silver in the ground.* Don't bet the farm on a company that "expects" to find high-quality gold and silver deposits. Put your cash in companies that have already PROVEN that they have quality property (either through positive soil samples or extensive drilling).

3) *A steady stream of press releases.* If a junior mining company is ever going to make it into production, it needs to plow ahead constantly – not be pre-occupied trying to raise cash. Look for companies that have money on hand and are using it to do active drilling (with positive results).

4) *Avoid stocks with extremely low volumes.* Investing in junior mining companies means you're going to be investing in thinly-traded stocks. That DOESN'T mean you should buy stock in a company whose shares haven't changed hands in weeks. Try to stick with stocks that trade at least a few thousand shares a day. That means there's interest in that company, and that you'll one day be able to sell your shares (rather than putting a sell order out that never gets filled since there aren't any buyers).

5) *Charts matter.* Beginning investors like to buy stocks that are going down out of the hopes of getting in "at the bottom." In fact, a stock that's going down is a stock no one wants at the moment. It's better to buy into strength. To paraphrase Warren Buffett: I'd rather get shares in a great company at a fair price than shares in a fair company at a great price.

CHAPTER 3
AN ALPHABETICAL GUIDE TO THE TOP 500 LARGEST
GOLD AND SILVER MINING STOCKS

Adventure Gold Inc. (PINK:AGONF) Adventure Gold Inc. holds rights to more than two dozen potential gold properties in the Abitibi Greenstone Belt located in north-western Quebec and north-eastern Ontario. The company plans to spend $14 million on exploration over the next five years. Most recently, Phase 2 drilling has begun on the Lapaska Property in Quebec. Highlights from previous drilling there showed 1.0 g/t gold over 103.4m including 10.3 g/t gold over 3.8m. http://www.adventure-gold.com/

African Gold Group Inc. (PINK:AGGFF) African Gold Group, Inc., holds rights to five projects: three in Ghana and two in Mali. The Company's most advanced asset is its Kobada gold project in Mali. The Kobada Trend contains an inferred mineral resource of 740,000 ounces of gold at a 0.3 g/t gold cutoff, and the company believes that Kobada could be a multi-million ounce deposit. African Gold's Ghana property also includes land abutting Keegan Resources' holdings. http://www.africangoldgroup.ca/

African Metals Corp. (PINK:AFMCF) A Canadian company currently exploring for copper and gold in the Democratic Republic of the Congo, African Metals has a 57 percent interest in the Luisha South Project in the Katanga Province. Grades returned from small scale mining at the site have been as high as 30 percent copper and 20 percent cobalt from selectively mined zones. http://www.africanmetals.com/

Africo Resources Ltd. (PINK:AFCRF) Africo Resources Ltd. has two projects, both of which are located in Africa: the Kalukundi Project in the

DRC and the Mporokoso Basin project, Zambia. The Kalukundi Project is expected to yield initial annual production of 16,400 tonnes copper and 3,800 tonnes cobalt. All told, the project could yield 164,296 tonnes copper and 38,485 tonnes of cobalt. The company is currently exploring for gold, nickel and copper at its Zambian project. http://www.africoresources.com/

EDITOR'S PICK: *Agnico-Eagle Mines Ltd. (NYSE:AEM)* Why we like it: 1.69% dividend; More than 21 million ounces of gold reserves. By market cap, Agnico is Canada's fifth-largest gold producer. In Q3 2011 alone, the company increased its production by 11 percent to 265,978 ounces of gold. According to their most recent numbers, they've got total proven and probable gold reserves nearing 21.3 million ounces. http://www.agnico-eagle.com/

AKA Ventures Inc. (PINK:AKAVF) AKA Ventures Inc. is currently focused on two projects: the Long Valley Gold project in Nevada and the Copper Joe project in Arizona. Grab samples at the Long Valley Gold project recently returned over 6 g/t of gold from the clay alteration in the northern portion of the property. Exploration at the Copper Joe property is in its early stages. http://www.akaventures.net/

EDITOR'S PICK: *Alacer Gold Corp. (PINK:ALIAF)* Why we like it: Looking to produce 800,000 ounces of gold a year by 2015; Shares up 31% in 2011. With gold reserves totaling 5.5 million ounces, Alacer Gold is forecasting gold production of 600,000 ounces in CY2013 and 800,000 ounces in CY2015. All told, the company holds interests in four operating gold mines in Australia and Turkey. http://www.avocaresources.com.au/

Alder Resources Ltd. (PINK:ARLSF) Alder Resources Ltd. is exploring the historic Mining Triangle in Northeast Nicaragua. Recent drilling at the company's 65-percent owned Santa Rita site returned trench intercepts of 1.06 g/t gold, 0.96% copper and 9.33 g/t silver over 12m and 3.26% copper, 55.82 g/t silver and 0.15 g/t gold over 8.30m. http://www.alderltd.ca/

Aldridge Minerals Inc. (PINK:AGMIF) Aldridge's flagship Yenipazar polymetallic VMS deposit in Turkey is advancing toward feasibility. Drill results announced in October 2011 graded as high as 7 g/t gold over 50m. All told, Yenipazar contains a resource base of 24 million tonnes containing gold, silver, zinc, lead and other metals. http://www.aldridge.com.tr/

Aldrin Resources Corp. (PINK:AOUFF) Drilling is underway at Aldrin Resource Corp.'s three Yukon projects. Each shows promising potential gold deposits. The original soil survey outlined at the Keystone property shows anomalous gold (2.6 g/t), arsenic (up to 10,000 ppm) and antimony (up to 2,000 ppm) in a trend that measures 3.2 kilometers long by 1,500m wide. http://www.aldrinresourcecorp.com/

Alexandria Minerals Corp. *(PINK:ALXDF)* Alexandria Minerals Corporation has a wide range of mineral claims throughout Canada. Worldwide, the company has measured and indicated gold resources of 446,891 ounces and 452,869 inferred ounces. That was intriguing enough to land partnerships with Agnico-Eagle (which holds 10 percent of the company) as well as Teck and IAMGOLD (which both hold 7 percent). http://www.azx.ca/

EDITOR'S PICK: *Alexco Resource Corp.* *(AMEX:AXU)* Why we like it: 1,000 g/t silver at Bellekeno in the Yukon. Alexco operates Canada's only primary silver mine at Bellekeno in the Yukon Territories, and the quality of the deposit there is world class with more than 1,000 g/t of silver. The company hopes to uncover more than 100 million ounces of silver in the Keno Hill Silver District, which includes Bellekeno. http://www.alexcoresource.com/

Alhambra Resources Ltd. *(PINK:AHBRF)* Alhambra Resources Ltd.'s primary asset is the 2.4 million acre Uzboy Project in north central Kazakhstan. Commercial operations at the 100 percent owned Uzboy heap leach mine kicked off on May 1, 2006. Exploration of more than 100 other targets within the project is ongoing. As of Dec. 15, 2009, the Uzboy gold deposit had a measured and indicated gold resource of 975,500 ounces and 421,700 ounces (inferred). http://www.alhambraresources.com/

EDITOR'S PICK: *Allied Nevada Gold Corp.* *(AMEX:ANV)* Why we like it: $190 cash cost per ounce of gold; Shares up 15% in 2011. The company's wholly-owned Hycroft gold mine was brought back online in 2009, and Allied Nevada expects production will double by 2013 to 300,000 ounces. Hycroft also has 400 million ounces of proven and probable silver, and that should help reduce cash costs per ounce of gold to $190 by 2015. All told, Allied Nevada has more than 100 exploration properties in Nevada. http://www.alliednevada.com/

Almaden Minerals Ltd. *(AMEX:AAU)* An explorer that drills underexplored projects then sells them for part of the future profits, Almaden recently did just that with its Caballo Blanco project in Mexico. Almaden sold their 30 percent stake in the site in exchange for 7 million shares in Goldgroup Mining Inc. (PINK:GGAZF). On Dec. 15, 2011, the company announced they'd intersected 28.96m of 2.44g/t gold and 103.1g/t silver at their Tuligtic project in Mexico. http://www.almadenminerals.com/

EDITOR'S PICK: *Alphamin Resources Corp. (PINK:AFMJF)* Why we like it: Good chart pattern with shares up 100%+ in 2011. Formerly La Plata Gold Corporation, Alphamin Resources Corp. holds rights to two gold properties in Argentina: the Sierra de las Minas project and the Neuquen Sedex Project. The company's prime asset, though, is its Violin 2 project in Guerrero, Mexico. Grab samples at one of the sites showed surface mineralization that assayed up to 2.8% copper, 54.8 g/t silver and 0.31 g/t gold. http://www.alphaminresources.com/

Altai Resources Inc. (PINK:ARSEF) Altai Resources Inc. holds a 50% joint venture interest in the Malartic gold property in Quebec. According to the company, the mine shows an historical (non 43-101 compliant) probable resource of 466,342 tonnes grading 7.11 g/t gold (513,909 tons grading 0.21 oz/ton gold). The company also holds interests in shale and natural gas resources in Canada. http://www.altairesources.com/

Alto Ventures Ltd. (PINK:ALVLD) Alto Ventures is actively exploring three projects in Quebec and Ontario. The Destiny project in Quebec has an NI 43-101 compliant indicated resource of approximately 10.8 million tonnes averaging 1.05 g/t gold (364,000 ounces) plus an inferred resource of approximately 8.3 million tonnes averaging 0.92 g/t gold (247,000 ounces). http://www.altoventures.com/

Amarillo Gold Corp. (PINK:AGCBF) Focused on developing gold resources in Brazil, Amarillo Gold Corp.'s prime asset is the Mara Rosa Gold Project. The 100-percent-owned project holds 1,174,900 ounces gold at 1.75 g/t (measured and indicated) and 156,400 ounces inferred gold at 1.34 g/t. A pre-feasibility study is nearing completion. http://www.amarillogold.com/

American Bonanza Gold Corp. (PINK:ABGFF) American Bonanza appears to be on the cusp of becoming a producer. The company announced that it had purchased mining equipment for its Copperstone gold mine in Arizona in October 2011. "The Copperstone property contains a 10.3 g/t oxide gold resource with 313,000 ounces of gold in the measured and indicated categories and 256,000 ounces of gold in the proven and probable mineral reserves category," according to the company. http://www.americanbonanza.com/

American Consolidated Minerals (PINK:AMERF) American Consolidated Minerals Corp. is exploring for gold and other metals in the Western United

States. The company's Toiyabe project in Nevada has an indicated mineral resource at a 0.01 oz/t gold cutoff of 173,562 contained ounces of gold. This equates to 4,975,000 tons at an average grade of 0.0349 oz/t. Samples at the company's Empress project in Nevada have graded as high as 1.848 oz/t over 2 feet. http://www.americanconsolidatedminerals.com/

Amerilithium Corp. (OTC:AMEL) Formerly Kodiak International Inc., AmeriLithium Corp. was established on March 9, 2010. The name change was part of an 8:1 forward stock split and a change of focus for the company, which is now dedicated to uncovering promising new lithium projects. Gold and silver are no longer primary minerals for the company. http://www.amerilithium.com/

Amerix Precious Metals Corp. (PINK:APMFF) Amerix Precious Metals Corp.'s flagship Limao project in Brazil has gotten promising results from 11 limited float samples at the site. Results ranged from 2.37 g/t gold to 106.6 g/t gold with an average of 38.5 g/t gold or 1.12 oz/t gold. More extensive drilling and geochemical sampling is in the works. http://www.amerixcorp.com/

Anaconda Mining Inc. (PINK:ANXGF) Anaconda Mining Inc. is transitioning into a full-fledged producer. For the first quarter of fiscal year 2012, ended August 31, 2011, the company sold 2,858 ounces of gold, generating over $4.5 million in revenue and approximately $1.1 million in earnings before interest, taxes, depreciation and amortization. The company's operational Pine Cove Mine hosts probable reserves of 175,000 ounces of gold. http://www.anacondamining.com/

Andes Gold Corp. (PINK:AGCZ) Andes Gold Corporation's Miranda Alto Mine is currently processing 20 tonnes of ore a day with 1 oz/t of gold and 15 g/t of silver. The company has 95,000 ounces of proven reserves on the Miranda vein. Other veins contain an inferred resource of 600,000 ounces. Efforts to ramp up production are underway. http://www.andesgoldmine.com/

EDITOR'S PICK: *Andina Minerals Inc. (PINK:ADMNF)* Why we like it: Nearing 20 million ounces of gold in Chile. Andina's flagship property is its Volcan Gold Project in the Maricunga Gold Belt in Chile. A pre-feasibility study at the site wrapped up on Feb. 14, 2011, and showed 8.9 million ounces of measured and indicated gold. The site also shows an indicated resource of 11.7 million ounces of gold. http://www.andinaminerals.com/

Anglo Swiss Resources Inc. (PINK:ASWRF) Anglo Swiss Resources Inc. is exploring the vast Nelson Mining Camp gold project in southeastern British Columbia. The site's home to the historic Kenville Gold Mine, which produced 181,395 tonnes of ore between 1890 and 1952. Nelson Mining Camp includes at least 10 other prospective properties. http://www.anglo-swiss.com/

Anglogold Ashanti Ltd. (NYSE:AU) AngloGold Ashanti should be producing 700,000 ounces of gold per year by 2016. That's after the company announced plans in September to invest $1.75 billion in Brazil to boost production there despite a murky political outlook on mining taxes. At the end of 2010, the company had gold reserves of 71.2 million ounces. http://www.anglogold.co.za/

Animas Resources Ltd. (PINK:ANIMF) Animas Resources Ltd. is exploring property in Mexico and Nevada. The company's Santa Gertrudis Gold Project in Mexico contains six separate projects, many of which were previously mined but still show potential for 100,000+ ounce resources (including Santa Gertrudis, which contains a non-NI 43-101 compliant 720,000 ounces of gold). On Oct. 6, 2011, the company announced it had acquired interests in the Desierto Project in Mexico. http://www.animasresources.com/

Arcus Development Group Inc. (PINK:ARCUF) Arcus Development Group Inc. shelled out $3.5 million for a 50 percent interest in the Dawson Gold Project in west-central Yukon. The project contains four claim blocks: the Touleary, Dan Man, Green Gulch and Shamrock mineral properties, which Arcus is actively exploring. Recent drill results at Touleary showed high-grade copper-silver-gold-zinc mineralization grading up to 7.18% copper, 116 g/t silver, 3.55 g/t gold and 4.30% zinc across 2.25m. http://www.arcusdevelopmentgroup.com/

Ardent Mines Ltd. (PINK:ADNT) Ardent Mines has two projects in Brazil: the Serra du Ouro project and the Serra do Sereno project in Brazil. The Serra du Ouro has a main vein that contains more than 1 million estimated ounces of gold. In September 2011, the company also announced the acquisition of mineral rights at the 10,000-hectare Misty Hills property in the state of Para. Exploration at the new property is expected to begin soon. http://www.ardentmines.com/

Argentex Mining Corp. (OTC:AGXMF) Focused on new properties in Southern Argentina, drill results have been impressive from the company's Pinguino property. Recent results include 6m of 2,428 g/t silver (78 ounces per short ton silver). Argentex owns 100 percent of the rights to the property. http://www.argentexmining.com/

EDITOR'S PICK: *Argonaut Gold Inc. (PINK:ARNGF)* Why we like it: A small-cap producer with nearly 3 million ounces of gold in the ground; Shares were up 51% in 2011. A small cap producer, Argonaut Gold posted a 33% increase in Q3 gold production. In all, the company mined 16,884 ounces of gold at its wholly owned El Castillo mine in Durango, Mexico, during the third quarter. Argonaut sold 7,994 ounces of gold in 2010. El Castillo hosts 1.23 million ounces of proven and probable gold reserves and 1.7 million ounces of measured and indicated resources. http://www.argonautgoldinc.com/

Armistice Resources Corp. (PINK:AISCF) Armistice Resources Corp. is focused on developing its McGarry Gold Project in Ontario. "Armistice has identified a mineralized system at a depth of 2,200 feet on the McGarry Project, which is geologically identical to that of the adjacent Kerr Addison property," the company writes. That's interesting as the Kerr Addison property produced 12 million ounces of gold from 41 million tons of ore over its 58 year operating life. http://www.armistice.ca/

Artha Resources Corp. (PINK:ATHCF) Artha Resources' flagship property surrounds Silver Standards' Pirquita's Mine in Argentina. Pirquita's is one of the largest primary silver mines in the world with reported reserves of just under 200 million ounces of silver. Early-stage exploration is underway. http://www.artharesources.com/

Artventive Medical Group, Inc. (PINK:AVTD) Formerly Uranium Plus Resource Corporation, the Artventive Medical Group, Inc. appears to have gotten out of the prospecting business to focus on creating medical devices, namely devices that unblock veins and arteries (endoluminal occlusion devices). Looks like the wrong stock to be holding if you're interested in gold or silver. http://www.artventivemedical.com/

EDITOR'S PICK: *Ascot Resources Ltd. (PINK:ASOLF)* Why we like it: Actively exploring a past-producing mine; Shares up 89% in 2011. Ascot Resources Ltd. signed an option agreement in 2009 to purchase all of the assets of the Premier Gold Mine held by Boliden Ltd. in the Cassiar Mining District in British Columbia. The historical Premier Gold Mine produced 2 million ounces of gold and 42.8 million ounces of silver before operations were suspended in 1996. Ascot is hoping to find more gold and silver at the site. The company also has four other projects or properties that it's exploring. http://www.ascotresources.ca/

Astur Gold Corp. (PINK:ATRGF) Astur Gold Corp. recently filed an application to develop its Salave Gold Project in northern Spain. Per the company: "Salave is one of the largest undeveloped gold deposits in Western Europe with an NI 43-101 compliant mineral resource estimate by Scott Wilson RPA containing 1,683,000 ounces of gold in the measured and indicated category (2,155,000 tonnes grading 3.88 g/t gold measured and 15,790,000 tonnes grading 2.79 g/t gold indicated) with an additional 338,000 ounces of gold in the inferred category (3,770,000 tonnes grading 2.8 g/t gold)." http://www.asturgold.com/

EDITOR'S PICK: *Athena Silver Corp. (OTC:AHNR)* Why we like it: Exploring the historic Langtry Mine, which produced 52 million ounces of silver. Athena Silver is focused on developing its historical Langtry resource. During the 1960s and 1970s, the property was drilled extensively by the Superior Oil Company, which found a 22 million ton ore body, with silver grading at an average of 2.37 oz/t for a total of 52.14 million ounces. Athena hopes to uncover new veins at the site. http://www.athenasilver.com/

EDITOR'S PICK: *Atna Resources Ltd. (OTC:ATNAF)* Why we like it: Early-stage gold producer; Expects to mine 50,000 ounces a year by 2015. Since re-starting production at the company's Briggs Mine in Inyo County, California, Atna's been prospecting for more gold at the site. The company already has 2.03 million ounces of total measured and indicated gold and 1.21 million inferred ounces of gold in its portfolio. Production is expected to hit 40,000 to 50,000 ounces per year by 2015. http://www.atna.com/

Augen Gold Corp. (PINK:AUGNF) Augen Gold Corp. was acquired by Trelawney Mining and Exploration Inc. on Nov. 4, 2011. Under the compulsory acquisition, Augen shareholders who did not elect to exercise dissent rights received 0.0862 of a common share of Trelawney for each Augen Gold Share they owned. http://augengold.ca/

Aura Silver Resources Ltd. (PINK:AUSVF) Pending acceptance, Aura Silver Resources Inc. submitted the final deliverables required for an option agreement on the Taviche Project in Mexico. If the deliverable is accepted, it will establish a joint venture on the property between Aura, Plata and Intrepid Mines to further develop Taviche. That would be good as Taviche shows an inferred silver resource of 865,000 tonnes at a grade of 119 g/t for 3.3 million ounces of contained silver and an inferred gold resource of 3.3 million tonnes at a grade of 0.51 g/t for 54,000 ounces of contained gold. http://www.aurasilver.com/

AuRico Gold Inc. (NYSE:AUQ) Formerly Gammon Gold, Q3 2011 production at AuRico was up 68 percent (per Reuters: http://www.reuters.com/article/2011/10/13/aurico-idUSL3E7LD3DN20111013). That doubled revenue to $112 million and brought their quarterly production up to 45,686 ounces. The company's primarily focused on mining operations in Mexico. All told, they boast 6.5 million ounces of pro forma gold reserves. http://www.auricogold.com/

Auriga Gold Corp. (PINK:AGRDF) Auriga Gold Corp. holds rights in the Flin Flon greenstone belt in Manitoba, Canada. The company's Maverick Gold Project looks particularly promising. The Puffy Lake Deposit there shows 174,000 ounces of indicated gold and 558,000 inferred ounces in an initial NI 43-101 report. http://www.aurigagold.ca/

Aurion Resources Ltd. (PINK:AIRRF) Prospecting for gold in Nevada and Mexico, Aurion Resources recently joint-ventured with AuRico to explore the company's La Bandera project in Mexico. The site is host to a 20+ km long, epithermal vein system with grades up to 74 g/t gold in early exploration. http://www.aurionresources.com/

EDITOR'S PICK: *Aurizon Mines Ltd. (AMEX:AZK)* Why we like it: A major producer with a bonanza-grade deposit. This active gold producer has a current mine life through 2020 at Casa Berardi in Quebec. The mine produced 141,000 ounces of gold in 2010 and estimated gold production of 160,000-165,000 ounces for 2011. The company's also drilling at promising sites including Marban Block in the Abitibi region of Quebec, which recently intersected grades as high as 906.2 g/t gold. Look for a resource estimate on the property early in 2012. http://www.aurizon.com/

Aurora Gold Corp. (PINK:ARXG) Aurora Gold is currently exploring two properties: the historic Gold Hill Mine in Colorado and the Tapajos Project in Brazil. The Gold Hill Mine produced more than 1,600 ounces of gold and 13,500 ounces of silver between 2007 and 2008. The San Domingo plot at the Tapajos Project has shown a JORC-compliant inferred resource of 130,000 ounces. http://www.aurora-gold.com/

Avala Resources Ltd. (PINK:AVLRF) Avala Resources Ltd. holds interests within and adjacent to the Timok Magmatic Complex (TMC) in the Republic of Serbia, and the company's actively exploring its claims. Avala planned to spend $20 million exploring the property in 2011 with the vast majority of that cash going toward exploring sediment-hosted gold targets. Early drilling has intersected 8.10 g/t gold over 17m. http://www.avalaresources.com/

Avino Silver & Gold Mines Ltd. (AMEX:ASM) Avino's optimistic over its Avino property in Durango, Mexico. Recent drilling in the Guadalupe Zone on the property returned 451 g/t silver over 1.35m. Avino knows there's silver there, too. The company first started mining the site in 1974. Over nearly three decades, they recovered 16 million ounces of silver, 96,000 ounces of gold and 24 million pounds of copper. They hope to add to those numbers with new mining soon. http://www.avino.com/

Axmin Inc. (PINK:AXMIF) Axmin Inc. is actively exploring for gold at the Komahun gold project in Sierra Leone. In 2008, the indicated mineral resources at Komahun were estimated to be 370,000 tonnes at a grade of 9.1 g/t gold and the inferred mineral resources were estimated to be 3.1 million tonnes at a grade of 4.3 g/t gold. A mine at the site could produce up to 50,000 ounces a year with an estimated mine life of six years. http://www.axmininc.com/

Azimut Exploration (PINK:AZMTF) Azimut has a knack for creating option agreements on the path to joint ventures. In just 8 years, the company has signed 29 strategic or option agreements with senior and junior partners, including Rio Tinto, Goldcorp, IAMGOLD and Aurizon Mines. Goldcorp recently exercised its second option on the company's Wabamisk property and has 10 years to complete a bankable feasibility study on the property. Azimut retains royalties on any property that reaches the production stage. http://www.azimut-exploration.com/

Balmoral Resources Ltd. (PINK:BALMF) A newcomer to the markets, Balmoral Resources was founded in 2010 by the team that led West Timmins Mining Inc. to a $424 million buyout by Lake Shore Gold Inc. the year before. The company's Martiniere Project in the Abitibi greenstone belt has shown encouraging drill results ranging from 0.94 g/t gold to 161 g/t gold. http://www.balmoralresources.com/

Banro Corp. (AMEX:BAA) Banro's Twangiza Congo mine poured its first gold on Oct. 11, 2011. The mine's expected to be on pace to churn out 120,000 ounces of gold per year by early 2012. All told, Twangiza should produce 1 million ounces of gold over seven years, and it will be joined by several other proposed mines in the area (the first of which is expected to begin production early in 2013). http://www.banro.com/

Barker Minerals Ltd. (PINK:BKMNF) Barker Minerals Ltd. holds claim to more than 300,000 acres of land in the historic Cariboo Placer Gold District in East-Central British Columbia, Canada. Drilling is currently underway on the company's 100% owned Frank Creek VMS project and will test near-surface targets that show the potential for copper, zinc, lead, silver and gold deposits. Grab samples reported up to 116 oz/t silver and 59 percent lead and 34 oz/t silver and 37.1% lead over 1m. Gold values in bedrock grab samples have graded as high as 7.5 g/t. http://www.barkerminerals.com/

Barkerville Gold Mines Ltd. (PINK:BGMZF) One of Canada's newest gold producers, Barkerville Gold Mines Ltd. started production at its QR Mine & Mill in September 2010. The company aimed to produce 50,000 ounces of gold by the end of 2011. Drilling is also ongoing at several of the company's other projects including Cariboo and Cow Mountain. Recent drill holes at Cow Mt. showed 21.5m of 9.97 g/t gold. http://www.barkervillegold.com/

Barrick Gold Corp. (NYSE:ABX) If you're looking to invest in the majors, Barrick should be near the top of the list. The company's the largest gold producer in the world with 26 operating mines spanning five continents. The company's portfolio is bulging with 140 million ounces of proven and probable gold reserves, 6.5 billion pounds of copper reserves and 1.07 billion (yes, with a "b") ounces of silver. Hedge funds poured a net $40 million into the company during Q2 2011. http://www.barrick.com/

Bayfield Ventures Corp. (PINK:BYVVF) Bayfield Ventures is exploring three properties that are entwined with the Rainy River Gold Project, a multi-million ounce gold deposit owned by Rainy River Resources. Recent drill holes at the project have yielded 14m of 35.35 g/t silver and 23.4m of 11.90 g/t silver. Thirty-seven more assays are pending at the time of this writing. http://www.bayfieldventures.com/

BCGold Corp. (PINK:BCGOF) BCGold Corp. has several prospective gold properties in the Yukon and British Columbia. The company's Engineer Mine in British Columbia has shown an inferred resource estimate of 25,000 ounces gold at an average grade of 19 g/t. http://www.bcgoldcorp.com/

EDITOR'S PICK: *Bear Creek Mining Corp. (PINK:BCEKF)* Why we like it: More than 500 million ounces of silver in Peru. Bear Creek Mining's Corani and Santa Ana Projects contain more than 500 million ounces of silver. According to the company, more than 320 million of those ounces are in reserves providing near-term production potential. A feasibility study at Santa Ana shows a 5-million-ounce per year silver mine with an 11 year mine life. http://www.bearcreekmining.com/

Bear Lake Gold Ltd. (PINK:BLGFF) Bear Lake Gold's primary project is the Larder Lake gold property in northeastern Ontario. The property has shown indicated gold resources of 43,800 ounces and 917,000 inferred ounces gold (at a grade of 5.55 g/t). A new drilling program to further explore the deposit is underway. http://www.bearlakegold.com/

Beaufield Resources (PINK:BFDRF) Beaufield Resources Inc. owns interests in several prospective properties in Ontario and Quebec. A 43-101 report is underway at the company's flagship Tortigny deposit, which has shown drill results with grades of 11.78% zinc, 5.70% copper, 128.76 g/t silver and 0.76 g/t gold over 18.95m. http://www.beaufield.com/

Bellhaven Copper & Gold Inc. (PINK:BHVCF) Bellhaven Copper & Gold Inc.'s flagship gold-copper project at La Mina in Colombia has shown an NI 43-101 resource of 1 million ounces gold (1.6 million ounces gold equivalent). Drilling to expand the resource is underway. http://www.bellhavencg.com/

Benton Resources Corp. (PINK:BNRJF) Benton Resources Corp. has invested in a wide web of projects and holds shares in a number of other mining companies. According to a recent press release, the company holds $11.5 million in cash, owns approximately 57.9 million shares in Coro Mining Corp., 348,000 shares of Stillwater Mining Company, 782,500 shares in Marathon Gold Corp., and 1.6 million shares in Puget Ventures among others. The company's in the process of spinning out its 42 percent investment in Coro Mining into a newly listed company. Benton is also exploring several properties. One – the Abernethy gold project – recently returned grades of 7.78 g/t over 1.5m. http://www.bentonresources.ca/

Big Bear Mining Corp. (OTC:BGBR) Big Bear Mining Corp. has interests in three mines: Lewiston, Wyoming, Rattlesnake Hills, Wyoming and Red Lake, Ontario. The Wolf mine in Lewiston yielded 3.6 g/t gold over 8m in sampling from 1984. http://bigbearminingcorp.com/

Bison Gold Resources Inc. (PINK:BGEZF) Bison Gold Resources Inc. is actively exploring several assets in Manitoba, particularly its flagship Central Manitoba property, which has shown promising drill results (one hole yielded 206 g/t over 1.91m). Much of Bison's holdings abut resources held by Canadian gold producer San Gold Corp. http://www.bisongold.com

Blue Note Mining Inc. (PINK:BLNMF) A prefeasibility study on Blue Note Mining Inc.'s Croinor Gold Project in Val D'Or Quebec was completed on July 19, 2010. The study showed a five-year mine life that could produce 185,260 ounces of gold. The company has received a permit to begin construction at the site and production could potentially start in 2012. http://www.bluenotemining.ca/

Bolero Resources Corp. (PINK:BRUZF) Bolero Resources Corp. is currently drilling the company's Carbonatite Syndicate rare earth element prospect in Northern British Columbia. In addition to that REE holding, the company is also exploring the "Red Chris South" copper-gold prospect in British Columbia and two separate prospective gold properties in the Yukon. Recent assays from the Carbonatite Syndicate property returned maximum concentrations of cerium and lanthanum as high as 1205 ppm and 663 ppm respectively. http://www.boleroresources.com/

Bonterra Resources Inc. (PINK:BONXF) BonTerra Resources Inc. is aggressively exploring the company's Eastern Extension project in the Urban-Barry Greenstone Belt in Québec. A chip sample at the property assayed 204.0 g/t gold and 25.8 g/t silver, and recent drill holes have assayed as high as 44.8 g/t gold over 1m. http://www.bonterraresources.com/

Bowmore Exploration Ltd. (PINK:BWMXF) Bowmore Exploration Ltd. has friends in high places. In 2009, Osisko Mining Corporation (a $4 billion+ mining company) acquired a 35 percent stake in Bowmore and named two of their top exec's to the company's board. Bowmore is exploring two projects in Quebec (St-Victor, Duverny) and three in Mexico (Chivas, Nueva Escondid, Paraje Azul). On Dec. 15, 2011, the company announced drilling at St-Victor had returned 0.35 g/t gold over 115m. http://bowmorexploration.com/

Bralorne Gold Mines (PINK:BPMSF) Bralorne Gold Mines has re-opened the historic Bralorne Gold Mine in British Columbia. The mine closed when the price of gold was fixed at $35 an ounce in 1971. Now, Bralorne's milling 500 tonnes per day and stockpiling reserves on top of that as the company further explores the gaps between the Bralorne, King and Pioneer gold mines. The company expects to produce 11,540 ounces of gold (at a grade of .38 oz/t) in 2011 and 2012. http://www.bralorne.com/

Bravada Gold Corp. (PINK:BGAVF) Bravada owns 22 exploratory projects in Nevada. The company is focusing most of its efforts on its Wind Mountain project where a pre-feasibility study is expected to be completed in Q1 2012. A 2007 43-101 report estimated a measured and indicated resource of 406,000 ounces of gold averaging 0.411 g/t, plus an inferred resource of 92,000 ounces of gold averaging 0.308 g/t gold. http://www.bravadagold.com/

Bravo Gold Corp. (PINK:BVGIF) Bravo Gold Corp.'s flagship gold property is the 100 percent owned Homestake Ridge Project in British Columbia. An updated NI 43-101 compliant mineral resource estimate in 2011 showed 191,000 ounces of gold and 1,350,000 ounces of silver indicated plus 530,000 ounces of gold and 13,470,000 ounces of silver inferred at a 3.0 g/t gold cut-off. http://www.bravogoldcorp.com/

Brazilian Gold Corp. (PINK:BGOZF) Brazilian Gold is actively exploring its Sao Jorge project in Brazil. According to the company, the deposit is host to an NI 43-101 compliant indicated mineral resource of 11.365 million tonnes grading 1 g/t gold (379,000 ounces of contained gold) and an inferred mineral resource of 20.673 million tonnes grading 0.8 g/t gold (558,000 ounces of contained gold) at a 0.3 g/t cut-off. http://www.braziliangold.ca/

Brigus Gold Corp. (AMEX:BRD) A prefeasibility study on Brigus's Goldfields project in northwestern Saskatchewan says the mine would produce 100,000 ounces of gold per year starting with its first year. According to the company, the project has a net present value of $144 million based on $1,250 gold. Brigus will decide whether or not to bring a mine online at Goldfields after its Black Fox project is steadily producing 25,000 ounces of gold per quarter. http://www.brigusgold.com/

Bryn Resources Inc. (PINK:BRYN) Currently exploring two properties in Eastern Canada, Bryn Resources' Wine Harbour claims are located on a historical gold mining site that produced 42,726 ounces of gold from 83,000 tons of ore, for an average content of 0.52 oz/t between 1862 and 1939. The company is also in the early stages of exploration on its Renfew claims in Nova Scotia. http://www.brynresources.com/

Buckingham Exploration Inc. (OTC:BUKX) Buckingham has 16 leases covering 360 hectares at its flagship Dome project in British Columbia. Located in the historic Beaverdell Mining Camp, the region does have a long history of gold and silver mining, but the company has released little information regarding the quality of its deposit. Aviador group (a gold and copper explorer) acquired 70% of Buckingham in late 2010. http://buckingham.com/

Bullion Monarch Mining Inc. (OTC:BULM) Currently looking at new avenues for financing, Bullion Monarch may issue up to 10 million common shares in the near future. The company is focused on five properties with two of the most prominent being the Carlin project in Nevada and the Tapajós project in Brazil. Bullion Monarch is entitled to a Gross Smelter Return ("GSR") Royalty of 1 percent on its Carlin Trend property. That's generated revenue of more than $10 million over the past three years and shows signs of continued growth, which should help Bullion Monarch finance new exploration projects. http://www.bullionmm.com/

Cadan Resources Corp. (PINK:CADAF) Cadan Resources Corp. expects to start commercial operations at its T'Boli gold-silver mine in Mindanao in the Philippines. The mine has deposits of 360,000 ounces of gold (indicated and inferred) and 1.6 million ounces of silver, according to the company. http://www.cadanresources.com/

Cadillac Ventures Inc. (PINK:CADIF) Cadillac Ventures has big backers in Trafigura AG (the parent company of Trafigura Beheer B.V.). Trafigura owns a 25 percent stake in the company. The company's exploration projects are wide-ranging and span numerous countries and royalty deals. Cadillac's flagship Thierry Property in Ontario hosts an NI 43-101 compliant resource of 8,281,000 measured and indicated tonnes grading 1.73% copper and 0.20% nickel, and 14,639,000 inferred tonnes grading 1.70% copper and 0.16% nickel. Most recently, Cadillac acquired a 30 percent indirect interest in the 51,000 hectare 'Lima Norte Property' in Peru. http://www.cadillacventures.com/

Calais Resources Inc. (PINK:CAAUF) Calais Resources is currently focused on re-opening its Cross/Caribou gold and silver mine in Nederland, Colorado. Mining there started more than 140 years ago, and the mine's estimated to have produced 500,000 ounces of gold and 20 million ounces of silver. An NI 43-101 shows 11,824 ounces of gold and 175,170 ounces of silver remaining at the site. http://www.calaisresources.com/

Caldera Resources, Inc. (PINK:CAEFF) Caldera Resources Inc. is in arbitration with Global Gold Corporation after Global Gold terminated its JV between the parties late in 2010. The outcome, which was expected in January 2012, will determine the ownership rights of the Marjan Project in Armenia. The Marjan Project has a historical resource equivalent to 405,147 ounces of gold and 14.2 million ounces silver (measured and indicated) and inferred resources of 647,152 ounces of gold and 37.1 million ounces of silver. http://calderaresources.com/

Caledonia Mining Corp. (OTC:CALVF) Caledonia Mining wholly owns and operates the Blanket Mine in Zimbabwe after the company acquired it from Kinross Gold Corporation in 2006. The mine currently has a production capacity of 40,000 ounces of gold per year. Ongoing talks over the indigenization of the mine, though, have some investors worried about the company's future. http://www.caledoniamining.com/

EDITOR'S PICK: *Calibre Mining Corp. (PINK:CXBMF)* Why we like it: Yamana holds a 7% interest in Calibre. Calibre Mining Corp.'s most promising project appears to be its 100%-owned Riscos de Oro high grade gold-silver prospect in Nicaragua. Phase III drilling is in the works after Phase II drilling intercepted grades as high as 10.25 g/t gold and 288.25 g/t silver over 5.4m. Yamana gold holds 7 percent of the company's shares. http://www.calibremining.com/

Canadian Orebodies (PINK:CNOBF) Canadian Orebodies Inc. has focused its energies on the Haig Inlet Iron Ore Project on the Belcher Islands in Nunavut. Drill results there have been encouraging with one hole showing 29.6% iron over 42m, including 34.7% iron over 16m (and that intersection occurred under just 13.1m of ground). The announcement of those results rocketed shares up 30 percent in one day of trading. The company also holds interests in gold and lithium projects in Canada. http://www.canadianorebodies.com/

Canadian Zinc Corp. (OTC:CZICF) Focused on bringing its Prairie Creek zinc, lead and silver mine online in the Northwest Territories, Canadian Zinc has uncovered high-grade deposits at the site. The Prairie Creek Property hosts measured and indicated resources of 5,840,329 tonnes grading 10.71% zinc, 9.90% lead, 161.12 g/t silver and 0.326% copper. http://www.canadianzinc.com/

Canarc Resource Corp. (OTC:CRCUF) Canarc's moving toward production at its New Polaris project in British Columbia. A past-producing, high-grade mine, New Polaris shows 1.1 million ounces of gold (at 13.56 g/t) still in the ground. The mine could potentially produce 80,000 ounces of gold per year. http://www.canarc.net/

Canasil Resources Inc. (PINK:CNSUF) Exploring in Canada and Mexico, Canasil Resources Inc. recently returned a chip sample of 2,150 g/t silver, 5.39% copper and 1.89% zinc over 0.90m from its Salamandra project in Mexico. The company's also actively exploring its Sandra-Escobar silver-gold project in Mexico with recent drill gradings of 19.09 g/t silver, 0.12% lead and 0.22% zinc over 52.5m, starting 7.50m below surface to a depth of 60m. http://www.canasil.com/

Candente Copper Corp. (PINK:CGDXF) Candente Copper's flagship property is the Canariaco Norte copper deposit in Northern Peru. The site shows a measured and indicated resource of 752.4 million tonnes grading 0.45% copper, 0.07 g/t gold and 1.9 g/t silver containing 7.533 billion pounds of copper, 1.7 million ounces of gold and 45.2 million ounces of silver. A feasibility study is underway. http://www.candentecopper.com/

Canstar Resources Inc. (PINK:CSRNF) Canstar Resources Inc. was in a "protracted" legal dispute over its Mary March property in Newfoundland. Rights to the property were granted to the company in November 2011, and Canstar's shares have shot up in response. Exploration should be aggressive in 2012. Canstar also has rights to the Slate Bay project in Red Lake. Past drilling there has graded up to 7.2 g/t gold, 5.81% copper and 183 g/t silver within "considerably longer sections of lower grade material attaining widths of over 100m." http://www.canstarresources.com/

Cantex Mine Development Corp. (PINK:CTXDF) Cantex Mine Development Corp.'s flagship project is in Yemen. Three sites there have shown nickel, copper, cobalt and platinum deposits, while a fourth project shows a gold deposit. The company signed a letter agreement with Vale International SA in November 2008 to further explore the property. Cantex is also moving ahead with exploration on its Yukon projects. Drilling at the Al Hariqah gold project has returned 7.5m of 3.53 g/t, 5.5m of 3.26 g/t, 12m of 2.79 g/t and 4.5m of 2.54 g/t gold. http://www.cantex.ca/

Cardero Resources Corp. (AMEX:CDY) Cardero's gradually transforming itself from a precious metals-centric company to one that focuses on bulk commodities including iron ore and coal. The company recently acquired Coalhunter Mining Corp., and it scored a big win early in 2010 when it sold its Pampa de Pongo iron deposit for $100 million. Cardero's Carbon Creek deposit in Canada contains 114 million tons of measured and indicated coal plus 89.1 million tons of inferred coal. http://www.cardero.com/

Carpathian Gold Inc. (PINK:CPNFF) Carpathian Gold Inc. hopes to produce 100,000 ounces of gold a year from its Riacho dos Machados Gold project in Brazil. Environmental concerns halted installation efforts at the site on Oct. 18, 2011, but the project's license to install has not been revoked. An updated timeline for the project is pending, but the company did receive financing of $97 million for the project (which was announced on Oct. 5, 2011). http://www.carpathiangold.com/

Cassidy Gold Corp. (PINK:CDXGF) Cassidy Gold Corp. is focused on further exploration at its Birimian gold fields site, Kouroussa, in Guinea (West Africa). Coffey Mining completed a resource estimate on the property in 2008 that showed an indicated resource of 680,000 ounces contained in 11,380,000 tonnes grading 1.9 g/t gold and an inferred resource of 363,000 ounces contained in 6,466,000 tonnes grading 1.7 g/t gold. http://www.cassidygold.com/

Caza Gold Corp. (PINK:CZGDF) Caza Gold Corp.'s Santiago Project is located in the Batopilas Silver District in Mexico, and the company hopes it will eventually uncover a 500,000 ounce gold deposit there. Chip samples have returned results as high as 30.3 g/t gold over 2.3m. The "property hosts multiple narrow high grade gold-quartz veins in the Cliff zone assaying up to 144 g/t gold over 1.5m within a 200m wide by 1000m long alteration zone," the company writes on its website. http://www.cazagold.com/

CB Gold Inc. (PINK:CBHDF) CB Gold Inc. is focusing on exploration in the Santander Province and the Norte de Santander Gold Project in Colombia. Early results from the Vetas Gold Project are promising. One sample (2.09m) graded as high as 316.67 g/t gold and 26.20 g/t silver. Former drill results have shown high grade gold and silver veins up to 667 g/t gold and 3,090 g/t silver. An NI 43-101 resource is expected in 2012. http://www.cbgoldinc.com/

Cedar Mountain Exploration (PINK:CDRMF) Cedar Mountain Exploration Inc. is exploring the Kelly Creek Gold Property on the Seward Peninsula of Alaska. The company planned 5,000m of diamond core drilling at the site in 2011. Kelly Creek was originally discovered by Anaconda Copper Mining Co., which drilled results of 1.07 g/t gold over 23.5m and 0.83 g/t gold over 32m in two separate holes. http://www.cedarmountainexp.com/

Century Mining Corp. (PINK:CMNZF) Century Mining Corporation became a subsidiary of White Tiger Gold Ltd. when the two companies combined on Oct. 20, 2011. With properties in Canada and Peru, Century Mining has been successfully producing gold and shows gold resources of 3.1 million ounces at its Lamaque Gold project in Canada and 175,125 inferred ounces at its San Juan project in Peru. http://www.centurymining.com/

Challenger Deep Resources (PINK:CNDRF) Challenger Deep Resources Corp. has a stated goal of assembling 100 million plus tonnes of coal reserves for production commencing in 2012 through several projects in East Kalimantan, Indonesia. Past interests in gold projects seem to have taken a back seat to coal as the company moves aggressively toward production. http://www.challengerdeep.ca/

Champion Bear Resources (PINK:CBRSF) Champion Bear Resources Ltd. has several exploration projects underway in Ontario including a joint-venture dig with Wallbridge Mining. A recent drill on the company's JV Sudbury property intersected 8m grading 4.11% nickel, 0.6% copper, and 4.32 g/t total precious metals, which was comprised of 1.40 g/t platinum, 2.68 g/t palladium, 0.23 g/t gold and 2.75 g/t silver. http://www.championbear.com/

Channel Resources Ltd. (PINK:CHJRF) Channel Resources Ltd. has its fingers in two very different projects: 1) the Tanlouka Gold Project in Burkina Faso, West Africa, and 2) the Fox Creek Lithium/Potash Brine Project in Alberta, Canada. The company's in the midst of a 15,000-metre drill campaign at Tanlouka, which has shown assays of 1.99 g/t gold over 70m (including 6.47 g/t over 13.5m). http://www.channelresources.ca/

China Ceetop.com Inc. (OTC:CTOP) Oregon Gold, Inc., a development-stage mining company, changed its name to China Ceetop.com Inc. in January 2011. The name-change led up to a merger with Surry Holding Limited, which also controls Hangzhou Ceetop Network Technology Co. Details are scant on the company's operations since the change. It's unclear if precious metals will remain a core part of the company's focus. Website n/a.

China Forest Energy Corp. (OTC:CFEC) An offshoot of China's Zhejiang Forest Bamboo Tech Co., China Forest Energy Corp. is (per Reuters) focused on acquiring a gold mining project in China. Scant information exists on the company, however, we do know Zhejiang Forest Bamboo Tech Co. produces carbonized bamboo as an energy source. http://www.cn-forest.com/

China TMK Battery Systems Inc. (OTC:DFEL) Formerly, Deerfield Resources, Ltd., an exploration-stage company, China TMK Battery Systems completed a reverse merger with Leading Asia Pacific Investment Limited (Leading Asia) in February 2010. The move gave Leading Asia access to public markets, but China TMK Battery's operations are unknown. The company's name indicates it has moved away from precious metals exploration. Website n/a

Claude Resources Inc. (AMEX:CGR) Claude's three main Canadian projects (Seabee, Amisk and Madsen) all boast multi-million-ounce ore bodies, and according to the company, each of the three have the potential to produce more than 100,000 ounces of gold per year. All told, the company has 1.23 million ounces of gold in the ground at Madsen. http://www.clauderesources.com/

Clifton Star Resources (PINK:CFMSF) Clifton Star Resources Inc. held rights to property in the Lac Dubonnet Mining District, which is northeast of Winnipeg, Manitoba, as of June 30, 2010. The company's web site is currently "under review," and trading in the shares appears to have concluded in July 2011. Little is known about Clifton Star's current operations. http://www.cliftonstarresources.com/

Cline Mining Corp. (PINK:CLNMF) As of August 31, 2011, Cline Mining Corporation had $57 million on hand, and that doesn't include the sale of $40 million in assets to Xstrata. The company's in the process of ramping up production at its New Elk coking coal mine in Colorado. Cline Mining expects to hit a production run-rate of 3 million tons a year early in 2012. Cline Mining also holds rights to its Cline Lake Gold Property in Northern Ontario, Canada. Drilling results show 2.10 oz/t over 23.7 feet; 0.29 oz/t over 10.4 feet; 0.9 oz/t over 9.0 feet; and 0.26 oz/t over 12.0 feet. http://www.clinemining.com/

CMC Metals Ltd. (PINK:CMCXF) CMC Metals Ltd. owns 100 percent of the rights to the Silver Hart mine in the Yukon. Non-NI 43-101 inferred resources are estimated at 56.5 oz/t silver. Per the company: "Chip samples taken along a 21m strike length averaged 1,187.8 g/t silver (38.2 ounces) across 1.5m (4.92 feet)." http://www.cmcmetals.ca/

CMQ Resources Inc. (PINK:CMQRF) CMQ Resources Inc. has leased three prospective gold properties in Nevada: the Red Canyon, The North Sleeper and the South Sleeper. The Red Canyon project has shown 95 feet of 0.117 oz/t gold from 20 to 115 feet and 85 feet of 0.046 oz/t. http://www.cmqresources.com/

EDITOR'S PICK: *Coeur D'Alene Mines Corp. (NYSE:CDE)* Why we like it: The largest primary silver producer in the US. Coeur d'Alene Mines is projected to produce 19.5 to 20.5 million ounces of silver in 2011. One top of that, they're expected to produce half a million ounces of gold. The company's three newest mines stretch from Boliva to Mexico and Alaska. Coeur currently holds over 278 million ounces of proven and probable silver reserves and 2.2 million in gold reserves. http://www2.coeur.com/

Cogitore Resources Inc. (PINK:CGORF) Cogitore Resources Inc. is currently exploring the Abitibi Belt in Quebec and Ontario as well as the Central Belt in Newfoundland. The company raised half a million dollars in October 2011 for further drilling. Two joint ventures (one with Inmet Mining Corporation and another with IAMGOLD) give Cogitore a partial claim in its flagship Estrades-Caribou project, the site of a former Agnico Eagle mine. A 2008 NI 43-101 report showed indicated resources of 709,172 tonnes with 9.8% zinc, 0.8% copper, 0.9% lead, 5 g/t gold and 163 g/t silver at Estrades. http://www.cogitore.com/

EDITOR'S PICK: *Colibri Resource Corp. (PINK:CRUCF)* Why we like it: Sprott and Agnico-Eagle hold 30% of Colibri. Colibri Resource Corp. is aggressively exploring properties in Sonora, Mexico, not far from Newmont's

La Herradura. "Agnico owns just under 20% of the company and Sprott Asset Management owns just under 20% and my wife and I own just under 10%," Ian Gordon said recently in an interview with Resource Investor (http://www.resourceinvestor.com/News/2011/10/Pages/Ian-Gordon-Hedging-Against-Imminent-Economic-Collapse.aspx). "You've got a major producer earning into that property and, if successful as Newmont and Fresnillo have been at La Herradura, it will take Colibri into production and hopefully find the 12 million ounces plus that they've found at La Herradura." http://www.colibriresource.com/

Colombia Crest Gold (PINK:ECRTF) Colombia Crest Gold Corp. got a huge vote of confidence on October 26, 2011, when IAMGOLD announced a $4.2 million stake in the company. That gives IAMGOLD a 20 percent stake in the company should they exercise all their warrants. Colombia Crest is focused on two gold projects in Colombia: the Fredonia and Venecia projects. Early exploration is underway on both. At its 100% owned San Simon project in Bolivia, the Company has an NI 43-101 indicated mineral resource of 262,300 tonnes grading 5.15 g/t gold and an inferred mineral resource of 251,800 tonnes grading 5.46 g/t gold, classified at a 3 g/t cut-off. http://colombiacrestgold.com/

Colombian Mines Corp. (PINK:CMBPF) Phase I drilling is underway at Colombian Mines Corporation's flagship Yarumalito gold-copper porphyry project in Colombia. 13,000 ounces of gold were mined from the site as small-scale, private miners stumbled upon a high-grade vein of gold there in 1988. Recent sampling at the company's El Dovio deposit returned results averaging 10.42 g/t gold, 20.7 g/t silver, 2.34% copper and 2.23% zinc over 9m. http://www.colombianmines.com/

Columbus Gold Corp. (PINK:CBGDF) Columbus Gold Corporation has stakes in impressive deposits in French Guiana and Nevada. In French Guiana, the company can earn 100 percent interest in the Paul Isnard gold project, which contains 1.9 million ounces of gold (inferred). The company also has 26 projects in Nevada, 13 of which are leased to major and junior mining companies including Agnico-Eagle Mines Limited. http://www.columbusgoldcorp.com/

Columbus Silver (PINK:CSLVF) Columbus Silver Corporation controls a 100% interest in 7 silver properties in Utah, Arizona, Nevada, and New Mexico. The company started Phase 1 drilling at its Mogollon Project in New Mexico in 2010. Drilling there in the 1980s "outlined a partially delineated deposit of 767,000 tonnes averaging 320 g/t silver and 5.1 g/t gold." http://www.columbussilvercorp.com/

Commander Resources (PINK:CMDRF) Commander Resources Ltd. has started an Induced Polarization (IP) survey at its Stump Lake gold property in British Columbia. The survey should identify drill sites after rock chip samples have shown gold grades ranging from 0.5 to 6 g/t. The company's key focus, though, is on its Baffin Gold Project on Baffin Island, which includes at least four identified gold zones. http://www.commanderresources.com/

EDITOR'S PICK: *Compania De Minas Buenaventura SA (NYSE:BVN)* Why we like it: Yielding 1.45%; Shares have returned 190% over past five years. Based in Peru, Buenaventura operates seven mines in the country. It's one of just four companies that largely dominate gold mining in Peru. The three others are Newmont (NEW), Barrick (ABX) and Gold Fields (GFI). Buenaventura, though, is the only one of the four companies that's actually based in Peru. The stock is currently yielding north of 1 percent, and the company has a market cap of $9.9 billion. http://www.buenaventura.com/

Comstock Mining, Inc. (AMEX:LODE) An updated technical report from the company in October 2011 bumped up gold estimates by nearly 1 million ounces. That's a 94 percent increase over the company's last NI 43-101 technical report. All told, the Comstock Mine Project in Nevada holds 1.5 million measured and indicated ounces of gold and 14.3 million measured and indicated ounces of silver. http://www.comstockmining.com/

Confederation Minerals Ltd. (PINK:CNRMF) Confederation Minerals Ltd. entered an option agreement with Redstar Gold Corp. to acquire up to 70 percent of the Newman Todd project in Northern Ontario. One recent drill hole there returned 7.06 ounces (242 g/t) gold over 0.5m. "Eight of the nine holes have intercepts of greater than 10 g/t gold, including a total of 9 intercepts greater than 20 g/t gold and 4 intercepts greater than 30 g/t gold," the company said in a press release. http://www.confederationmineralsltd.com/

Conquest Resources (PINK:CQRLF) Conquest Resources Limited is in the midst of a three-year exploration project at the company's Alexander Project in the Red Lake Gold Mining District of northwestern Ontario. Favorable geography there has management optimistic that the land holds large gold deposits, much like Goldcorp's high grade Red Lake and Campbell mines, which lie just 400m to the west. 2009 drilling at the site intersected gold mineralization ranging from 1 to 9 g/t over 0.30m to 2m widths. http://www.conquestresources.net/

Coral Gold Resources Ltd. (OTC:CLHRF) Coral Gold is focused on exploring its Robertson project in Nevada. Their holdings there show an inferred gold resource estimate of 3.4 million ounces, and the property abuts Barrick Gold Mines' Cortez Mine. http://www.coralgold.com/

Corex Gold Corp. (PINK:CGEKF) Corex Gold Corporation is focused on its Santana and Zuloaga properties in Mexico. Recent drilling at the Santana project has returned "up 457.6 g/t silver." Trenching samples at the company's nearby Seis Gramos target showed gold values ranging from 0.3 g/t to 6.73 g/t. http://www.corexgold.com/

Cornerstone Capital Resources Inc. (PINK:CTNXF) Cornerstone Capital Resources is exploring gold and copper sites in Ecuador, Chile and Newfoundland. Cornerstone has an option agreement with Intrepid Mines of Australia, which could earn a 60 percent interest in the property by spending $6 million on exploration over five years. One hole during Phase 1 drilling intersected 45m of 0.71 g/t gold within a broader zone of 101m of 0.41 g/t gold. http://www.cornerstoneresources.com/

Coro Mining Corp. (PINK:CROJF) Coro Mining Corp.'s stated goal is to become a "mid-tier copper producer." On the way to that goal, the company's fighting a legal battle over its San Jorge copper-gold development project in Mendoza, Argentina. In the meantime, they're focused on potential copper projects in Chile. Recent drilling at the Chacay porphyry copper project in Chile intersected 0.15% copper, 0.05 g/t gold, 0.004% molybdenum and 0.23% copper equivalent over 50m. http://www.coromining.com/

Corona Gold Corp. (PINK:CRGAF) The President and Chief Executive Officer of Corona Gold Corporation also sits on the board of directors for another Canadian mining exploration company: Dundee Resources Limited. Corona doesn't appear to have a Web site, but the company's focused on exploring properties near Dayohessarah Lake in northwestern Ontario. Little else is known about Corona's operations. Website n/a

Coyote Resources, Inc. (OTC:COYR) Coyote Resources is concentrating efforts on exploration at its Tonopah Extension Mine in Nevada. The mine was active between 1900 and 1940 when a fire at the mill shut down the operation. During that 40-year span before the mine was closed, 174 million ounces of silver and 1.8 million ounces of gold were mined at Tonopah. Historical estimates say the mine could yet hold another 40+ million ounces of silver and 430,000 ounces of gold (although it's very important to note that those number are not NI 43-101 compliant). http://www.coyoteresourcesinc.com/

Cream Minerals Ltd. (OTC:CRMXF) Cream Minerals' flagship project is its 100-percent owned Nuevo Milenio silver-gold tract in Mexico. The plot has an inferred mineral resource of 54.6 million ounces silver equivalent. http://www.creamminerals.com/

Crown Gold Corp. (PINK:CWMZF) Crown Gold Corporation was formed by the merger of Crown Minerals and Gold Summit. The new company is pursuing gold and silver targets in Nevada and Ontario with an emphasis on the Monte Cristo and Sugarloaf projects in Nevada. Crown Gold currently claims NI 43-101 resources of 367,000 ounces of gold "with upside in excess of 1 million ounces." http://www.crowngoldcorp.com/

Crystallex International Corp. (PINK:CRYXF) 16.8 million proven and probable gold ounces lie under the ground at the Las Cristinas Project in Venezula. The Venezuelan government nationalized Las Cristinas, though, on October 2010 (effectively breaking its contract with Crystallex). Since then, Crystallex's been working the international court system to try to regain its rights to mine the site. Early in October 2011, the International Centre for Settlement of Investment Disputes informed Crystallex that its arbitrated case against the Venezuelan government had begun. The outcome is still pending. http://www.crystallex.com/

Currie Rose Resource (PINK:CUIRF) Currie Rose Resources Inc. is exploring the Lake Victoria Gold Fields in Tanzania. Drill results released on Oct. 25, 2011, included one hole showing 2.68 g/t gold. Investors didn't like the results, though, and pushed shares down 35 percent in one day of trading. Further drill results are pending. http://www.currierose.com/

Dajin Resources Corp. (PINK:DJIFF) Dajin Resources Corp. is exploring for gold in British Columbia and potash and lithium in Argentina. The company has a 65 percent interest in the Cowtrail property in B.C. - a site where they've intersected 1.16 g/t gold and 0.043% copper over 18.3m. http://www.dajin.ca/

Dakota Gold Corp. (OTC:DAKO) Dakota Gold is currently exploring the Caldera property in Nevada. The property covers 1,780 acres and the company believes the tract could contain one or more economic gold-silver deposits as it's located in an area with several past and current producing mines. Historic drill results from the Caldera property include an intercept that assays 25 feet at 0.243 oz/ton gold. http://dakotagoldcorp.com/

Dalradian Resources Inc. (PINK:DRLDF) Dalradian Resources Inc.'s flagship project is the 84,000-hectare Tyrone Project in Northern Ireland. Recent step-out drilling at the site has intersected grades as high as 5.84 g/t gold over 8.34m. The Curraghinalt Deposit at the project shows indicated mineral resources of 0.95 million tonnes grading 13.24 g/t gold for 0.40 million contained ounces, and an inferred mineral resource of 1.16 million ounces. http://www.dalradian.com/

Decade Resources (PINK:DECXF) Drill results are rolling in from Decade Resources Ltd.'s Red Cliff project in Northwestern British Columbia. The latest numbers show anywhere from 2.7 g/t to 43.7 g/t gold over 7.4m. The Red Cliff project is operated by Decade under a 60/40 joint venture agreement with Mountain Boy Minerals Ltd. http://www.decaderesources.ca/

Dia Bras Exploration Inc. (PINK:DBEXF) Dia Bras Exploration Inc. has two main properties: the operational Yauricocha Mine (gold-copper-zinc-lead) in Central Peru and the Bolivar Property (copper-zinc-silver) in Chihuahua State, Mexico. The Yauricocha Mine produced 837kt of ore grading 4.74 opt silver, 3.44% lead, 0.95% copper and 3.16% zinc in 2010. Pilot mining is also underway at the company's Bolivar Property. http://www.diabras.com/

DNI Metals Inc. (PINK:DMNKF) DNI Metals Inc. has uncovered some promising results at the Buckton Mineralized Zone on its Alberta polymetallic black shale projects. An initial report showed an inferred resource of 250,092,000 short tons containing molybdenum, nickel, uranium, vanadium, zinc, copper, cobalt and lithium. That includes 66 million pounds of nickel, 16.5 million pounds of uranium (U3O8) and 75.5 million pounds of lithium (Li2CO3). http://www.dnimetals.com/

Dolly Varden Resources (PINK:DVRRF) Dolly Varden Resources Inc. got its name from one of two former producing silver mines that the company holds claims on: the Dolly Varden mine and the Torbrit mine. There's been very little news from the company since it appointed Clinton Smyth as President and Chief Executive Officer (CEO) in April 2010. Current operations are unknown. Website n/a

Douglas Lake Minerals Inc. (OTC:DLKM) Focused on gold exploration in the Republic of Tanzania, Douglas Lake is exploring two recently-purchased properties in the country: the Handeni Gold Project and the Mkuvia Alluvial Gold Project. The company's Handeni Gold Project abuts a property owned

by Canaco and has shown rock samples with grades as high as 16.8 g/t gold.
http://www.douglaslakeminerals.com/

EDITOR'S PICK: *DRDGold Ltd. (NASDAQ:DROOY)* Why we like it:
No more strikes in South Africa. DRDGold recently negotiated a new
contract with its miners at the company's Blyvoor mine in South Africa. The
three-year contract should alleviate some uncertainty there. All told,
DRDGold has 7.3 million ounces of gold reserves and 60 million ounces of
gold resources. http://www.drd.co.za/

EDITOR'S PICK: *Dynacor Gold Mines (PINK:DNGDF)* Why we like it:
Production rose 34% in 2011. Dynacor Gold Mines' custom milling plant in
Peru helps finance the company's exploration activities. According to
Dynacor, the company "generated $3.1 million of cash flow from operations
on record gold sales of $43.7 million" last year. They also expected
production to rise 34 percent in 2011, and that should help fund a $5.5
million exploration campaign underway at the Tumipampa gold-copper
project in Peru. http://www.dynacorgold.com/

Eagle Hill Exploration Corp. (PINK:EHECF) Eagle Hill Exploration
Corporation's flagship property is the Windfall Lake Property, which covers
12,000 hectares in the Abitibi mineralized belt in Quebec. The most
promising drill hole so far intersected 14.2m of 7.5 g/t gold. A mineral
resource announced in November 2011 shows an indicated resource of 1.144
million tonnes at 9.10 g/t gold (344,000 ounces) and an inferred resource of
1.690 million tonnes at 6.70 g/t of gold (364,000 ounces).
http://www.eaglehillexploration.com/

Eagle Plains Resources Ltd. (PINK:EGPLF) Eagle Plains Resources Ltd.'s
CEO also served as director for Aben Resources, which is exploring the
Yukon and Northwest Territories. Eagle Plains currently controls over 35
gold, silver, uranium, copper, molybdenum, zinc and rare earth mineral
projects. On Sept. 29, 2011, the company announced it was considering
spinning out its Yellowjacket Gold Project into a separate company:
Yellowjacket Resources Ltd. In addition to mining claims, Eagle Plains holds
16 million shares of partner companies including Alexco Resource Corp.,
NovaGold Resources Inc., Giyani Gold Corp., Aben Resources Ltd. and
others. Drill results announced in November 2011 from the company's
Dragon Lake gold project in the Yukon graded as high as 1.57 g/t gold over
3.0m. http://www.eagleplains.ca/

East Asia Minerals Corp. (PINK:EALAF) East Asia Minerals Corporation is
focused on a gold-copper project in Indonesia and uranium projects in

Mongolia. In Indonesia, the Company has a 70 to 85% interest in six advanced gold and gold-copper properties covering 440,000 hectares. On top of that, they have 100 percent interest in seven uranium and two phosphate properties in Mongolia. Historic trench results at the company's Kelapa project have graded as high as 14m of 34.8 g/t gold and 10m of 9.11 g/t gold. http://www.eaminerals.com/

Eastfield Resources Ltd. (PINK:ETFLF) Eastfield Resources Limited options its properties to other companies as a vehicle for funding its own exploration efforts. That approach has given rise to at least two companies: Cariboo Rose Resources (TSX:CRB) and Lorraine Copper (TSX:LLC). The company's currently exploring projects in British Columbia and Nevada. Recent drilling at their Zymo copper and gold project in B.C. has intersected 72m of 0.72% copper and .54 g/t gold. http://www.eastfieldresources.com/

Eastmain Resources Inc. (PINK:EANRF) Eastmain Resources Inc. has two substantial gold properties in their 100-percent owned Eau Claire and Eastmain gold deposits. Eau Claire in Quebec contains an estimated resource of 310,000 ounces of gold (indicated) and 680,000 ounces of gold (inferred). The Eastmain Mine holds some 250,000 ounces. http://www.eastmain.com/

El Capitan Precious Metals, Inc. (OTC:ECPN) Currently engaged in exploring the El Capitan property in New Mexico, ECPN is optimistic that the property could one day support a low-cost, long-life gold, silver and platinum mine. The company is currently seeking permits for sub-surface exploration on the property and plans further drilling to outline the existing 141 million tons of measured resource with a gold equivalent grade of 0.044 opt. http://www.elcapitanpmi.com/

Eldorado Gold Corp. (NYSE:EGO) Eldorado has six mines in operation in China, Turkey, Brazil and Greece. The company's stated goal is be producing 1.5 million ounces of gold a year in 2015. According to forecasts for 2011, the company expected to produce 650,000 ounces of gold at a cost of $400 per ounce. http://www.eldoradogold.com/

Eloro Resources Ltd. (PINK:ELRRD) Eloro Resources recently acquired a 100% interest in the Simkar Gold Project, a historic mine located in the prolific Val d'Or gold mining camp in Quebec. The company kicked of diamond drilling at the site in February 2011. Phase one drilling intersected 3.14 g/t gold over 7m and included an interval of 8.1 g/t gold over 1.9m. http://www.elororesources.com/

Ely Gold & Minerals Inc. (PINK:ELYGF) Ely Gold & Minerals Inc. is working toward production at its Centennial Gold Deposit on the 100-percent owned Mount Hamilton property in Nevada. A Preliminary Economic Assessment shows the mine could produce 40,000 ounces of gold equivalent per year over eight years at a cost of $450 an ounce. http://www.elygoldandminerals.com/

EMC Metals Corp. (PINK:EMMCF) Formerly Golden Predator Mines Inc., EMC Metals Corp. is focused on the "application of technology for specialty and exotic metals." This includes the company's soon-to-be-operational tungsten mill (the Springer Tungsten Facility), which will be the only tungsten mill in the U.S. when it's completed. "This mill will also have the capability of concentrating precious and other base metals," the company writes. EMC also has interests in its own tungsten projects as well as scandium and vanadium projects. http://www.emcmetals.com/

EDITOR'S PICK: *Endeavour Silver Corp. (NYSE:EXK)* Why we like it: Surging revenue; Shares were up 48% in 2011. Focused primarily on silver mining in Mexico and Chile, Endeavour Silver has two mines in operation and is showing promising exploration results at its Guanajuato Mines project in Mexico. Drilling highlights in the Daniela vein include 448 g/t silver and 14.0 g/t gold over 4.61m. Q3 2011 revenue at the company surged 93 percent and silver production rose 8 percent. http://www.edrsilver.com/

Endurance Gold Corp. (PINK:ENDGF) Endurance Gold Corporation is focused on developing its nickel and copper discovery in the Yukon. The Bandito Ree project could hold up to 11% nickel and 2.07% copper (based on grab samples). The company also has 100 percent interest in the Rattlesnake Hills property in Nevada. Surface samples have shown gold grades up to .66 g/t gold. http://www.endurancegold.com/

Entree Gold Inc. (AMEX:EGI) Entree Gold has large copper interests in several countries, including Mongolia, Australia, Peru and the U.S. Underexplored potential gold deposits range from New Mexico to Mongolia and the company's Mystique property in Australia. Rio Tinto and Ivanhoe Mines are major shareholders in Entree holding approximately 13% and 12% respectively. Entree's primary asset in Nevada is the Ann Mason deposit which has an inferred resource totaling approximately 7.1 billion pounds of copper. http://www.entreegold.com/

Equitas Resources Corp. (PINK:EQTRF) Equitas Resources Corp. recently acquired the Day Copper-Gold Porphyry Project in British Columbia. The deposit was first discovered in the 1970s. Drilling then intersected 0.67%

copper and 0.84 g/t gold across 58.83m. Equitas is in the early stages of exploration at the site. http://www.equitasresources.com/

Erin Ventures Inc. (PINK:ERVFF) Erin Ventures Inc. completed a technical report at its Deep River gold deposit in North Carolina on Feb. 28, 2011. The report shows an inferred gold resource of 708,000 ounces at a grade of 0.012 ounces per ton and 59 million tons of ore material. Erin Ventures also has interests in exploratory projects in Serbia and the Yukon. http://www.erinventures.com/

Eskay Mining Corp. (PINK:ESKYF) Eskay Mining Corp. holds "some 130,000 acres surrounding Barrick Gold Corporation's prolific Eskay Creek Mine in British Columbia, Canada." The most interesting plot in their portfolio is probably the land that lies immediately adjacent to the Pretium Snowfield deposit, which is owned by Pretium Resources. 2010 drilling at Eskay Creek showed an intercept of 0.65 g/t gold, 0.26% lead, 0.38% zinc and 6 g/t silver over 10m. http://www.kenrich-eskay.com/

Eurasian Minerals Inc. (PINK:ESMNF) Eurasian Minerals Inc. has interests around the world from Turkey, Haiti, the Kyrgyz Republic, Europe, the Southwest United States and the Asia Pacific. And that's landed them quite a few joint ventures with some big names including Newmont Mining Corporation, Vale S.A. and Freeport-McMoran Copper & Gold Inc. On Oct. 26, 2011, the company announced it was added to the Standard & Poor's S&P/TSX Venture Select Index. The company's Savane La Place Prospect in Haiti is particularly promising, as they've identified 243m at 1.71 g/t gold and 96m at 2.5 g/t gold. http://www.eurasianminerals.com/

Evolving Gold Corp. (PINK:EVOGF) Evolving Gold Corp. currently has a joint venture with Agnico Eagle to advance its discovery at Rattlesnake Hills, Wyoming. In another good sign, the company's largest shareholder is Goldcorp. Evolving Gold's Carlin-Humboldt, Nevada, deposit has shown intersections of 18.3m at 11.7 g/t gold, 14.7m of 8.8 g/t gold and 15.7m of 5 g/t gold. http://www.evolvinggold.com/

Excel Gold Mining (PINK:EGMXF) Excel Gold Mining Inc. intersected near-surface gold at the former Montauban Mine in Quebec. The company's concessions there cover 76,840 hectares and exploration kicked off late in 2010. There hasn't been much news from the company since they announced Phase II drilling at the site on October 21, 2010, though. http://www.excelgoldmining.com/

EDITOR'S PICK: *Exeter Resource Corp. (AMEX:XRA)* Why we like it: Sitting on a huge deposit in Chile. A tightly-focused company, Exeter's aggressively exploring its Caspiche property in Northern Chile. Recent results show 21.3 million ounces of gold (plus 5.1 million inferred ounces), 5.3 billion pounds of copper (plus 1.4 billion pounds of inferred copper) and 48.4 million ounces of silver (plus 14.5 million ounces of inferred silver) in the ground. http://www.exeterresource.com/

Firesteel Resources Inc. (PINK:FIEIF) Firesteel Resources Inc.'s flagship property lies at Copper Creek in British Columbia. The company envisions three working mines on the property, which has shown grades as high as 0.85% copper and 12.5m of 0.24 g/t gold. They believe the property contains a minimum of 220 million tonnes of copper/gold ore. http://www.firesteelresources.com/

Firestone Ventures (PINK:FSVEF) Firestone Ventures is currently exploring for silver, lead and zinc in Nevada and Guatemala. The company's Torlon Hill zinc-lead-silver project in Guatemala has a preliminary 43-101 compliant resource showing 330 million pounds of zinc, 114 million pounds of lead and 978,000 ounces of silver. http://www.firestoneventures.com/

First Mexican Gold Corp. (PINK:FMGXF) First Mexican Gold Corp.'s Guadalupe Property in Sonora, Mexico, is in the early stages of exploration. The company could earn up to an 80 percent interest in any minerals on the property should they hit paydirt. Drilling was underway as of August 2011 with results grading as high as .77 g/t gold and 105 g/t silver over 15.7m. http://www.fmgoldcorp.com/

First Point Minerals Corp. (PINK:FPOCF) First Point Minerals Corp. is focused predominantly on stainless steel nickel-iron alloy deposits worldwide. The company's flagship Decar property in British Columbia boasts a 300-million tonne exploration target containing a nickel-iron alloy. In the past, the company had explored for gold in Honduras, but the emphasis appears to have shifted toward base metals. http://www.firstpointminerals.com/

Fjordland Exploration Inc. (PINK:FEXXF) Fjordland Exploration has interests in 37 properties in British Columbia, four of which are undergoing drilling in 2011. The company's successful drilling at its Woodjam Joint Venture with Cariboo Rose Resources Ltd. has led to a spinoff company (Consolidated Woodjam Copper Corp.) that was announced on Oct. 5, 2011. 2011 drilling at the Red Lobster SEDEX Target returned assays of 0.22% zinc and 0.17% lead over 17.1m. http://www.fjordlandex.com/

FLM Minerals Inc. (PINK:FLMS) Very little is known about China-based FLM Minerals Inc. The company had no ore bodies as of Nov. 30, 2008, although they do mention an agreement with Altair Minerals, which gives FLM mineral exploration rights to four claims. The location of those claims and whether or not they're still valid is unknown. Website n/a

Foran Mining Corp. (PINK:FMCXF) Foran Mining Corporation's flagship McIlvenna Bay Project in Saskatchewan shows an indicated mineral resource of 6.7 million tonnes grading 0.87% copper, 6.51% zinc and 26.0 g/t silver and a further 6.0 million tonnes grading 0.83% copper, 5.89% zinc and 24.8 g/t silver in the inferred category. http://www.foranmining.com/

Fortress Minerals Co. (PINK:FTMNF) Fortress Minerals Corp. is exploring Russia for gold and base metals projects. There hasn't been much news from the company since they reported the start of drilling at their Malmyzh project (a prospective copper-gold project), which was acquired through a 51% Share Purchase Agreement with Freeport-McMoRan Exploration Corporation. That drilling intersected 414.2m grading 0.36% copper and 0.07 g/t gold including 102.8m grading 0.58% copper and 0.15 g/t gold for a copper equivalent of 0.66%. http://www.fortressminerals.com/

Fortune Minerals Ltd. (PINK:FTMDF) Fortune Minerals Limited is slated to have two producing mines up and running in 2014: NICO in the Northwest Territories (which contains gold, cobalt, bismuth and copper) and the Mount Klappan project in British Columbia (anthracite coal). Mt. Klappan shows 107.9 million tonnes measured coal, 123 million indicated tonnes and 359.5 million inferred tonnes. The NICO project has proven and probable reserves of 907,000 ounces gold, 82 million pounds cobalt, 109 million pounds bismuth and 27 million pounds copper (per ResourceClips.com). http://www.fortuneminerals.com/

Franklin Mining, Inc. (PINK:FMNJ) On Oct. 13, 2011, Franklin Mining, Inc. announced its first sale and shipment of gold-bearing ore from its Escala Mine in Bolivia. Entitled to 50 percent of the mine, Escala is expected to produce 2,000-5,000 tonnes of ore per day. Grades are unknown, but the company plans to "disclose the details shortly." http://www.franklinmining.com/

Freegold Ventures Limited (PINK:FGOVF) Freegold Ventures Limited completed an NI 43-101 compliant resource on its Dolphin Zone deposit in Golden Summit, Alaska. That showed 174,000 indicated ounces of gold and 526,000 ounces inferred. Phase I drilling has kicked off at the site with highlights of 207.4 m at 1 g/t gold and 24.8m at 34.7 g/t gold. The company's

Vinasale project, also in Alaska, shows an inferred resource of 1.33 million ounces of gold. http://www.freegoldventures.com/

Full Metal Minerals (PINK:FLMTF) Full Metal Minerals Ltd. has joint venture agreements with Anglo American/Northern Dynasty Minerals and Antofagasta Minerals on the strength of the company's three main projects: The Pyramid Porphyry Project, the Rolling Thunder Property and the 40 Mile Property, all of which are in Alaska or Yukon. 2011 highlights from the Pyramid Project include intercepts of 155.94m of 0.97% copper equivalent and 117.54m of 0.81% copper equivalent. http://www.fullmetalminerals.com/

GWR Resources Inc. (PINK:GWRRF) GWR Resources Inc. is focused on two gold projects in Canada: 1) Lac La Hache in British Columbia; and 2) Sainte Sabine in Quebec. Recent drilling at their flagship Lac La Hache project "intersected variable widths exceeding 0.5% copper with a maximum value in hole SL11-117 of 2.23% copper (plus 0.34 g/t gold, 9.2 g/t silver) over 2m, within a wider true thickness grading 0.7% copper over 12m." http://www.gwrresources.com/

Galore Resources Inc. (PINK:GALOF) Exploration is underway at Galore Resources Inc.'s Dos Santos project in Mexico. They're focused on two targets there: the El Alamo Target, which has shown results as high as 54m of 0.97 g/t gold, and the Los Gemelos Target, which has shown assay results up to 34.3 g/t gold over 1.7m. http://www.galoreresources.com/

Galway Resources Ltd. (PINK:GWYRF) Galway Resources Ltd. is focused on gold and silver projects in Columbia and the Victorio Molybdenum-Tungsten Project in New Mexico. A preliminary NI 43-101 resource estimate on the California project in Columbia is expected in Q1 2012. The Vetas property in Columbia is also promising with results including 21.9 g/t gold over 6.7m, 82.4 g/t gold over 2.7m, 9.7 g/t gold over 9.4m and 138.0 g/t gold over 1.1m. http://www.galwayresources.com/

General Metals Corp. (OTC:GNMT) General Metals' Independence Project in Nevada is surrounded by Newmont Gold's Phoenix Mine holdings. The Independence Mine was in operation from 1938-1987 and produced 750,000+ ounces of silver and 11,000+ ounces of gold. "Current NI 43-101 compliant resource estimate stands at 207,500 ounces of gold and 3.6 million ounces of silver in measured and indicated resource categories, with additional inferred resources of 65,500 ounces of gold and 268,000 ounces of silver," the company writes. http://www.generalmetalscorporation.com/

Geo Minerals Ltd. (PINK:GMNRF) Gold producer New Gold (TSE:NGD) announced on Oct. 17, 2011, that it will pay $17 million cash, or 16 cents per share, to acquire Geo Minerals (CVE:GM). The deal was a 33% premium to company's closing price of 12 cents at the time of the announcement. New Gold will retain Geo's Blackwater gold project. http://www.geominerals.ca/

Geologix Explorations Inc. (PINK:GXEXF) Geologix Explorations Inc. is targeting production by 2014 at the company's Tepal Gold-Copper Porphyry Project in Michoacán State, Mexico. A pre-feasibility study is underway. Currently, the project shows an indicated resource of 311.1 million pounds of copper and 800,000 ounces of gold (at .42 g/t). The project also shows an inferred resource of 800,000 ounces of gold (at .28 g/t) and 414.8 million pounds of copper. http://www.geologix.ca/

Geopulse Exploration Inc. (OTC:GPLS) Geopulse is exploring gold, silver, copper and potash properties in Mexico, Ecuador, Colombia and the United States. In May, the company acquired rights to land in the La Sal Mountains region of San Juan County, Utah, an area rife with gold and copper deposits. The company also holds rights to the past-producing Lisbon Valley Copper Mine. At full production, Lisbon Valley was producing over 27,000 tonnes of copper ore annually. http://www.geopulseinc.com/

Ginguro Exploration Inc. (PINK:GNGXF) Ginguro Exploration Inc. is focused on exploring two properties: 1) the Pardo Property in Ontario; and 2) the El Alto Property in San Felipe, Chile. Initial grab sampling at the Pardo property shows "several samples >1 g/t" gold. A recent drill hole at El Alto intersected 28.88m of mineralization grading 0.5% copper, 18.8% iron and 1.8 g/t silver. http://www.ginguro.com/

Giyani Gold Corp. (PINK:CATPF) Formerly 99 Capital Corporation, Giyani Gold Corp. changed its name to emphasize a strategic shift toward gold exploration. The company is exploring the Giyani Greenstone Belt in South Africa, and in June 2011, acquired a 74 percent interest in the historic Madonsi Gold Mine for $2 million. An NI 43-101 technical report is forthcoming, but the quality of the remaining deposit is unknown. http://www.giyanigold.com/

Glass Earth Gold Ltd. (PINK:GELGF) New Zealand-based Glass Earth Gold is actively producing 2,500 ounces of gold a year with the potential to expand to 7,500 ounces a year in 2012. A joint venture with Newmont could give Glass Earth a cut of the 10 million ounce Waihi Martha Hill Mine. The company also owns 100 percent of the rights to the 390,000 ounce (1.5 g/t) deposit at Muirs Reef. The area has the potential to hold more than 1 million ounces according to the company. http://www.glassearthgold.com/

Glen Eagle Resources Inc. (PINK:GERFF) Glen Eagle Resources Inc. shows an indicated resource of 4.1 million tonnes of ore containing 1.04% lithium at its Authier lithium project. The property also holds an inferred resource of 2.2 million tonnes of ore at 1% lithium. The company's Souart project shows estimated historical resources (non NI 43-101 compliant) of 110,000 ounces at 6.17 g/t gold. http://www.gleneagleresources.com/

Global Gold Corp. (PINK:GBGD) Global Gold Corporation is operating three properties in Armenia and holds a 100% interest in an alluvial gold property in Chile. The company's biggest gold project in Armenia (Toukhmanuk) is on schedule to produce 130,000 ounces of gold per year within 3 years at a cash cost of approximately $350 per ounce. The Global Gold Valdivia property in Chile contains an estimated 7.4 million ounces of gold. Production there could hit 200,000 ounces per year by 2012. http://www.globalgoldcorp.com/

EDITOR'S PICK: *Global Minerals Ltd. (PINK:GMLFF)* Why we like it: Sitting on 23 million ounces of silver and 78 million pounds of copper. Global Minerals Ltd.'s flagship property is the Strieborna silver/copper project in Roznava, Slovakia. The site contains 14.3 million ounces of silver and 48.1 million pounds of copper in the measured and indicated categories plus an additional 8.7 million silver ounces and 29.8 million pounds of copper in the inferred category. Esperanza Resources Corp. has a 28 percent stake in property. http://www.globalminerals.com/

Global Security Agency Inc. (OTC:GSAG) Formerly a precious metals exploration company known as Belvedere Resources Corporation, Global Security Agency Inc. took on the name of a subsidiary. Since then, it appears the company has concluded exploring on its Spanish Gold property and focused instead on security services unrelated to mining. http://www.globalsecurityagency.org/

GMV Minerals Inc. (PINK:GMVMF) GMV Minerals Inc. holds rights to 535,000 acres in Guyana, South America. The properties are all located in close proximity to major South American deposits including Las Cristinas and Las Brisas. The company is in the process of identifying targets on its claims. Sampling grades were unknown at the time of this writing. http://www.gmvminerals.com/

Gogold Resources Inc. (PINK:GLGDF) Gogold Resources Inc. commenced drilling at its San Diego Project in Durango, Mexico, on August 15th, 2011. Recent drill results have shown 95m of 1.48 g/t gold equivalent. The company hopes to generate a resource at its Breccia Hill target by 2012. http://www.gogoldresources.com/

Gold American Mining Corp. (OTC:SILA) A partnership with Yale Resources Ltd. gives Gold American Mining Corp. a 90 percent interest in two mining concessions in Zacatecas State, Mexico. Exploration on the property began on June 30, 2011, and is expected to continue through the end of 2013 so long as the validity of the mining claims stands. The company's website is "under construction" and investors have no information on the quality of its deposits. http://www.gold-american.com/

EDITOR'S PICK: *Gold Canyon Resources Inc. (PINK:GDCRF)* Why we like it: An initial resource estimate is on its way. Gold Canyon Resources Inc.'s Springpole Gold Project in Ontario is working on an initial resource estimate. Drilling there has shown samples up to 45 ounces of gold per ton. Results announced in December 2011 showed Gold Canyon had intersected 257m at 1.48 g/t gold at Springpole. "We are big believers in this deposit," Marshall Auerback of Pinetree Capital told BusinessInsider.com recently. "The initial resource should be out by the end of this year (2011) and is promising to be several million ounces with grades exceeding most other bulk tonnage deposits in Canada." http://www.goldcanyon.ca/

EDITOR'S PICK: *Gold Fields Ltd. (NYSE:GFI)* Why we like it: Suring earnings. Gold Fields produces 3.5 million gold equivalent ounces from eight mines spanning from South Africa to Australia and Peru. All told, the company has gold equivalent reserves of 76.7 million ounces. Things look great in the near-term. Gold Fields was expected to grow earnings by 155 percent in 2011, per Forbes. http://www.goldfields.co.za/

Gold Reach Resources (PINK:GRVJF) Gold Reach Resources is exploring two properties in British Columbia: 1) the 19,000 hectare Ootsa Property and 2) the 22,319 hectare Auro Property. Ootsa is adjacent to the copper producing Huckleberry Mine and has shown 86 million tonnes of porphyry (copper/moly) mineralization. Auro lies next to Richfield Ventures Ltd.'s Blackwater Gold Project. Gold Reach is in the early stages of exploration as it's attempting to identify targets at both sites. http://www.goldreachresources.com/

Gold Reserve Inc. (AMEX:GRZ) Gold Reserves' Brisas deposit in Venezuela is locked up in the courts. The massive deposit has reserves of 10.2 million ounces of gold and 1.4 billion pounds of copper. Hugo Chavez's ban on gold exports could keep that ore out of Gold Reserves' hands. The case is currently pending at the World Bank. http://www.goldreserveinc.com/

EDITOR'S PICK: *Gold Resource Corp. (AMEX:GORO)* Why we like it: Aggressively buying back shares. With mines in Mexico, Gold Resource Corporation swung to a profit in Q2 2011. Faced with slumping share prices, the company also bought back $20 million in shares in 2011. Gold Resource's flagship El Aguila Project commenced commercial production July 1, 2010. Drilling there has yielded a 36 g/t gold sample and a 3,100 g/t silver sample. http://www.goldresourcecorp.com/

Gold World Resources Inc. (PINK:GLWDF) Gold World Resources Inc. is focused on exploring the Mount Anderson Yukon gold/silver, polymetallic Project. The company believes the property includes a body of mineralization that is more than 6,000 meters across with a gold-enriched core that's 1,750m by 400m wide. Grab sampling has returned grades of 10.7 g/t gold, 1,554 g/t silver, 3.27% copper, 47.63% lead and 8.92% zinc. http://www.goldworldresources.com/

Goldbank Mining Corp. (PINK:GLBKF) Goldbank Mining Corporation bumped up its stake in the Leota Gold Property in Yukon to 75 percent on Oct. 7, 2011, when the company issued an additional 3 million shares to vendors. Goldbank is in the early stages of exploration on its Leota Gold Property in the Yukon. Soil samples were unknown at the time of this writing. http://www.goldbankmining.com/

Goldcliff Resource Corp. (PINK:GCFFF) Goldcliff Resource Corporation is exploring for gold, silver and base metals in British Columbia. Surface samples at the company's Copper Mountain Mine have graded as high as 0.655% copper and 1.3 g/t silver. The company kicked off new silver exploration at its Ainsworth project in August 2011. http://www.goldcliff.com/

EDITOR'S PICK: *Goldcorp Inc. (NYSE:GG)* Why we like it: Stability from a major; Monthly dividends. A gigantic company with more than 11,500 employees, Goldcorp is currently paying out a monthly dividend, and that's good reason to consider holding their shares over gold bullion. Deutsche Bank recently upgraded the stock from a "hold" to a "buy" with a $54 price target, and HSBC gives the stock a $79 price target (per LocalizedUSA). Goldcorp currently holds 62 million ounces of proven and probable gold reserves and 1.3 billion ounces of silver. http://www.goldcorp.com/

Golden Arrow Resources Corp. (PINK:GARWF) Golden Arrow Resources Corporation is already generating cash thanks to royalty income from its 1% NSR on Yamana Gold Corp.'s Gualcamayo Gold mine in San Juan, Argentina. They've also got a JV with Vale on two properties, and they're using that cash to further new exploration projects. Most recently, the company announced chip samples with grades of 11.2% copper, 9.7 g/t gold and 221g/t silver at their 100% owned Don Bosco property in La Rioja Province, Argentina. http://www.goldenarrowresources.com/

Golden Band Resources (PINK:GBRIF) Golden Band Resources Inc. completed its first full quarter of gold production on July 31, 2011. For that quarter, the company produced 10,933 ounces of gold from its 100 percent-owned La Ronge Gold Belt project in Saskatchewan. The deposit has shown measured and indicated gold resources of more than 200,000 ounces. http://www.goldenbandresources.com/

Golden Dawn Minerals Inc. (PINK:GDMRF) Golden Dawn Minerals is exploring the Greenwood Mining District in British Columbia. Already, they've shown an inferred resource estimate of 279,300 troy ounces of gold on the Wild Rose, Tam O'Shanter property there. Further assay results and land-use permits at Tam O'Shanter are expected soon. http://wp.goldendawnminerals.com/

Golden Goliath Resources Ltd. (PINK:GGTHF) Golden Goliath Resources Ltd. has claims on several past-producing gold and silver mines in Mexico. That makes Ian Gordon of Longwave Analytics and Longwave Strategies optimistic about the company's future. "Agnico-Eagle owns about 8% of the company's shares and Sprott Asset management owns a little less than 20%," Gordon told ResourceInvestor.com recently. "The company is working towards a joint venture agreement with Agnico-Eagle on its Las Bolas property." Drilling below the Las Bolas Tunnel hit 1.235m of 3,735 g/t silver recently. http://www.goldengoliath.com/

EDITOR'S PICK: *Golden Minerals Company (AMEX:AUMN)* Why we like it: More than 200 million ounces of silver. A junior silver producer, Golden Minerals has 25 million ounces of measured and indicated silver and 187 million ounces of inferred silver in the ground. Tack onto that 1.8 million ounces of inferred gold, 1 billion pounds of inferred lead and 1.24 billion pounds of inferred zinc, and you've got an interesting company with operations mainly focused in Mexico and South America. The company recently brought in $30.6 million in a private offering of common stock. http://www.goldenminerals.com/

Golden Peaks Resources (PINK:GDPEF) Golden Peaks Resources Ltd. has been busy. The company recently acquired Reliance Resources Limited, an Australian company which owns mineral properties located in Indonesia. Indonesia is the company's main digging ground, and Golden Peaks' most advanced project there is the Tanoyan on Sulawesi Island. The project has an inferred gold resource estimate of 91,100 ounces of gold at a grade of 1.3 g/t. http://www.goldenpeaks.com/

Golden Phoenix Minerals, Inc. (OTC:GPXM) Golden Phoenix appears to have re-aligned itself as a mining royalty company. Their stated objective is to analyze up to 50 prospective properties, narrow those down to five projects that can be advanced toward production, then invest in the startup of those projects. The company would retain up to a 30 percent interest leveraged to the price of gold in each of those projects. One of Golden Phoenix's partners (Scorpio Gold) recently uncovered initial drill results grading 15.85 g/t gold over 3.05m (per MarketWire). http://goldenphoenix.us/

EDITOR'S PICK: *Golden Predator Corp. (PINK:GPRXF)* Why we like it: Moving toward a production decision. Golden Predator Corp.'s flagship Brewery Creek Project in the Yukon is moving toward a production decision. The former mine site produced 278,484 ounces of gold between 1996 and 2002 before shutting down due to low gold prices. Ongoing drilling at the site is identifying new targets. Recent holes have intersected grades as high as 26.72m of 1.28 g/t gold and 21.56 g/t silver from a depth of 66.24m. http://www.goldenpredator.com/

Golden Reign Resources Ltd. (PINK:GRGNF) Golden Reign Resources, Ltd. has optioned the San Albino-Murra Gold Concession in north central Nicaragua. Several drill holes there have returned promising gold intervals including: 3.83m of 24.98 g/t gold and 17.65 g/t silver and 2m of 39.30 g/t gold and 21.0 g/t silver. http://www.goldenreignresources.com/

Golden River Resources Corp. (OTC:GORV) Currently exploring claims in Nova Scotia and Nunavut, Canada, Golden River Resources holds a 71.48% interest in Acadian Mining Corporation. Acadian has a portfolio of 70,000 hectares in Nova Scotia. Acadian's Beaver Dam property shows nearly 160,000 ounces of measured and indicated gold per the company's latest estimates. http://www.goldenriverresources.com/

EDITOR'S PICK: *Golden Star Resources Ltd. (AMEX:GSS)* Why we like it: Growing revenue in Ghana. Golden Star Resources' operations are primarily concentrated in Ghana, West Africa. The company's Wassa mine there had 830,000 ounces of proven and probable gold reserves at the start of 2011.

The company generated $125 million in revenue during the 3 months ending Sept. 30, 2011. http://www.gsr.com/

Golden Tag Resources Ltd. (PINK:GTAGF) Drilling is underway at Golden Tag Resources Ltd.'s San Diego Joint Venture Project in Durango State, Mexico. An agreement with Golden Minerals Company gives Golden Tag a 50 percent stake in San Diego. A recently completed NI 43-101 resource estimate showed an indicated resource of 4,250,000 ounces of silver equivalent and an inferred resource of 214,300,000 ounces silver equivalent. http://www.goldentag.ca/

Golden Touch Resources Corp. (PINK:GNHRF) Golden Touch Resources Corp. recently anointed a new CEO in Ken Chapple, the former chief geologist for Union Resources. Golden Touch is actively exploring three projects in Albania, most notably in the Rubik Gold District where a recent drill hole intersected 37m of gold mineralization averaging 1.67 g/t gold from 63–100m. http://www.goldentouchresources.com/

Golden Valley Mines (PINK:GLVMF) Golden Valley Mines Ltd. holds a 66.3% interest in Abitibi Royalties Inc., a 70.4% interest in Nunavik Nickel Mining Ltd. and a 37.6% interest in Uranium Valley Mines Ltd. That's part of the company's growth strategy as it acquires mining targets, then finds partners to carry on exploration. Golden Valley is currently exploring the Abitibi Greenstone Belt in Ontario. http://www.goldenvalleymines.com/

Goldrich Mining Company (OTC:GRMC) Goldrich Mining Company owns 100 percent of the Alaskan Chandalar property. In 2009, the company installed a test mine on the property and successfully produced 1,500 ounces of gold there a year later. Further drilling is planned on the company's 7,000 hectares. http://www.goldrichmining.com/

Goldsands Development Co. (OTC:GSDC) Goldsands is actively exploring some 175 square miles of land that hugs the Maranon river system in Peru. "This immense braided river system has the potential of developing into a multi-million ounce world class dredging operation," according to the company's senior technical consultant. Test mining could start as early as 2012. http://www.goldsandsco.com/

Gowest Gold Ltd. (PINK:GWSAF) Gowest Gold Ltd. is focused on developing its North Timmins Gold Project in Timmins, Ontario. The project includes the 100 percent-owned Frankfield East gold deposit, which contains an NI 43-101 resource of 1.2 million ounces of +6 g/t gold (348,000 oz. indicated ounces plus 839,000 ounces inferred). Drilling in 2011 should increase the deposit's indicated ounces. http://www.gowestgold.com/

EDITOR'S PICK: *Great Basin Gold Ltd. (AMEX:GBG)* Why we like it: 30 million ounces of gold and a COO from Gold Fields Limited. Great Basin Gold recently named Dana Roets as COO. Roets comes from Gold Fields Limited (NYSE:GFI) - a $10 billion company. Great Basin has two emerging mines (one in Nevada and one in West Africa) with a total resource base of 23.4 million gold ounces and 7.3 million gold ounce reserves. http://www.greatbasingold.com/

EDITOR'S PICK: *Great Panther Silver Ltd. (AMEX:GPL)* Why we like it: An early-stage silver producer. Great Panther already has two silver mines in production in Mexico. Cash costs per ounce of silver range from $6.50 to $7.50 per ounce,. and the company currently has CA$38 million on hand. Great Panther's Guanajuato property contains 5.46 million ounces of measured and indicated silver equivalent and 2.77 million ounces of inferred silver. http://www.greatpanther.com/

Great Quest Metals Ltd. (PINK:GQMLF) Great Quest Metals Ltd. is exploring for phosphate and gold in Mali, West Africa. The company's two gold projects, Sanoukou and Bourdala, cover 254 sq km in the western Mali gold belt. Great Quest appears to be increasingly focusing on phosphate deposits. Grab samples from the Tin Hina concession ranged from 5.11-33.05% phosphate. http://www.greatquest.com/

Guyana Frontier Mining Corp. (OTC:SHESF) Guyana Frontier Mining Corp. is exploring for gold in Guyana, where the company holds interests in more than 320,000 acres. The Company's flagship property is the Marudi Mountain Project where new diamond drilling is underway. A historical hole at the site was re-confirmed to grade 2.61 g/t gold over 151.80m and 2.96 g/t gold over 111.05m in July 2011. http://www.guyanafrontier.com/

Guyana Goldfields Inc. (PINK:GUYFF) Guyana Goldfields Inc. holds 5.71 million ounces of measured and indicated gold resources. That's thanks to their Aurora gold project in Guyana, South America. On Oct. 5, 2011, the company announced it had signed a memorandum with the Guyana government, which should soon lead to a mining agreement. A feasibility study for the project is expected early in 2012. http://www.guygold.com/

Habanero Resources (PINK:HBNRF) Habanero Resources Inc. is in the early stages of exploring two projects: 1) The White Gold Prospect in the Tintina gold province in the Yukon; and 2) the Haldane Silver Prospect in the Keno

Hill Silver district of the Yukon. Habanero also has land holdings prospective for lithium in Alberta and has significant acreage in the Alberta Oil sands. Grades on Habanero's projects were unknown at the time of this writing. http://www.habaneroresources.com/

Hana Mining Ltd. (PINK:HNMFF) Hana Mining Ltd. is developing its Ghanzi Copper-Silver Project in Botswana, Africa. An NI 43-101 technical report estimates that the project has indicated resources of 762.3 million pounds of copper and 16.1 million ounces of silver from 37.4 million tonnes. A new technical report is in the works. http://www.hanamining.com/

Handy and Harman Ltd. (NASDAQ:HNH) A diversified global company, Handy and Harman operates in five business segments, one of which includes precious metals. Their Lucas-Milhaupt division fabricates brazing alloys (typically using gold, silver, palladium and base metals) for a wide range of industries. The company doesn't profit off the purchase and resale of precious metals, but rather the fabrication of specialty parts. Investors shouldn't think of the company as a play on precious metals. http://www.handyharman.com/

Happy Creek Minerals (PINK:HPYCF) Happy Creek Minerals Ltd. is exploring for copper, molybdenum, tungsten, gold and silver, in British Columbia, Canada. The company has two main projects: the Cariboo Properties and the Rateria Property. Both projects are in the early stages of exploration, though initial drilling has shown results of 120m of 0.38% copper starting at the surface, 95m of 0.67% copper, 3.6 g/t silver and 250m of 0.25% copper. http://www.happycreekminerals.com/

EDITOR'S PICK: *Harmony Gold Mining Co. (NYSE:HMY)* Why we like it: Expanding reserves, more than 200 million ounces of gold in the ground. Harmony produced 1.43 million ounces of gold last year. The company mines predominantly in South Africa and Papua New Guinea although its recently looked at new projects in the Philippines. As of June 2010, the company held mineral reserves of 48.1 million ounces and mineral resources of 189.2 million ounces. http://www.harmony.co.za/

Harte Gold Corp. (PINK:HRTFF) Harte Gold Corp.'s flagship Sugar Zone Property in Ontario contains an NI 43-101 compliant indicated resource of 1,117,000 tonnes grading 8.41 g/t gold for 302,000 ounces and an inferred resource of 417,000 tonnes grading 7.13 g/t (95,000 ounces). Harte currently owns a 49% interest in the property with the option to acquire the remaining 51%. http://www.hartegold.com/

Heatherdale Resources Ltd. (PINK:HTRRF) On Oct. 26, 2011, Heatherdale Resources Ltd. announced it was buying Niblack Mineral Development Inc. (TSX:NIB) in a deal worth $10.4 million. The deal gives Heatherdale access to the Niblack Project, a copper-gold-zinc-silver project in Alaska. As of March 2011, Niblack shows an indicated resource of 308,000 ounces gold, 207 million pounds of zinc and 5.1 million ounces of silver as well as an inferred resource of 142,000 ounces of gold, 126 million pounds zinc and 2.1 million ounces silver. http://www.heatherdaleresources.com/

EDITOR'S PICK: *Hecla Mining Company (NYSE:HL)* Why we like it: Negative cash costs; High-volume stock. A silver-focused miner that's expected to see double-digit earnings growth in 2012, Hecla recently linked its dividend payout to the price of silver. If silver averages $30 an ounce, Hecla will pay $0.01 per share and go up from there (per Forbes). Last year alone, the company produced 10.6 million ounces of silver at an average total cash cost of negative $1.46 per ounce. http://www.hecla-mining.com/

EDITOR'S PICK: *Huldra Silver Inc. (PINK:HUSIF)* Why we like it: Coeur d'Alene holds a 7% interest in Huldra. Coeur d'Alene recently took a 7 percent interest in Huldra Silver Inc. on the strength of Huldra's high-grade Treasure Mountain silver property in British Columbia. Huldra's already processing ore from Treasure Mountain and expects to be in full production by Q1 2012. The deposit contains an indicated 880,000 ounces silver, 3,030,000 pounds of lead and 2,760,000 pounds zinc (on top of an inferred resource of 3.5 million ounces of silver). http://www.huldrasilver.com/

Huntmountain Resources Ltd. (PINK:HNTM) HuntMountain Resources Ltd. holds a majority stake in Hunt Mining Corp., which is exploring projects in the Santa Cruz province, Argentina. The La Josefina Gold-Silver Project is the company's flagship property with a preliminary economic assessment underway. Assays at the site have graded as high as 12.2m of 23 g/t gold, 3.1m of 94.44 g/t gold and 56.6 g/t silver. http://www.huntmining.com/

Hy Lake Gold Inc. (PINK:HYLKF) Hy Lake Gold Inc. owns the rights to 3,300 hectares in west Red Lake, Ontario, and it's property that includes three past-producing gold mines. The grades at those mines ranged historically from 0.65 ounces to 1.82 ounces per tone. Hy Lake is digging further with Goldcorp at the company's JV Rowan Property. Recent results there intersected a 6m zone of 69.34 g/t gold with three high-grade intercepts: 362 g/t gold, 34.50 g/t gold and 16.90 g/t gold, each over 1m. http://www.hylake.com/

EDITOR'S PICK: *IAMGOLD Corp.* *(NYSE:IAG)* Why we like it: Looking to spend $1 billion on new gold assets. IAMGOLD made headlines recently on news that the company's ramping up to invest as much as $1 billion to add to its portfolio of gold assets. The company will focus in the Americas and, perhaps, West Africa (per Reuters). IAMGOLD expected to produce 870,000-930,000 ounces of gold in 2011. http://www.iamgold.com/

Imperial Metals Corp. *(PINK:IPMLF)* Imperial Metals Corporation generated $69.4 million in revenue during the quarter ended September 2011. The explorer/producer is regularly shipping concentrate from its Mount Polley and Huckleberry mines in British Columbia. Mount Polley is producing 20,000 tonnes per day and has a reserve estimate of 309.1 million pounds copper and 386,000 ounces gold with a mine life through Q3 2016. The Huckleberry mine is producing 15,000 tonnes per day. http://www.imperialmetals.com/

Indigo Exploration Inc. *(PINK:IGXEF)* Indigo Exploration Inc. is currently exploring for gold in Burkina Faso, West Africa. Early drilling at the company's Moule Project has shown promise, and the company expected to drill 20,000m (150+ holes) in 2011. Drill results were unknown at the time of this writing. http://www.indigoexploration.com/

Integra Gold Corp. *(PINK:KALRF)* Integra Gold Corp.'s shares shot up 33 percent on Nov. 16, 2011, when the company upgraded its resource estimates for its flagship Lamaque Gold project in Val d'Or, Quebec by 40 percent. The NI 43-101 compliant resource increased the total resource at Lamaque to 518,643 ounces inferred and 162,962 ounces indicated. http://www.integragold.com/

International Minerals Corp. *(PINK:IMZLF)* International Minerals Corporation owns a 40 percent stake in the Pallancata silver-gold mine in Peru. 2009 production at the mine was expected to reach 7 million ounces of silver and 25,000 ounces of gold. On Dec 19, 2011, the company released a preliminary economic assessment for its 100%-owned Converse gold deposit in Nevada. The site could return a pre-tax non-discounted cash flow of approximately $494 million over a 14 year mine-life assuming production of 217 million tonnes at 0.52 g/t gold and 3.9 g/t silver. All told the company claims 12.3 million ounces gold equivalent resources in 6 properties. http://www.intlminerals.com/

EDITOR'S PICK: *International PBX Ventures Ltd.* *(PINK:IPBXF)* Why we like it: An NI 43-101 Technical Report is in the works. International PBX Ventures Ltd. is exploring for gold, silver, copper and molybdenum in Chile.

The Copaquire project contains 308 million pounds of in-situ molybdenum and 1.2 billion pounds of in-situ copper surrounded by a large porphyry copper system (sulfato) with grades of up to 2% copper. An NI 43-101 report is underway. http://www.internationalpbx.com/

International Silver Inc. *(PINK:ISLV)* International Silver, Inc. holds the rights to explore the historic Prince Mine in Nevada. The former silver mine reportedly contains over 2 million tons of historically measured in-situ ore-grade mineralization accessible through existing workings, according to the company. International Silver also has interests in the Leviathon Mine in California, which has an inferred mineral resource historically stated to be 1,800,000 tons with a grade of 1.6 ounces of silver and 60% barite. http://internationalsilverinc.com/

EDITOR'S PICK: *International Tower Hill Mines Ltd.* *(AMEX:THM)* Why we like it: A potential takeover target? International Tower Hill was one of six companies recently named to Mining MarketWatch Journal's "Top Takeover Targets" (per Baystreet.ca). That's largely due to its massive Livengood Surface Mine where the company holds 20 million ounces of measured, indicated and inferred gold. A prefeasibility study is expected in the first half of 2012. http://www.ithmines.com/

INV Metals Inc. *(PINK:ILNLF)* INV Metals Inc. is exploring for precious and base metals in Brazil, Namibia and Ontario. The company's Okohongo target in Nambia shows an inferred resource of 10.2 million tonnes at 1.12% copper and 17.75 g/t silver. That's good for $1.2 billion in situ value. The company plans to spend $3 million exploring its potential iron-oxide-copper-gold deposit at Rio Novo, Brazil. http://www.invmetals.com/

EDITOR'S PICK: *Ireland Inc.* *(OTC:IRLD)* Why we like it: Shares up more than 5,000% over the past five years. Ireland Inc. is focused on its Columbus Project in Nevada. The company has outlined seven mineralized zones there with a total inferred geological resource of 343.9 million tons with an average grade of 0.040 opt gold equivalent (calculated at gold plus .013 silver). http://www.irelandminerals.com/

Iron Creek Capital Corp. *(PINK:INCKF)* Iron Creek Capital Corp. is exploring for copper, gold and silver in Chile. The company has joint ventures With Andina Minerals and Hochschild Mining as it explores the Dominador Fault Zone in Chile. Right now, the company is focused on drilling near Yamana's El Penon and Fortuna deposits (which hold 7 million+ ounces gold and 200 million+ ounces silver). Vein float samples have returned values from trace up to 9.97g/t gold and 22.4g/t silver. http://www.ironcreekcapital.com/

EDITOR'S PICK: *Jaguar Mining Inc. (NYSE:JAG)* Why we like it: Nearing production in Brazil. With gold mining operations focused in Brazil, Jaguar Mining has measured and indicated gold resources of 6.2 million ounces and 1.5 million inferred ounces. The company's goal is be producing 400,000 ounces of gold per year by 2013. http://www.jaguarmining.com/

Jasper Mining Corp. (PINK:JAMGF) Jasper Mining Corporation is exploring more than 15 properties for precious and base metals in British Columbia. Efforts seem to be focused on the company's Isintok property, although, Jasper has went back and forth on whether or not they're working on an NI 43-101 technical report for the project. "Conceptual" quantity and grades range from 50 million to 110 million tonnes of .12 percent copper and 0.03 g/t gold. Those conceptual numbers have drawn heat from regulators. http://www.jaspermining.com/

EDITOR'S PICK: *Jayden Resources, Inc. (PINK:PNMLF)* Why we like it: Expect a prefeasibility study in 2012. Jayden Resources is focused on its gold and silver project in the Stewart Camp in British Columbia. The so-called Silver Coin project is a historic mine that's expected to yield a prefeasibility study in 2012 en route to re-entering production. Over its mine life, the Silbak-Premier Mine produced 4.7 million tons yielding approximately 1.8 million ounces gold, 41 million ounces silver, 4.2 million pounds copper, 62 million pounds lead and 20 million pounds zinc. Recent drill results at the site have graded as high as 7.97 g/t over 14.3m. http://www.jaydenresources.com/

Jinhao Motor Co., Ltd. (PINK:GIMC) Formerly Georgia International Mining Corporation, Jinhao Motor Company appears to have completely changed the company's focus from mining and exploration to manufacturing parts for vehicles. It's unclear whether or not the company retains any mining claims. "From our inception, we were engaged in various business endeavors, including mining. Prior to the end of our fiscal year ended December 31, 2009, we decided to redirect our business focus towards identifying and pursuing options regarding the development of a new business plan and direction," the company wrote in an SEC filing at the start of 2011. Website n/a

Kalimantan Gold Corp. (PINK:KMGLF) Kalimantan Gold Corporation Limited is exploring for copper and gold in Kalimantan, Indonesia, under a joint venture with a subsidiary of Freeport-McMoRan. Exploration is focused on the company's Jelai property, which was explored at one point by an earlier incarnation of Ivanhoe Mines. Recent drill holes there have shown grades as high as 5.6 g/t gold over an interval of 5.6m. http://www.kalimantan.com/

EDITOR'S PICK: *Kaminak Gold Corp. (PINK:KMKGF)* Why we like it: Analyst approved. Kaminak Gold Corporation holds prospective land in the Yukon. The company's Coffee Gold Project "could become a low-cost, multimillion-ounce deposit in an emerging new gold camp," according to Rob Chang, an analyst at Versant Partners. Drill results have ranged from 15.5m at 17.1 g/t gold to 83.93m at 1.08 g/t gold to 35m at 6.3 g/t gold. A resource estimate has not yet been defined. http://kaminak.com/

Karmin Exploration Inc. (PINK:KRMEF) Karmin Exploration Inc. is exploring for gold and base metals in Brazil. The company's Aripuana Property shows indicated and inferred resources of 21,850 tonnes of concentrate at a grade of 4+ percent zinc, .18 to .25 g/t gold and 33-41 g/t silver. http://www.karmin.com/

Kat Gold Holdings Corp. (PINK:BVTG) Kat Gold Holdings Corporation acquired 100 percent of the mineral rights to the Handcamp gold and base metal property in Newfoundland, Canada, in 2010. Rock samples from the property have shown grades as high as 158 g/t gold. The president of KAT Gold Holdings Corp., Ken Stead, also heads up the Canadian company Kat Exploration Inc. Website n/a

EDITOR'S PICK: *Keegan Resources Inc. (AMEX:KGN)* Why we like it: More than 5 million ounces in West Africa. A disappointing pre-feasibility study at Keegan's Esaase gold project in West Africa has punished shares. And yet the deposit holds 3.64 million ounces measured and indicated and 1.55 million ounces inferred. Higher than expected cash costs may have frightened some investors, but I don't expect they'll stay gone for good. http://www.keeganresources.com/

Kenai Resources Ltd. (PINK:KAIFF) Kenai Resources Ltd.'s Sao Chico gold project in Brazil has shown average gold grades of 17.7 g/t, and the company's working on an updated NI 43-101 on the project now. A decision on whether or not to move ahead is expected in September 2012. The company's also exploring the Hope Butte gold project in Oregon - a site that shows historical resource estimates of 8 million tons of mineralized material with a grade of 0.94 g/t gold. http://kenairesources.net/

Key Gold Holding Inc. (PINK:KGHZF) Key Gold Holding Inc. is exploring for gold and copper in Quebec. On Dec. 6, 2011, Key Gold appointed Steve Barrett as the Interim President and Chief Executive Officer. The company also announced it would no longer pursue the Souart Gold Property. In another sign that the company is re-focusing its energies, Key Gold's website is under construction. Investors may want to move on until Key Gold announces its new strategy. http://www.keygoldholding.com/

Kilo Goldmines Ltd. (PINK:KOGMF) Kilo Goldmines Ltd. announced an initial inferred resource of 2 million ounces of gold at its Adumbi Deposit in the Democratic Republic of the Congo early in 2011. New drilling continues to show promising results including 7.71 g/t gold over 12.60m. http://www.kilogold.net/

Kimber Resources, Inc. (AMEX:KBX) Kimber's flagship mine, Monterde, is situated in a well-known high-grade silver belt in Mexico. Right now the company's sitting on 510,000 ounces of indicated gold and nearly 20 million ounces of indicated silver (on top of another 10 million inferred ounces of silver). http://www.kimberresources.com/

King's Bay Gold Corp. (PINK:KBGCF) King's Bay Gold Corporation is exploring for gold in Northwest Ontario. Efforts are focused on the Menary Gold Project, which recently returned drill results of 40.52 g/t gold in grab samples. Historical processing of 1,000 tonnes at the site showed grades of 10.73 g/t gold. http://www.kingsbaygold.com/

EDITOR'S PICK: *Kinross Gold Corp. (NYSE:KGC)* Why we like it: "A once-in-a-generation gold discovery." Kinross is sitting on top of what it calls "a once-in-a-generation gold discovery" at its Tasiast project in Mauritania. The company got 100 percent interest in the mine when it acquired Red Back Mining in 2010 at a lofty price upwards of $1,000 an ounce. All told, though, Tasiast alone could hold more than 21 million ounces of gold. Kinross was on pace to produce 2.6 to 2.7 million ounces of gold a year in 2011 and expects to be producing 4.5-4.9 million ounces a year by 2015. http://www.kinross.com/

Kobex Minerals Inc. (AMEX:KXM) Kobex is currently on the prowl for promising exploration properties. The company has $38 million on hand to buy property rights. Landing the right tract of land could send shares higher. The company also holds right in southeast Yukon. http://kobexminerals.com/

La Quinta Resources Corp. (PINK:LQRCF) La Quinta Resources Corporation is actively exploring its Carruthers Pass property in British Columbia. Recent drilling has returned weighted average assays of 2.37 g/t gold, 192 g/t silver, 6.24% copper and 5.87% zinc. The Company is also focused on exploring for gold and silver on the Easter Project and on its Black Jack properties in Nevada. The Easter Project has a base resource of 2.6 million tons at 1.3 g/t gold and 14 g/t silver within an area of gold mineralization with a strike length of at least 6,450 feet with widths up to 90 feet. http://www.laquintaresources.com/

Lake Shore Gold Corp. (AMEX:LSG) Lake Shore aimed to produce 85,000 to 100,000 ounces in 2011 from its Timmins Mine in Ontario. Two more mines are in development, and it's likely they'll enter production soon as it took the company just 2.5 years to get Timmins online. The average grade for the company's ore is 4.16 g/t gold. http://www.lsgold.com/

Lake Victoria Mining Company, Inc. (OTC:LVCA) Lake Victoria Mining Company is currently exploring projects in the Lake Victoria Greenstone Belt in Tanzania, East Africa. Results from the company's Singida-Londoni gold project have graded as high as 37.30 g/t gold over 1m. http://www.lakevictoriaminingcompany.com/

Legend Gold Corp. (OTC:NOATF) Legend Gold Corp. has interests in three gold projects in Mali, West Africa. Drilling is ongoing at all three sites. The company's Tiekoumala deposit alone contains an NI 43-101 compliant resource of 600,000 ounces gold. http://www.legendgold.com/

EDITOR'S PICK: *Levon Resources Ltd. (PINK:LVNVF)* Why we like it: More than 450 million ounces of silver. Levon Resources Ltd. is exploring its Cordero Project in northwest Mexico. The project is promising, with indicated resources of 310 million ounces of silver, 900,000 ounces of gold and inferred resources of 140 million ounces of silver and 229,000 ounces of gold. http://www.levon.com/

Liberty Gold Corp. (OTC:LBGO) Liberty Gold currently holds rights to three properties: the Moneyrock Property in Alaska, the Monte del Favor Property in Mexico and the Domestic Portfolio in Arizona. Arizona holdings are estimated to contain some 9.7 million gold equivalent ounces (including rare earth metals). The Mexico project adds another 4.2 million ounces of gold equivalent resources. http://www.libertygoldcorp.com/

Lincoln Mining Corp. (PINK:LNCLF) Lincoln Mining Corporation is focused on past-producing precious metals projects in California and Nevada.

Specifically, they're pushing their Pine Grove Property in Nevada and the Oro Cruz Property in California toward production. Pine Grove shows an indicated resource of 177,000 ounces of gold at 0.033 ounces per tone, and Oro Cruz shows an inferred gold resource of 341,800 ounces gold at 0.07 ounces per tonne. http://www.lincolnmining.com/

LKA International Inc. (PINK:LKAI) LKA International, Inc.'s Golden Wonder mine near Lake City, Colo., is currently in exploration mode, but its already started generating the company cash from the sale of exploratory ore. The company hopes it will be able to bring the historic Golden Wonder mine back into production. From 1998 through the second quarter of 2006, the Golden Wonder mine produced over 133,701 ounces (82% of which came during the period of 2002-2006) from ore with an average grade of 16.01 ounces (454 g/t) gold. http://www.lkaintl.com/

Loreto Resources Corp. (OTC:LRTC) Loreto Resources purchased Peruvian company Minera Huallanca S.A. in 2009. At the time, Huallanca was operating two mines and producing 500,000 metric tons of mined ore a year. Little more is known about Loreto's current operations, although a Sept. 2, 2011, press release from the company described Loreto as an early-stage oil and gas exploration company (per PRNewsWire). http://www.loretoresources.com/

Lounor Exploration Inc. (PINK:LOUXF) Lounor Exploration Inc. has extensive experience exploring for gold and base metals projects in Canada's Abitibi Greenstone Belt. The company's main focus now is the Harker Gold Property in the Timmins/Kirkland Lake area in Ontario. Early stage drilling has been encouraging with grades as high as 2.66 g/t gold over 5.09m and 5.92 g/t gold over 2.01m. http://www.lounor.com/

Lucky Boy Silver Corp. (PINK:LUCB) There's been little trading or news out of Lucky Boy Silver Corp. recently. The company did announce results in February 2011 from its Silver Strike and Silver Summit Projects in Nevada. Silver, gold and base metal values along a target zone ranged from 249 ppm (7.26 opt) to 11 ppm (0.32 opt) with gold up to 1.25 ppm (0.04 opt). http://www.luckyboysilver.com/

Luna Gold Corp. (PINK:LGCUF) Luna Gold Corp. has been producing gold at its Aurizona Gold Mine in Brazil since Feb. 2011. The property has a 2009 NI 43-101 resource estimate of 909,000 ounces gold measured and indicated and 403,000 ounces inferred and should be producing 60,000 ounces of gold a year in the near-term. By 2013, the company could be producing as much as 100,000 ounces a year. http://www.lunagold.com/

EDITOR'S PICK: *Mag Silver Corp. (AMEX:MVG)* Why we like it: More than 90 million ounces of silver in Mexico. Mag Silver's got 44 percent of the rights to a large silver deposit at its Juanicipio property in Mexico. Resource estimates for the company's share of the deposit show 90 million ounces of indicated and inferred silver and 311,000 ounces of indicated and inferred gold as well as additional lead and zinc. All told, the company's got more than 100 square miles of prospective ground in Mexico. http://www.magsilver.com/

Magellan Minerals (PINK:MAGNF) Two of Magellan Minerals Ltd.'s properties already show impressive gold and silver deposits. The Cuiu Cuiu Deposit and the Coringa Deposit are both based in Brazil. Cuiu Cuiu shows indicated gold reserves of 100,000 ounces and inferred reserves of 1.2 million ounces. Coringa shows indicated resources of 100,000 ounces and 300,000 ounces inferred. http://www.magellanminerals.com/

Malbex Resources Inc. (PINK:MXRSF) Malbex Resources Inc. released a technical report on its gold-silver oxide discovery at Del Carmen in Argentina in September 2011. The report showed 816,600 ounces of contained gold (at 1 g/t) and 10.9 million ounces of contained silver (at 13.3 g/t). The inferred resource puts the total for the project over 1 million ounces of gold. http://www.malbex.ca/

Manitou Gold Inc. (PINK:MNTUF) Manitou Gold Inc. reported positive results from drilling at its Gaffney Extension project in Lower Manitou Lake, Ontario, in October 2011. One hole averaged 18m of 2.6 g/t gold, including a higher grade section of 2.8m at 14.6 g/t gold. Later, the company drilled 75.1m at 2.4 g/t gold at the same site. Manitou also claims "significant ownership by Goldcorp, Inc." http://www.manitougold.com/

Mansfield Minerals Inc. (PINK:MFMNF) Mansfield Minerals Inc.'s flagship project is the Lindero gold deposit which hosts an NI 43-101 compliant gold reserve of 1.92 million ounces of gold within a 2.95 million ounce resource. Lindero is capable of producing 161,000 ounces of gold per year at a cash cost of US$373 over the initial five years of production. http://www.mansfieldminerals.com/

Manson Creek Resources (PINK:MCKRF) Manson Creek Resources Ltd. is focused on the Tell Project in the Yukon and the Virgin Arm Gold Project in Newfoundland. Drilling at the Newfoundland site has returned gold assays ranging from 0.5 g/t gold to more than 10 g/t gold. http://www.manson.ca/

Marifil Mines Ltd. (PINK:MFMLF) Focused on mineral properties in Argentina, Marifil Mines Ltd.'s flagship property is the San Roque project in the Rio Negro province. The property is under a joint venture with NovaGold Resources Inc. NovaGold could earn up to a 70 percent interest in the project. Phase II drilling has returned grades of 143m at 0.74 g/t gold, 27.2 g/t silver, 0.37% lead and 0.55% zinc as well as 11.7m of 174 g/t indium. An NI 43-101 resource report is currently underway. http://www.marifilmines.com/

EDITOR'S PICK: *Maudore Minerals Ltd. (PINK:MAOMF)* Why we like it: Potential for a high-grade deposit in Quebec. Maudore Minerals Ltd. has more than 1.2 million ounces of inferred gold resources in Quebec. Small samples have show high grades of gold including 398.8 g/t gold over 1.3m. http://www.maudore.com/

Maya Gold & Silver Inc. (PINK:MYAGF) Maya Gold & Silver Inc. filed an NI 43-101 technical report on its Amizmiz Gold property in Morocco on Nov. 7, 2011. The total inferred resource for the project stands at 342,094 ounces gold. Recently, the company acquired rights to a historic mine as well at Zgounder (also in Morocco). In 2004, the mine showed historical resources of 582,000 tonnes at 361 g/t silver (good for 7.5 million ounces of silver). http://www.mayagoldsilver.com/

Mazorro Resources Inc. (PINK:MZRRF) Mazorro Resources Inc. entered into an option agreement with Adventure Gold Inc. in December 2010 to acquire up to a 70% interest in the Lapaska property in Quebec. The project has inferred resources of 220,000 metric tonnes grading 3.14 g/t gold for a total of 22,197 ounces at a cut-off grade of 2.0 g/t gold. Exploration is ongoing at the company's other projects. http://www.mazorro.com/

MDN Inc. (PINK:MDNNF) MDN Inc. is profitable thanks to a 30% participating interest in African Barrick Gold's (ABG) Tulawaka gold mine in Tanzania. Tulawaka grew gold production by 29 percent during Q3 2011 to 20,160 ounces. The company also owns a 72.5 percent interest in Crevier Minerals Inc. which owns an NI 43-101 niobium-tantalum resource in the Lac-Saint-Jean area of Quebec. http://www.mdn-mines.com/

Mega Precious Metals Inc. (PINK:MPRXF) Mega Precious Metals Inc. shows measured and indicated gold reserves of 600,000 ounces and another 1.2 million ounces of inferred gold reserves at their Monument Bay project in Manitoba, and they're continuing exploration there with the goal of producing 150,000 ounces a year (at full production) starting in 2014. http://www.megapmi.com/

Merc International Minerals (PINK:MIMZF) Merc International Minerals Inc. holds rights to 84,888 hectares in the Indian Lake Gold Camp in the Northwest Territories, much of which contains historically identified gold deposits. The company's Treasure Island Corridor has shown historical grades from 5.1 g/t gold up to 12.7 g/t gold. Drilling is ongoing. http://www.mercinternational.ca/

Merrex Gold Inc. (PINK:MXGIF) Merrex Gold Inc. has an NI 43-101 resource estimate of 308,200 ounces of gold (2.39 g/t measured and indicated) and 69,500 ounces inferred (2.29 g/t) at their Siribaya Gold Project in Mali, West Africa. Ongoing drilling confirms the "potential for a 2 to 4 million ounce deposit." http://www.merrexgold.com/

Metanor Resources Inc. (PINK:MEAOF) Metanor Resources Inc. is entering into gold production at its Bachelor Lake Mine and Mill in Quebec. In late October 2011 that prompted Industrial Alliance Securities to give the stock a near-term 12 month price target of C$0.95. The company's Barry Project also shows a resource of 771,000 ounces of gold. http://www.metanor.ca/

Mexus Gold U.S. (OTC:MXSG) A partnership with Mexus Gold Mining S.A. DE C.V. gives Mexus Gold U.S. the option to acquire ninety-nine percent of the outstanding shares of Mexus Gold Mining. The agreement was driven by the promise of gold and silver deposits at Mexus Gold Mining's Guadalupe de Ures project in the State of Sonora, Mexico. Mexus is currently awaiting a blasting permit before exploring the property. http://www.mexusgoldus.com/

Microelectronics Technology Co. (PINK:MELY) Microelectronics Technology Company has been all over the map. Formerly named China YouTV Corp., the company was evaluating "an Internet media venture in China" and acquiring mineral claims. Late in 2011, though, the company purchased Cloud Data Corporation and has shifted gears to focus on cloud computing. No word on what happened to the company's mineral claims. http://www.microelectronicstechnology.com/

Midland Exploration Inc. (PINK:MIDLF) The king of joint ventures, Midland Exploration has granted options to some major mining companies including Osisko Mining Corporation, North American Palladium Limited, and Agnico-Eagle Mines Ltd. Should those projects go into production, Midland stands to make a lot of cash. "The company has some $4.5M in cash, which is small, but all of its properties are joint-ventured out, and it has an extremely low burn rate," Adrian Day, an investor who's bullish on the stock, told BusinessInsider.com in a recent interview. "It won't need to raise money this year or next year — and certainly not on arduous terms." http://www.midlandexploration.com/

EDITOR'S PICK: *Midway Gold Corp. (AMEX:MDW)* Why we like it: Momentum on their side with shares up more than 150% in 2011. Midway's Pan Project in Nevada contains 1.13 million ounces of measured and indicated gold. The company has five other gold projects in Nevada, and share prices shot up more than 150 percent in 2011. http://www.midwaygold.com/

Minaurum Gold Inc. (PINK:MMRGF) Minaurum Gold Inc. is advancing a number of gold and silver projects in Mexico. The company announced initial drilling at the Capilla Silver project in Sinaloa state, Mexico, in November 2011. Drilling is ongoing at the company's Aurena project in Oaxaca. So far, the best drill results from Aurena have shown 6.46 g/t gold. http://www.minaurum.com/

EDITOR'S PICK: *Minco Gold Corp. (AMEX:MGH)* Why we like it: Sprott-approved mining in the PRC. Based in Canada, Minco's set its sights on China where the company recently acquired a 1 million-ounce+ gold deposit at Changkeng as well as 13 other promising gold projects. Sprott's among the company's major shareholders. Minco Gold also holds 13 million shares in Minco Silver Corporation. http://www.mincogold.com/

Minefinders Corp. Ltd. (AMEX:MFN) Minefinders is on pace to produce up to 70,000 ounces of gold and 3.5 million ounces of silver from its flagship Dolores Mine in Northern Mexico in 2011. That's just the beginning. The company expects to be able to increase production by 80% to 90% by 2015. http://www.minefinders.com/

Mines Management, Inc. (AMEX:MGN) Mines Management is currently focused on developing its massive Montanore silver/copper project, which the company claims is the largest silver-copper deposit in the U.S. with some 63 million ounces of silver measured, indicated and inferred. Mine Management's market cap per ounce of silver reserves and resources stood at less than $0.30 per ounce at the time of this writing. http://www.minesmanagement.com/

Miranda Gold Corp. (OTC:MRDDF) A network of joint ventures has allowed Miranda Gold Corp. to be active on 12 projects. Earlier this year (2011), the company signed a joint-venture agreement with Agnico-Eagle to explore the Ester Dome project located in Alaska. The company has also built up a portfolio of stock in four other junior mining companies. During 2011 drilling at Angel Wing in Nevada, maximum gold values were 0.3m at 0.045 oz/t gold and maximum silver values were 1.5m of 147 g/t silver. http://www.mirandagold.com/

Monster Mining Corp. (PINK:MMNGF) Monster Mining Corp. is exploring in the Keno Hill area in the Yukon. The company's flagship Keno-Lightning property has not seen enough drilling for a resource calculation. The Caribou vein has returned the best results so far with 116 g/t silver over 2.0m. http://www.monstermining.com/

Moss Lake Gold Mine (PINK:MLGXF) Moss Lake Gold Mines Ltd. is a subsidiary of Wesdome Gold Mines Ltd. Moss Lake holds rights to a low-grade gold deposit in Thunder Bay, Ontario. The deposit shows an inferred resource of 56.1 million tons grading 0.027 oz/ton gold for a total of 1.51 million ounces. http://www.mosslakegold.com/

Mountain Lake Resources Inc. (PINK:MLKRF) Mountain Lake Resources is focused on exploring for gold and base metals in Newfoundland, Canada. The company's Leprechaun Deposit shows a measured and indicated resource of 277,000 ounces of gold and an additional 285,000 ounces of inferred gold. Historic resource estimates at Glover Island show total gold resources north of 250,000 ounces. http://www.mountain-lake.com/

Murgor Resources Inc. (PINK:MGRRF) Murgor Resources Inc. is exploring several of the most prolific mining regions in Canada. Late in 2010, the company acquired up to a 70% interest on the Golden Arrow Gold Mine; a gold deposit that produced 279,000 tons at 2.1 g/t in 1981-82 by open pit. Production was eventually halted due to falling gold prices, but Murgor's continuing to drill there out of the hopes of bringing the mine back online. http://www.murgor.com/

Namibia Rare Earths Inc. (PINK:NMREF) Namibia Rare Earths Inc. is focused on its Lofdal Rare Earths Project in Namibia. The deposit shows high grades of heavy rare earth-enriched carbonatite deposits. A mineral resource should be defined by mid-2012. There's been little news of other exploration projects outside of the REE deposit. http://www.namibiarareearths.com/

Nevada Exploration Inc. (PINK:NVDEF) Nevada Exploration Inc. (NGE) is using a "new and unique exploration technology" that analyzes groundwater chemistry to point toward gold deposits. NGE is in the early stages of exploration on 9 projects covering more than 20,000 hectares in Nevada. In

June 2010, the company entered into a JV agreement with Northgate minerals Corp. on its Awakening Project. Northgate can earn 50 percent by spending $4.1 million on exploration. http://www.nevadaexploration.com/

EDITOR'S PICK: *Nevsun Resources (AMEX:NSU)* Why we like it: Recent stock upgrade. Nevsun's Bisha Mine in Eritrea, East Africa, holds more than 1.14 million ounces of gold, 11.9 million ounces of silver, 821 million pounds of copper, and over 1 billion pounds of zinc. Shares were recently upgraded to a buy at TheStreet. http://www.nevsun.com/

New Dimension Resources (PINK:NWDMF) New Dimension Resources Ltd. is focused on potential bulk tonnage gold and silver deposits throughout North and South America. Phase I exploration kicked off at the Lansing Project in the Yukon in the summer of 2011. Soil samples returned grades as high as 8.32 g/t gold. New Dimension has an option to earn up to a 100% interest in the Lansing Project (as well as the Mars Project) from Strategic Metals. http://www.newdimensionresources.com/

EDITOR'S PICK: *New Gold Inc. (AMEX:NGD)* Why we like it: New mine online soon. New Gold currently has three mines in operation: the Mesquite Mine in the U.S., the Cerro San Pedro Mine in Mexico, and the Peak Gold Mine in Australia. All three combined were expected to produce between 380,000 and 400,000 ounces of gold in 2011. A new mine (New Afton) is scheduled to start adding to their production numbers this year. http://www.newgold.com/

New Guinea Gold Corp. (PINK:NGUGF) At the time of this writing, New Guinea Gold Corp. and PNG Gold Corp. are negotiating a potential merger. That makes sense, as both companies are focused on exploration in Papua New Guinea. PNG is principally interested in New Guinea's Sinivit mine, which is already in production and shows an indicated and inferred resource of more than 180,000 ounces of gold. http://www.newguineagold.ca/

New Jersey Mining Company (PINK:NJMC) New Jersey Mining Company is focused on the Coeur d'Alene Mining District in Idaho and Montana. The company's Golden Chest deposit contains 27,885 ounces of proven and probable gold with new drill results coming out regularly. Chip samples from the company's Silver Strand Mine show gold grades of 5.43 g/t gold and silver grades of 361 g/t. http://newjerseymining.com/

New Oroperu Resources (PINK:NOPUF) New Oroperu Resources Inc. is focused on exploration in Peru, particularly on the Tres Cruces Project, which was optioned in part to Barrick Gold. Barrick is actively exploring the land on the strength of a historical measured and indicated resource of 34.5 million tonnes grading 1.59 g/t gold. That's good for 1.7 million ounces of gold. New Oroperu retains a 30% interest in the project. http://www.oroperu.com/

New World Resource (PINK:NWFFF) New World Resource Corp. is focused primarily on two large projects in Bolivia: the Lipena/Bonete copper-gold project (a JV with COMIBOL) and the Pastos Grandes lithium brine project. Drill holes at Lipena have returned grades ranging from 0.94 g/t gold to 7.48 g/t gold. http://www.newworldresource.com/

Newcastle Minerals Ltd. (PINK:NCMBF) Newcastle Minerals Ltd. is exploring for gold in Ontario. The company's Pickle Crow Project is home to the former Central Patricia Gold Mine, which produced 621,000 ounces of gold from 1.7 million tons between 1934 and 1949. Newcastle's initial drilling at the site intersected a 15 foot section which averaged 2.63 g/t gold. http://www.newcastleminerals.com/

EDITOR'S PICK: *Newmont Mining Corp. (NYSE:NEM)* Why we like it: Rapidly-growing dividends. An aggressive dividend policy at Newmont seems to have spared the company from a major share sell-off when the gold price collapsed in September 2011. Shares in Newmont stayed the course. Newmont is among the biggest mining companies in the world with proven and probable gold reserves of 93.5 million ounces. In terms of market cap, it falls behind only Barrick Gold Corp. and Goldcorp Inc. http://www.newmont.com/

EDITOR'S PICK: *Newstrike Capital Inc. (PINK:NWSKF)* Why we like it: Experienced management. Newstrike's management team doesn't lack for experience. In the past, they discovered more than eight million ounces of gold in the Guerrero Gold Belt in Mexico. Now, the company's looking for new deposits there. In June 2010, Newstrike acquired 100% of the Ana Paula Project from Goldcorp. 2005 drill results at the site returned gold grades between 1.175 g/t and 5.55 g/t. http://www.newstrikecapital.com/

EDITOR'S PICK: *NGEx Resources Inc. (PINK:NGQRF)* Why we like it: More than 4 million ounces of gold in the ground. NGEx Resources Inc. holds rights to several promising copper-gold projects in Chile. The Los Helados project contains more than 700m at 0.67% copper and 0.3 g/t gold. The Josemaria project contains 4.4 million ounces of gold, and the company's actively exploring several early-stage projects in Chile. http://www.ngexresources.com/

Niblack Mineral Development, Inc. (PINK:NIBMF) Heatherdale Resources Ltd. announced it was acquiring Niblack Mineral Development Inc. on October 26, 2011. The deal valued Niblack at $10.4 million. At the time of this writing, Niblack shares are still trading. Niblack's self-named Niblack project in Alaska includes an indicated resource of 4,136,000 tonnes grading 2.32 g/t gold, 38.70 g/t silver, 1.13% copper and 2.27% zinc and an inferred resource of 2,493,000 tonnes grading 1.77 g/t gold, 25.90 g/t silver, 1.21% copper and 2.29% zinc. http://www.niblack.com/

North American Palladium Ltd. (AMEX:PAL) Sprott Resource Lending Corp. ponied up $25 million when North American Palladium recently sold CA$70 million in senior notes. That's a decent endorsement in the company, even after PAL announced in September it could soon face a class action lawsuit for alleged misrepresentations in the company's public disclosure. PAL's been producing gold at its Sleeping Giant Mine in Quebec for more than 20 years and it operates one of just two primary palladium mines in the world at its Lac Des Iles Mine in Ontario. http://www.napalladium.com/

EDITOR'S PICK: North Country Gold (PINK:NCGDF) Why we like it: Rated outperform. North Country Gold Corp. is currently rated "outperform" by RBC Capital Markets. The company's Three Bluffs deposit is in the Greenstone Belt in Canada and contains a total of 750,000 ounces of gold at 6 g/t (measured, indicated and inferred). The company is focused on delivering a substantially updated resource estimate in Q1 2012. http://northcountrygold.com/

Northern Abitibi Mining Corp. (PINK:NOMNF) Northern Abitibi Mining Corp.'s most advanced project is the Viking Gold deposit in Newfoundland. The property shows an inferred resource of 131,511 ounces of gold (at a grade of 0.65 g/t). Exploration in 2011 is focused on expanding the size of the resource. http://www.naminco.ca/

Northern Dynasty Minerals Ltd. (AMEX:NAK) Northern Dynasty's Pebble deposit in southwest Alaska is massive. Resource estimates peg the property as holding 55 billion measured and indicated pounds copper, 66.9 million measured and indicated ounces of gold and 3.3 billion pounds of measured and indicated molybdenum. The mine should last some 45 years, and is estimated to be the largest undeveloped copper-gold-moly porphyry system in the world. http://www.northerndynastyminerals.com/

Northern Gold Mining Inc. (PINK:NTGMF) Northern Gold Mining Inc. is focused on exploring the Kirkland Lake and Timmins areas in Ontario. The company's flagship Garrcon Deposit showed an indicated resource of 3.78

million tonnes of ore at a grade of 1.2 g/t gold (for 144,000 ounces of gold) and an inferred resource of 18.5 million tonnes of ore at a grade of nearly 1 g/t gold (for 530,000 ounces of gold) as of November 2010. Including the Jonpol Deposit, the Garrison Gold Property hosts a resource of 207,000 ounces of gold in the indicated category and 776,500 ounces of gold in the inferred category in its two advanced stage exploration projects. http://www.northerngold.ca/

Northern Superior (PINK:NSUPF) Northern Superior Resources Inc. has entered into a joint venture with Rainy River Resources Ltd. to further explore the company's Ti-pa-haa-kaa-ning (TPK) gold property in Ontario. Drilling in 2010 was highlighted by an intersection of 25.9 g/t gold over 13.5m. http://www.nsuperior.com/

Northern Tiger Resources, Inc. (PINK:NTGSF) Northern Tiger Resources Inc. is exploring the Yukon for gold and copper. At the moment, the company's focused on its 3Ace project where it identified new mineralization in 2011. Drilling highlights include: 35.0m of 4.6 g/t gold, 30.3m of 4.3 g/t gold and 1.05m of 145.2 g/t gold. The nearby Sprogge Project has returned samples up to 34.8 g/t gold. http://www.northern-tiger.com/

Northgate Minerals Corp. (AMEX:NXG) Northgate expected to produce up to 205,000 ounces of gold in 2011. The company hoped to produce 300,000 ounces of gold in 2012 and 350,000 ounces of gold in 2013. The company's reserves and resources stand at 2,726,000 ounces gold, and that was good enough to convince AuRico to acquire Northgate in October 2011. http://www.northgateminerals.com/

EDITOR'S PICK: *Novagold Resources Inc. (AMEX:NG)* Why we like it: More than 50 million ounces of gold. NovaGold's stated goal is to become a low-cost million-ounce-a-year gold producer. Costs to get their Donlin Gold mine up and running in Alaska were recently revised up dramatically from $4.5 billion to $7 billion. Once the mine's operational, though, the company should produce some 800,000 ounces of gold a year. Galore Creek contains 12 million ounces of gold and Donlin Gold contains 39 million ounces. http://www.novagold.com/

Odyssey Resources Ltd. (PINK:ODXSF) There hasn't been much news out of Odyssey Resources Limited since the company was scheduled to begin exploring its FCI and Auclair projects in the James Bay region of Quebec in the winter of 2010. The 50% joint venture interest with Virginia Mines Inc. was expected to spend $1.9 million on exploration. http://www.odysseyresources.com/

EDITOR'S PICK: *Olympus Pacific Minerals Inc. (OTC:OLYMF)* Why we like it: Up and coming gold producer. An up-and-coming gold producer, Olympus Pacific expects to produce 46,000 ounces of gold in 2011. Production should grow to 70,000 ounces by the end of 2012, and the company expects Vietnamese production alone could reach 170,000 ounces by 2015. Altogether, Olympus has reserves and resources of 3,870,506 ounces gold. http://olympuspacific.com/

Orex Minerals Inc. (PINK:ORXIF) Orex Minerals' flagship project is its Barsele Gold project in Sweden. Barsele has an NI 43-101 compliant resource estimate of 382,000 ounces of gold indicated at 1.2 g/t (9.97 million tonnes) and 648,000 ounces of gold inferred at 1.0 g/t gold (21.04 million tonnes). http://www.orexminerals.com/

EDITOR'S PICK: *Orezone Gold Corp. (PINK:ORZCF)* Why we like it: A growing deposit in Burkina Faso. Orezone Gold Corporation has 2.3 million ounces of measured and indicated gold and 2.2 million ounces of inferred gold at its three, 100%-owned projects in Burkina Faso. The company's Bombore gold deposit alone contains 1.6 million ounces measured and indicated gold and 1.9 million ounces inferred gold. Drilling to expand the resource is ongoing. http://www.orezone.com/

EDITOR'S PICK: *Orko Silver Corp. (PINK:OKOFF)* Why we like it: More than 150 million ounces of silver. Orko Silver Corp. is developing its large La Preciosa silver deposit in Durango State, Mexico. The deposit holds 113 million ounces of indicated silver and 46 million ounces of inferred silver. The scale of the deposit drew a JV with Pan American Silver Corp. "Pan American will contribute its demonstrated mine development expertise, as well as 100% of the funds necessary to develop and construct an operating mine, in consideration for a 55% interest in the joint venture. Orko Silver retains a 45% interest fully carried to production." http://www.orkosilver.com/

Oro Mining Ltd. (PINK:OMRGF) Oro Mining Ltd.'s flagship project is the Trinidad property in Sinaloa, Mexico. As of 2010, the project showed 187,000 indicated gold ounces and 118,000 inferred gold ounces. On top of that, the company's El Compas project in Zacatecas State also has a substantial deposit with 74,000 indicated ounces gold and 1,103,000 indicated ounces silver. There's another 54,000 inferred ounces gold and 641,000 inferred ounces of silver at the site. http://www.oromining.com/

OroAndes Resource Corp. (PINK:OARFF) OroAndes Resource Corp. is focused on its Kilometre 26 Nickel-Gold Project in British Columbia. In 1983, Cominco discovered a quartz-ankerite-magnesite-mariposite boulder at Kilometre 26 that "repeatedly graded 8.1 g/t gold." Rocks newly-tested in 2011 have contained up to 0.21% nickel. http://www.oroandes.com/

Oroco Resource Corp. (PINK:ORRCF) Oroco Resource Corp. released its second NI 43-101 compliant resource estimate for its Cerro Prieto project in Sonora State, Mexico. Envisioned as an open pit oxide gold mine, the project has a measured and indicated resource of 14,740,000 tonnes grading 0.71 g/t gold and 12.83 g/t silver with a contained 383,833 ounces of gold and 6,080,000 ounces of silver. The deposit boasts an additional 5,900 inferred ounces of gold and 113,000 inferred ounces of silver. Construction on a mine at the site started in August 2011. http://www.orocoresourcecorp.com/

Orofino Gold Corp. (PINK:ORFG) Based in Colombia, Orofino Gold Corp. is currently operating a mine at its La Azul project in the Senderos de Oro area in Colombia. The company claims samples from La Azul have graded as high as 253 g/t gold and 255 g/t silver. Per the company's web site, "Orofino Gold Corp. will become a 100,000-ounce-per-year gold producer from its first mine within five years of formation." http://www.orofinogoldcorp.com/

Oromin Explorations Ltd. (OTC:OLEPF) Oromin is currently focused on the Sabodala gold concession (the OJVG project) in Senegal, West Africa, and the Santa Rosa Dome oil prospect in Argentina. The OJVG shows 3.3 million ounces of measured and indicated resources in addition to over 400,000 ounces of inferred resources. A 2010 feasibility study showed the mine could produce 174,000 ounces of gold a year in the first three years and support a total of 9 years of mining. Oromin has at least two major backers in IAMGOLD (which holds 11.9 percent of the company's shares) and Teranga Gold Corp. (13.8 percent). http://www.oromin.com/

Orosur Mining Inc. (PINK:OROXF) Orosur Mining Inc. is already producing nearly 60,000 ounces of gold a year from its San Gregorio operation in Uruguay. More output is expected in the coming years, too, as the company works to bring its Arenal Deeps project online. Arenal Deeps holds 96,000 measured ounces of gold and 153,000 indicated ounces of gold. The company's also excited about its Talca project in Chile, which they've estimated could potentially hold up to 500,000 ounces of gold. http://www.orosur.ca/

Orvana Minerals Corp. (PINK:ORVMF) Orvana Minerals Corp. has two mines in production: the El Valle-Boinas/Carle's gold-copper project in northern Spain, and the Don Mario Mine in Bolivia. The El Valle-Boinas mine should generate approximately 105,000 ounces of gold, 8.6 million pounds of copper and 160,000 ounces of silver over seven years. The Don Mario Mine holds more than 282,000 ounces of gold. Orvana's also developing the Copperwood copper project in the Upper Peninsula of Michigan. http://www.orvana.com/

Pacific Gold Corp. (PINK:PCFG) Pacific Gold Corp. operates four mining-related subsidiaries: Nevada Rae Gold, Inc., which owns and operates the Black Rock Canyon gold mine in Nevada, Pilot Mountain Resources Inc., which owns Project W, a tungsten-based deposit, Fernley Gold, Inc., which has acquired the exclusive lease rights to mine the Lower Olinghouse Placers, and Pacific Metals Corp., which owns mining claims in San Juan and Dolores Counties, Colorado. http://www.pacificgoldcorp.com/

Pacific Ridge Exploration (PINK:PEXZF) Pacific Ridge Exploration Ltd. has started early-stage drilling at its Mariposa Gold Project in the Yukon White Gold District. A recent discovery drill hole intersected 2.44 g/t gold over 39m. Expect more drilling to further define the resource. http://www.pacificridgeexploration.com/

Pacific Rim Mining Corp. (PINK:PFRMF) Pacific Rim Mining Corp.'s flagship property is the El Dorado gold project in El Salvador. A 2008 resource estimate for the project estimated 1.4 million measured and indicated gold equivalent ounces and a further 300,000 inferred gold equivalent ounces. Permitting issues have suspended drilling at the site, but international arbitration is ongoing and should wrap up in 2012. http://www.pacrim-mining.com/

Paget Minerals Corp. (PINK:PGTMF) Paget Minerals Corp. is exploring for precious and base metals in British Columbia, Mexico and Colombia. Five projects in British Columbia are under development with active drilling ongoing at the company's Ball Creek project. Surface sampling at Ball Creek has shown grades with highs of 19 and 59 g/t gold and 106 and 169 g/t silver. http://www.pagetminerals.com/

Pan American Goldfields Ltd. (OTC:MXOM) The first phase of production at Pan American's Cieneguita Project in Mexico kicked off in November 2010. The tract shows an indicated and inferred resource of 33.4 million ounces of silver and 474,000 ounces of gold. The company should soon launch a feasibility study on a mine there. http://www.panamgoldfields.com/

EDITOR'S PICK: *Pan American Silver Corp. (NASDAQ:PAAS)* Why we like it: Investor overreaction? Shares in the world's second largest primary silver producer got slammed on news that Peru was raising taxes on miners by 5 percent. It's an overreaction, according to the company which produces some 29 percent of its silver in Peru. Bank of America-Merrill Lynch downgraded the stock from "neutral" to "underperform" in October. Canaccord Genuity upgraded shares around the same time from a "hold" to a "buy." http://www.panamericansilver.com/

Paragon Minerals Corp. (PINK:PAONF) Paragon Minerals Corporation is exploring for gold and base metals in Newfoundland and Ontario. The company's Huxter Lane JV Project in Newfoundland contains an indicated 11.18 million tonnes averaging 0.546 g/t gold for 196,257 ounces gold and an inferred resource of 38.76 million tonnes averaging 0.457 g/t gold for 569,496 ounces gold. Drilling is ongoing at the company's South Tally Pond Project, too, where recent drill holes have intercepted grades as high as 1.65% copper, 12.74% zinc, 3.27% lead, 185.75 g/t silver and 10.13 g/t gold over 7.0m. http://www.paragonminerals.com/

Paramount Gold and Silver Corp. (AMEX:PZG) A recent resource estimate on Paramount's Sleeper Gold Project in Nevada showed 2.6 million ounces of measured and indicated gold and 25.3 million ounces of silver. Tack onto that another 1.1 million ounces of inferred gold and 8.2 million ounces of inferred silver and you've got a stock that could be undervalued. An engineering study is due in 2012. http://paramountgold.com/

PCGold Inc. (PINK:PCGLF) PC Gold Inc. owns rights to the historic Pickle Crow mine in northwestern Ontario. New exploration at the site has uncovered 1.26 million inferred ounces of gold (10,150,000 tonnes averaging 3.9 g/t gold). Further exploration at the site is underway as the company moves toward a pre-feasibility study. http://www.pcgold.ca/

EDITOR'S PICK: *Pelangio Exploration Inc. (PINK:PGXPF)* Why we like it: Approaching 30 million ounces of gold. Pelangio Exploration Inc. has a great track record. The company acquired, explored and sold the Detour Lake deposit in Ontario (and it currently boasts an indicated resource of over 20 million ounces). Pelangio's now focused on its Obuasi and Manfo Properties in Ghana, West Africa. The historic Obuasi mine has produced over 30 million ounces of gold since 1897 and currently hosts an 8.92 million ounce reserve grading 7.05 g/t gold in a measured and indicated resource of 18.13 million ounces and a further 11.40 million ounces of inferred resource. http://www.pelangio.com/

Peregrine Metals Ltd. (PINK:PTTDF) Peregrine Metals Ltd. was acquired by Stillwater Mining Company on October 4, 2011. The company had a 100% interest in the Altar porphyry copper-gold deposit in San Juan Province, Argentina. A 2010 resource estimate at Altar showed a measured and indicated resource of 802 million tonnes grading 0.44% copper equivalent containing 7.41 billion pounds of copper and 1.53 million ounces of gold. The inferred resource included 4.32 billion pounds of copper and 880,000 ounces of gold. http://www.peregrinemetals.com/

EDITOR'S PICK: *Pershimco Resources (PINK:RSPRF)* Why we like it: A good chart pattern with shares up more than 100% in 2011. Pershimco Resources Inc. is focused on the Cerro Quema Gold-Copper Project in Panama. The deposit contains reserves of 372,500 ounces of proven and probable gold, and 451,400 ounces of measured and indicated resources (from a 2009 report). http://www.pershimco.ca/

Petaquilla Minerals Ltd. (OTC:PTQMF) Petaquilla Minerals brought its 100-percent-owned Molejon Gold Mine in Panama online in January of 2010. The Molejon project has a total measured resource of 532,801 ounces of gold and an indicated resource of 223,785 ounces. http://www.petaquilla.com/

Pilot Gold Inc. (PINK:PLGTF) Formed as a spin-out from Fronteer Gold after its acquisition by Newmont Mining Corporation, Pilot Gold Inc. currently holds projects in Nevada and Turkey. Drilling at the Halilaga project in Turkey has returned grades as high as 0.26 g/t gold and 0.33% copper over 646.50m. The TV Tower project, also in Turkey, has intersected 57.8m of 9.51 g/t gold within a broader interval of 136.2m of 4.28 g/t gold. http://www.pilotgold.com/

Plato Gold (PINK:PTOZF) Plato Gold Corp. has an NI 43-101 report showing indicated resources of 30,212 ounces of gold and inferred resources of 146,315 ounces of gold at the company's Nordeau West project in Val d'Or, Quebec. Plato also holds a 75 percent interest in the Lolita Property in Argentina. http://www.platogold.com/

Plexmar Resources Inc. (PINK:PLLGF) Plexmar Resources Inc. is focused on developing gold properties in Peru including the Almirante Miguel Grau mining property. Plexmar raised $417,000 in a private offering in July of 2011, but that's been the last big news out of the company. Soil grades at Almirante Miguel Grau were unknown at the time of this writing. http://www.plexmar.com/

EDITOR'S PICK: *PMI Gold Corp. (PINK:PMVGF)* Why we like it: A ballooning gold deposit in Ghana. PMI Gold Corp. recently tripled the company's gold resource at its Obotan gold project in Ghana when it announced a new NI 43-101 resource estimate. Obotan now shows 3.22 million ounces of measured and indicated gold and 1.29 million ounces of inferred gold. Figures are expected to be revised higher in 2012. Altogether, PMI owns four historic gold mines in Ghana. http://www.pmigoldcorp.com/

Polar Star Mining (PINK:POSRF) Polar Star Mining Corporation entered production at its Chepica, Chile, gold-silver-copper mine in central Chile in October 2011. "The mine's initial throughput is targeted at approximately 5,000 tonnes per month, with a monthly production objective of 1,000 ounces of gold and 50,000 pounds of copper," the company wrote in a press release at the time. The plan is to use profits from the mine to finance further exploration at the company's flagship Montezuma property in Chile. http://www.polarstarmining.com/

EDITOR'S PICK: *Premier Gold Mines (PINK:PIRGF)* Why we like it: $8.50 price target. Premier Gold Mines Limited earned an "outperform" rating and a 12-month price target of $8.50 from Stonecap Securities in November 2011. Premier's Trans-Canada project includes the 3.6 million ounce gold Hardrock deposit and represents one of the "most significant undeveloped gold projects in Canada," Stonecap told ProactiveInvestors. Stonecap believes Premier's holdings could be acquisition targets for bigger miners (i.e. Newmont and Goldcorp) in the years to come. http://www.premiergoldmines.com/

EDITOR'S PICK: *Pretium Resources Inc. (NYSE:PVG)* Why we like it: A world class deposit. Pretium Resources Inc. was formed explicitly to acquire the Snowfield and the Brucejack Projects from Silver Standard Resources Inc. That move has proved to be extremely prescient with Pretium identifying a large deposit at Brucejack. The property now shows 9.3 million tonnes at 16.92 g/t gold and 105.6 g/t silver, for a total of 5.06 million ounces of contained gold, and 31.6 million ounces of contained silver. In the inferred category, resources stand at 3.3 million ounces of contained gold and 2.7 million ounces of contained silver. http://www.pretivm.com/

EDITOR'S PICK: *Probe Mines Ltd. (PINK:PROBF)* Why we like it: Royalties and a growing resource. Probe Mines Limited's getting a steady influx of cash thanks to a 5% net smelter royalty on a portion of Agnico Eagle's Goldex Mine in Quebec. Probe is using that cash to further explore its Borden Lake Property where an NI 43-101 resource estimate shows an indicated resource of 300,000 ounces (0.82 g/t gold) plus an inferred resource of 3.8 million ounces (0.69 g/t gold). http://www.probemines.com/

Puma Exploration (PINK:PUXPF) Puma Exploration's focused on its Nicholas-Denys project in New Brunswick where a preliminary NI 43-101 compliant mineral resource showed 1 million ounces of indicated silver. Ongoing drilling at the site has yielded more high-grade results including 225 g/t silver and 1.2 g/t gold over 29.1m and 130 g/t silver and 0.9 g/t gold over 31.0m. http://www.explorationpuma.com/

EDITOR'S PICK: *Rainy River Resources (PINK:RRFFF)* Why we like it: Lots of cash and lots of drilling. Rainy River Resources started trading on the TSX on November 23, 2011. Rainy River's self-named Rainy River project in Quebec has defined measured and indicated resources of 4.4 million ounces gold and 2.33 million ounces inferred gold. Aggressive drilling was planning throughout 2011 when the company started out the year with $100 million in its treasury. http://www.rainyriverresources.com/

EDITOR'S PICK: *Randgold Resources Ltd. (NASDAQ:GOLD)* Why we like it: Ahead of schedule on a very large mine. When Randgold acquired a 45 percent interest in the Kibali Project in the Democratic Republic of Congo, the company thought it could be 2015 before production started. Recently, though, the company announced the mine could be operational by the end of 2013. With 10 million ounces of reserves, the mine is one of the largest undeveloped gold deposits in Africa. http://www.randgoldresources.com/

REBgold Corp. (PINK:RBGCF) REBgold Corporation owns bioleaching technology that frees metals from rock that would normally be sent to a smelter or roaster. That's drawn interest from companies like Yamana Gold Inc. REBgold's conducting bioleach test work for Yamana's Jeronimo project. If the results are satisfactory, Yamana will pay a 1% net smelter returns royalty to REBgold on gold production generated from REBgold technology at the Jeronimo Project. http://www.reb-gold.com/

EDITOR'S PICK: *Red Metal Resources Ltd. (OTC:RMES)* Why we like it: Promising gold and copper deposits in Chile. Red Metal Resources holds rights to four copper-gold projects in Chile's III Region. The company's four largest projects have shown promising copper and gold deposits. To name two: the Farellon project included 2.57% copper and 4.16 g/t gold over 5m, and the Mateo project has shown 16,000 tonnes mined grading an average of 3.15% copper, 45.2 g/t silver and .74 g/t gold. http://www.redmetalresources.com/

EDITOR'S PICK: *Redstar Gold Corp. (PINK:RGCTF)* Why we like it: A good chart pattern with shares up more than 80% in 2011. Redstar Gold Corp. has been getting encouraging results from its Unga project, on the Unga and Popof Islands in Alaska. Late in November 2011, the company announced it had intersected 1m grading 43.8 g/t gold and 18.5 g/t silver. That came inside a wider 21m interval of 4.02 g/t gold and 5.4 g/t silver. A non-compliant resource estimate done in the 1980s showed 225,000 ounces of contained gold and one million ounces of contained silver. http://www.redstargold.com/

Renaissance Gold Inc. (PINK:RNSGF) Confidence in Renaissance Gold's Spruce Mountain Property in Nevada landed the company a spot on Alan Coyner's Nevada Top Ten Exploration Projects List (per MineWeb.com). All told, Renaissance has 24 early-stage projects in Nevada and Utah, one project in Spain and five in Argentina. Ten of the company's projects feature earn-in agreements with major companies including Agnico-Eagle and Newmont Mining. http://www.rengold.com/

Reunion Gold Corp. (PINK:RGDFF) Reunion Gold Corporation is focusing exploration efforts on land surrounding an abandoned manganese mine in the Guiana Shield region in Guyana. "This company has a major manganese deposit in the northwest district of Guyana," investment banker Michael O'Brian told The Gold Report on Nov. 9, 2011. "The company has 12 kilometers (km) of strike in a 40km zone and has large widths of high-grade mineralization. ... The company raised $41M in a private placement priced at $1.79 per share this past April through BMO Nesbitt Burns. The shares are currently substantially below this price. I am looking for serious appreciation as the results become known." http://www.reuniongold.com/

Reva Resources Corp. (PINK:RVARF) Reva Resources Corp. is currently focused on base metals exploration at the company's Chu Chua Massive Sulfide Deposit Project in British Columbia. A resource calculation conducted by Mintec Inc. in 1989 quoted a resource of 2.9 million tonnes at 1.6% copper, 0.26% zinc, and 6.9 g/t silver. Using a 2% copper cut-off grade, a resource was estimated at 798,611 tonnes at 3.87% copper, 0.45% zinc and 12.8 g/t silver. Those numbers are not NI 43-101 compliant. http://www.revaresources.com/

Revett Minerals Inc. (AMEX:RVM) Revett's sitting on an estimated 300 million ounces of silver and 2.5 billion pounds of copper at its Rock Creek Project in Montana. That's driven a large influx of institutional buying (per SeekingAlpha) with nearly 28 percent of the company's shares landing in institutional hands in Q2 2011. http://www.revettminerals.com/

EDITOR'S PICK: *Richmont Mines Inc. (AMEX:RIC)* Why we like it: An early-stage gold producer. Richmont has 14 active projects in Ontario and Quebec. The company's three active mines are expected to produce between 80,000 and 85,000 ounces of gold in 2011 (compared to the 68,123 ounces the company produced across two mines in 2010). Very promising results are coming out of the company's multi-million-ounce Wasamac property as well. All told, the company has reserves and resources of 1,987,984 ounces gold. http://www.richmont-mines.com/

Riverside Resources Inc. (PINK:RVSDF) Riverside Resources Inc. has three fully-owned gold and silver projects in Mexico. The Tajitos Gold Project has previously produced an estimated 50,000 ounces of high-grade gold. The company has JV projects underway as well. Riverside and partner Sierra Madre Developments are working to delineate a resource at the Penoles Gold-Silver Project. Recent assays there returned a highlight of 1,757.7 g/t silver from a 0.2m wide interval. http://www.rivres.com/

RJK Exploration Ltd. (PINK:RJKAF) RJK Explorations Ltd. is exploring Blackwater West and Blackwater East in British Columbia, Canada. Both properties are contiguous to New Gold Inc.'s Blackwater project, which holds 6.52 million ounces of gold and 36.3 million ounces of silver. RJK has filed for drilling permits and intends to begin an initial drilling program as soon as the permits are approved. http://www.rjkexplorations.com/

Robex Resources (PINK:RSRBF) Robex Resources Inc. completed a feasibility study for its 100%-owned Mininko/Nampala project in Mali on Nov. 8, 2011. The site showed proven and probable open-pit reserves of 17.3 million tonnes at 0.70 g/t gold for a total of 392,520 ounces of gold (345,418 ounces of recoverable gold at 88% average recovery rate). Robex's Mininko project is also host to a resource of 713,065 ounces of measured and indicated gold and 815,870 ounces of inferred gold. http://www.robexgold.com/

Rochester Resources Ltd. (PINK:RCTFF) Rochester Resources Ltd. is focused on its Mina Real gold/silver project in Mexico. 2010 drilling at the site intersected grades as high as 7.37 g/t gold and 78 g/t silver over 1.14m and 0.11 g/t gold and 189.6 g/t silver over 10.4m. http://www.rochesterresources.com/

Rockcliff Resources Inc. (PINK:RKLFF) Rockcliff Resources Inc. expects to kick off diamond drilling at the company's Snow Lake Project in 2012. Rockcliff has rights to more than 500 sq km there, including two former copper mines. The Rail deposit on the property shows 822,000 tonnes with 3.04% copper, 0.90% zinc, 9.25 g/t silver and 0.6 g/t gold. http://www.rockcliffresources.com/

Rockhaven Resources (PINK:RKHNF) Rockhaven Resources Ltd. is currently focused on its Klaza property, a gold-silver prospect in Mt. Nansen in the Yukon. Shallow drill holes and trenching at the site have yielded promising results including 6.27 g/t gold and 18.94 g/t silver over 8.9m and 6.86 g/t gold and 157.71 g/t silver over 2.5m. http://www.rockhavenresources.com/

Rockridge Capital Corp. (PINK:RRCPF) Rockridge Capital Corp. is exploring southern Mali for gold. The company's Fatou Gold Project has intersected 213.97 g/t gold over 4m. That drew the interest of Highland Park SA, which acquired 7.1 million units in Rockridge at a cost of $0.64 on Nov. 30, 2011. http://www.rockridgecapitalcorp.com/

Rogue Resources (PINK:GCRIF) Rogue Resources Inc. has interests in several joint venture gold-copper projects that are currently undergoing exploratory drilling. The company's two most advanced projects are the Langmuir nickel project and the Radio Hill iron project. Langmuir in Quebec is in the pre-feasibility process and has shown an indicated nickel resource of 12 million pounds, 2.4 million inferred pounds and 1.9 million indicated pounds. http://www.roguemining.com/

EDITOR'S PICK: *Romarco Minerals Inc. (PINK:RTRAF)* Why we like it: Looking to pour their first gold in 2014. Romarco Minerals Inc. re-opened the Haile Gold Mine in South Carolina in 2011, and the company expects to pour its first gold from the site in 2014. The mine's expected to produce 150,000 ounces of gold over five years and the deposit is estimated to contain 3.1 million ounces of gold. The discovery has sparked renewed interests in mining in the Southern United States. http://www.romarco.com/

Rome Resources Ltd. (PINK:RMRSF) Rome Resources Ltd. is exploring for copper, tungsten, silver and gold in Argentina and Mexico. The company's currently drilling its silver-gold-tungsten Don Luis Property in Sonora, Mexico, where it believes a bulk tonnage mine is feasible. Drilling results so far have yielded silver averages of 9.82 g/t over 2,748m and 0.117 g/t gold over 2,748m. http://romeresources.com/

EDITOR'S PICK: *Roxgold Inc. (PINK:ROGFF)* Why we like it: A growing deposit in Burkina Faso; Shares up 3,500% in 2011. High grade gold intersections of 53.56 g/t gold over 8m, 47.41 g/t over 8.5m and 31.90 g/t over 16m from Roxgold Inc.'s Burkina Faso projects have lit a fire under this stock. Shares rocketed up 3,500% in 2011. http://www.roxgold.com/

EDITOR'S PICK: *Royal Gold, Inc. (NASDAQ:RGLD)* Why we like it: A gold-streaming company. Royalty companies like Royal Gold make their money by fronting miners the cash to get mines operational. Then, they take a cut of the mine's future profits. Royal's one of the leading companies in the sector with 33 producing properties and more than 150 development-stage and exploration-stage properties. http://www.royalgold.com/

Royal Mines and Minerals Corp. (PINK:RYMM) Royal Mines and Minerals Corporation is focused on refining the precious metal extraction process. The company claims its process "is up to 70 times more efficient than that of a traditional cyanide process and is environmentally friendly and features a zero discharge closed loop circuit." The company also acquired rights to the Golden Anvil project in Mexico late in 2011. Limited samples from Golden Anvil project have graded as high as 140 g/t gold and 2,384 g/t silver. http://www.royalmmc.com/

EDITOR'S PICK: *Royal Standard Minerals Inc. (OTC:RYSMF)* Why we like it: Moving toward feasibility. Royal Standard Minerals Inc. is moving toward feasibility at its Goldwedge property in Nevada. The project boasts current gold resources of 600,000 ounces. The company also believes its Pinon-Railroad Project in Nevada shows "high potential for multimillion ounce deposit open-pit and underground gold (silver) oxide resources." http://www.royalstandardminerals.com/

EDITOR'S PICK: *Rubicon Minerals Corp. (AMEX:RBY)* Why we like it: Agnico-Eagle owns a 9% stake in Rubicon. Rubicon has good backing after Agnico-Eagle Mines Ltd. (AEM) purchased 9.2 percent stake in the company in September 2011. That totals a C$70 million investment in Rubicon. Rubicon has begun mine construction at its Red Lake Phoenix target. Drilling at the Phoenix target has intercepted grades as high as 156.0 g/t gold over 4m. http://www.rubiconminerals.com/

EDITOR'S PICK: *Ruby Creek Resources Inc. (OTC:RBYC)* Why we like it: Recently acquired a mining license. In September, Ruby Creek Resources, Inc. acquired 95 percent ownership in Gold Standard Tanzania. A month later, the company officially received a 10 sq km mining license, an established mining camp and "all Gold Standard Tanzania's mining equipment." It was another big step toward production at Ruby Creek's Tanzania Gold Plateau Project. "Previous exploration of a very small area (< 0.4% of the Gold Plateau) and shallow depth (~6m) yielded 27,500 of NI 43-101 inferred gold ounces grading 0.30 g/m3," according to the company. http://www.rubycreekresources.com/

Rugby Mining Ltd. (PINK:RBMNF) Rugby Mining Limited is developing three distinct projects in three different countries: the Mabuhay Gold Copper Project in the Philippines, the Comita Copper Gold Project in Colombia and the Interceptor Copper Gold Project in Argentina. Intersections at the Mabuhay project have graded 1.2 g/t gold and 0.16% copper over 254m. In late November 2011, the company announced it had acquired an option agreement on the Rio Chico gold-platinum-copper project and the Zonda porphyry gold-copper project in Argentina. http://www.rugbymining.com/

Rupert Resources Ltd. (PINK:RUPRF) Rupert Resources Ltd. is exploring its Gold Centre property, which lies 600m from Goldcorp's Red Lake Gold Mine in Ontario. Little is known about the company's progress, though, as it hasn't issued a news release since appointing a new CFO in July 2010. Rupert announced a $3.8 million drill project at Gold Centre in 2008. http://www.rupertresources.com/

Rusoro Mining Ltd. (PINK:RMLFF) Rusoro Mining Ltd. operates the Choco 10 mine (formerly operated by Goldfields) and the Isidora Mine, which are located in the El Callao district in Venezuela. Production guidance for the two mines for 2010 was 90,000 ounces of gold. The company got some bad news on September 16, 2011 when they were told they could no longer export their gold, though. The mines were slated to be nationalized within 90 days of the announcement and Rusoro's stake in the mines was to be reduced to at least 45 percent. http://www.rusoro.com/

Ryan Gold Corp. (PINK:RYGZF) Ryan Gold Corp. is in the early stages of exploration at several sites in the Yukon. The company's Ida Oro Project has shown promising results from drilling that started in August 2011. Highlights include Hole IODD002, which intersected 99.50m grading 0.62g/t gold from 77.50m including 3.65m grading 2.43 g/t gold from 127.75m. http://www.ryangold.com/

EDITOR'S PICK: *Sabina Gold and Silver Corp. (PINK:SGSVF)* Why we like it: Sitting on more than 6 million ounces of gold. Sabina Gold and Silver Corp. is exploring three properties in Nanavut, Canada: the Back River Project, the Hackett River Project and the Wishbone Project. The company has more than doubled its resource estimate at Back River in the past two drilling campaigns. The site now comprises indicated resources of 22.3 million tonnes grading 5.62 g/t for 4.03 million ounces of gold and additional inferred resources of 10 million tonnes grading 6.23 g/t for 2.02 million ounces   gold.   http://www.sabinagoldsilver.com/

Sacre-Couer Minerals (PINK:SCRMF) Sacre-Coeur Minerals, Ltd.'s flagship project is its Million Mountain project in north-central Guyana. The 21,768-acre site contains an NI 43-101 compliant resource estimate of 451,397 troy ounces gold. The company is currently constructing a gravity processing plant designed to treat 1000 cubic meters per day at the site. http://www.scminerals.com/

Sage Gold Inc. (PINK:SGGDF) Sage Gold's Clavos Mine hosts a resource of 143,000 tonnes at 10.27 g/t gold for 37,100 ounces (measured and indicated), and an inferred resource of 529,000 tonnes at 6.7 g/t gold for 110,300 ounces of gold. The company has completed 12,500m of drilling and an updated resource estimate and preliminary economic assessment are in the works. http://www.sagegoldinc.com/

Sagebrush Gold Ltd. (OTC:SAGE) Earlier this year, Empire Sports & Entertainment Holdings Company changed its name to Sagebrush Gold when it acquired rights to two potential gold deposits at Red Rock and North Battle Mountain in Nevada. Soon after, the company acquired the formerly-operational Relief Canyon mine in Nevada. Relief Canyon shows 42,000 inferred ounces of gold and 113,000 indicated ounces. http://www.sagebrushgold.com/

Sama Resources Inc. (PINK:LNZCF) Sama Resources Inc. is exploring nickel-copper projects in West Africa. The company's actively drilling at its Samapleu Project in Cote D'Ivoire. A recent hole intersected 20.65m of 1.17% nickel and copper. Another drill hole showed 17.6m of 1.95% nickel, 1.95% copper, 0.07% cobalt, 1.5 g/t palladium, 0.13 g/t platinum and 0.27 g/t gold. http://www.samaresources.com/

Samex Mining Corp. (OTC:SMXMF) Samex is currently exploring the Andean Cordillera of Chile. The company is actively looking to joint-venture or sell its INCA-area copper project there as it focuses predominantly on its Los Zorros Gold Property. The Los Zorros property has shown an average grade of 1.5% copper, 0.2-0.6 g/t gold and 2.0-8.0 g/t silver. http://www.samex.com/

San Marco Resources Inc. (PINK:SMREF) San Marco Resources Inc. is exploring for gold and base metals in British Columbia and Mexico. The company's Alwin Copper Project in British Columbia was home to a former mine that produced 155,000 tonnes grading 1.54% copper. The company's

Tecomate Project in Mexico has returned trenching results as high as 0.60 g/t gold and 1.65 g/t silver over 37.5m. http://www.sanmarcocorp.com/

EDITOR'S PICK: *Sandstorm Gold Ltd. (PINK:SNDXF)* Why we like it: A gold-streaming company. Something of a gold-streaming company, Sandstorm helps companies finance the development of mines in exchange for future gold production. On Dec. 15, 2011, Sandstorm Gold Ltd. announced that it had entered production at its JV Ming Copper-Gold Mine in Newfoundland. Sandstorm is entitled to receive 25%-32% of the first 175,000 ounces of payable gold, and 12% of the payable gold produced thereafter from the Ming Mine. http://www.sandstormgold.com/

Santa Fe Gold Corp. (OTC:SFEG) Santa Fe Gold Corp.'s Summit silver-gold project has already begun processing ore and was slated to achieve commercial production by the end of 2011. Operating costs are estimated at $364 per ounce of gold equivalent. Funds from the mine should help bankroll three more advanced projects in the Southwestern United States. http://santafegoldcorp.com/

Saturn Minerals Inc. (PINK:SAEUF) Saturn Minerals, Inc. has evolved to focus largely on coal and oil projects in Saskatchewan and Manitoba. The company's Saskatoba Project has yielded two coal discoveries since 2010 "including one of the thickest coal seam intersections ever encountered in Canada at 88m," the company says of its Overflowing Property in Manitoba. http://www.saturnminerals.com/

EDITOR'S PICK: *Scorpio Gold Corp. (PINK:SRCRF)* Why we like it: An early-stage silver producer with a nice chart pattern. Scorpio Gold Corporation and Golden Phoenix Minerals, Inc.'s "Mineral Ridge" Joint Venture has a mineral resource estimate of 221,000 ounces of gold (measured and indicated) and 136,000 ounces of gold (inferred) within the area of the Drinkwater and Mary pits. Current mine plans are looking at 3.2 million tons of mineralized material being mined over a period of 41 months, according to Marketwatch. http://www.scorpiogold.com/

Scorpio Mining Corp. (PINK:SMNPF) Scorpio Mining Corporation is already producing precious metals at its Nuestra Senora silver-lead-zinc-copper mine in Cosala, Mexico. Production from Nuestra Senora was estimated to exceed 3 million silver equivalent ounces in 2011, and the resource estimate at the site (which is already north of 350,000 ounces) is expected to grow significantly. http://www.scorpiomining.com/

Seabridge Gold, Inc. (AMEX:SA) Proven and probable reserves for Seabridge Gold total 38.5 million ounces of gold and 10 billion pounds of copper. The company expects to complete a preliminary feasibility study at its Courageous Lake mine in the Northwest Territories in the second quarter of 2012. http://www.seabridgegold.net/

Seafield Resources Ltd. (PINK:SRLTF) Seafield Resources Ltd. upped its gold resources at its Dosquebradas gold-copper prospect in Colombia on Dec. 13, 2011. To date, the Dosquebradas prospect contains inferred resources of 57.79 million tonnes grading 0.5 g/t gold and 0.04% copper, at a cutoff grade of 0.3 g/t gold, for a total of 920,772 ounces of gold, per ProactiveInvestors. http://www.sffresources.com/

Search Minerals Inc. (PINK:SHCMF) Search Minerals Inc. released its first mineral resource estimates for its rare earth elements Foxtrot Project in southeastern Labrador, Canada, in December 2011. Highlights include 3,410,000 tonnes of indicated mineral resources with a grade of 0.18% heavy rare earth elements and 0.89% total rare earth elements (TREE+Y), including 189 ppm dysprosium and 1,442 ppm neodymium. The company also holds rights to a potential gold deposit at its Katie project in Newfoundland. http://www.searchminerals.ca/

Searchlight Minerals Corp. (OTC:SRCH) Searchlight Minerals Corp. holds interests to two mineral projects: the Clarkdale Slag project in Clarkdale, Arizona, and the Searchlight Gold Project in Nevada. At Clarkdale, the company is planning to reclaim precious and base metals from the former United Verde Copper Mine in Jerome, Arizona. Early-stage sampling has yielded 0.5 opt gold via extraction processes. http://www.searchlightminerals.com/

Sennen Resources Ltd. (PINK:SNNJF) Sennen Resources Ltd. is drilling at its Hope Bay Oro Gold Property in Western Nunavut, Canada. Drill results announced in November 2011 returned intersections of 7.55m grading 4.91 g/t gold (including 8.00 g/t gold over 4.20m), and 2m grading 20.22 g/t gold. http://www.sennenresources.com/

Serengeti Resources Inc. (PINK:SGRNF) Serengeti Resources Inc. has rights to a large copper-gold deposit in British Columbia. The company's Kwanika project is the most advanced with a measured, indicated and inferred resource of 2.48 million pounds of copper, 2.5 million ounces of gold and 17.6 million ounces of silver at a $7.50 cut-off. http://www.serengetiresources.com/

Shoshone Silver Mining Co. (PINK:SHSH) Shoshone Silver had produced test runs of concentrate at its Lakeview Mill project in northern Idaho. The Lakeview District has produced more than 1 million ounces of silver in the past, and Shoshone has re-started production there thanks to higher silver prices. Concentrate sales generated $47,885 during fiscal 2011. http://shoshonesilvermining.com/

Sienna Gold Inc. (PINK:SNNGF) Sienna Gold Inc. is exploring for gold and silver at its Igor project in northern Peru. A 15,000m drill campaign was planned for November 2011. Before that, drill holes had intercepted grades as high as 13 g/t gold and 2,112 g/t silver over 4m. http://www.siennagold.com/

Siga Resources Inc. (OTC:SGAE) In March 2011, Siga Resources acquired 100 percent of the rights to the Lucky Thirteen Gold Project outside of Hope, British Columbia. "An empirically derived but realistic estimate of the average gold value encountered (at Lucky Thirteen) by reported testing to date, is on the order of $42 per cubic yard at 2007 gold price of $675 per oz.," the company writes. "This extends to about $75 per cubic yard at recent prices of $1200 per ounce." http://sigaresourcesinc.com/

EDITOR'S PICK: *Silver Bear Resources Inc. (PINK:SVBRF)* Why we like it: A large silver deposit in Russia. Silver Bear Resources Inc. is primarily focused on silver properties in Russia. The company's flagship Mangazeisky silver project hosts an NI 43-101 resource estimate of 1.1 million tonnes averaging 514 g/t silver fot 18 million ounces and an additional inferred mineral resource of 1.7 million tonnes averaging 554 g/t silver for 31 million ounces. http://www.silverbearresources.com/

Silver Bull Resources Inc. (AMEX:SVBL) Formerly Metalline Mining Company, Silver Bull has shown promising results at its flagship Sierra Mojada Project in Coahuila, Mexico. The Shallow Silver Zone there has "an Indicated silver resource of 28.564 million tonnes at an average grade of 50.4 g/t - equivalent to 46.313 million troy ounces of silver." http://www.silverbullresources.com/

EDITOR'S PICK: *Silver Dragon Resources Inc. (OTC:SDRG)* Why we like it: Silver mines behind the Great Wall. Focused on silver plays in China and Mexico, Silver Dragon Resources has rights to seven projects behind the Great Wall. Already, their Erbahuo silver mine has yielded more than 3,000 tonnes of silver ore as the company develops tunnels on the site. Currently, the Erbahuo and Dadi properties have 45–50 million silver-equivalent ounces of indicated and inferred resources. http://www.silverdragonresources.com/

EDITOR'S PICK: *Silver Falcon Mining Inc. (PINK:SFMI)* Why we like it: On the cusp of production. Silver Falcon Mining, Inc. expects to start initial production at War Eagle Mountain in southern Idaho during fiscal year 2011. The 15-20 year mine is estimated to yield "$6.6 million (per year) at the price of gold of $1,650," according to the company's Web site. "The owner believes at least 500,000 ounces of gold equivalent can be mined, milled and poured into dore over the next ten years." Mining and milling costs are expected to be under $200 per ounce. http://www.silverfalconmining.com/

Silver Predator Corp. (PINK:SVROF) Silver Predator Corp. has interests in 20 properties in Nevada and the Yukon. The company's Taylor Silver Project in Nevada shows 14.9 million ounces of measured and indicated silver at 79.2 g/t. The site also boasts 1.9 million inferred ounces of silver. http://www.silverpredator.com/

EDITOR'S PICK: *Silver Standard Resources Inc. (NASDAQ:SSRI)* Why we like it: A potential takeover target? Silver Standard lays claim to having the largest silver resource of any publicly-traded silver company. Their Pirquitas Mine in Argentina is projected to produce 8.5 million ounces of silver in 2011. As of the end of 2010, Silver Standard had measured and indicated silver resources of 993 million ounces. Credit Suisse recently named the company as a prime takeover target (per TheStreet). http://www.silverstandard.com/

EDITOR'S PICK: *Silver Wheaton Corp. (NYSE:SLW)* Why we like it: A silver-streaming dream. A silver-streaming company, Silver Wheaton loans miners cash to get mines operational in exchange for rights to all or some of the silver that comes from those mines. The company expects attributable production to be north of 25 million ounces of silver in 2011. By 2015, the company should be producing 43 million silver equivalent ounces. http://www.silverwheaton.com/

Silverado Gold Mines Ltd. (OTC:SLGLF) Silverado's Ester Dome property outside of Fairbanks, Alaska, shows indicated gold resources of 126,700 ounces and 214,000 inferred ounces. The company's poured most of its funds into further exploring its Nolan Creek Gold and Antimony Project, though – a tract that has shown promising antimony and gold deposits. 2009 drilling intercepted 0.64 feet of 0.57 oz/t gold and 55.4% antimony. http://www.silverado.com/

EDITOR'S PICK: *Silvercorp Metals Inc. (NYSE:SVM)* Why we like it: Negative cash costs. China's largest primary silver producer, the company was recently the target of what's increasingly looking like false allegations of fraud and a massive short position against the stock. Shares briefly fell as low as $6.30, and the company decided to buy back some $35 million worth of stock. In the quarter ended June 30, 2011, Silvercorp produced 1.6 million ounces of silver at a cash cost of negative $6.12 per ounce. http://silvercorpmetals.com/

Silvercrest Mines (OTC:STVZF) SilverCrest Mines Inc. has already begun production at its Santa Elena Mine in Mexico. The company believes that by pumping 2,500 tonnes per day through its processing facility, the mine will ultimately produce 800,000 ounces of silver and 30,000 ounces of gold per year. http://www.silvercrestmines.com/

Silvore Fox Minerals (PINK:SVFMF) Silvore Fox Minerals Corp. is in the process of doing its due diligence drilling as it acquires two gold/copper properties in Chile. The first drill hole returned 1.3 g/t gold and 1.49% copper over 1.4m. http://www.silvorefox.com/

Sintana Energy Inc. (PINK:DRFLF) Since changing names on Oct. 12, 2011, Sintana Energy Inc. (formerly Drift Lake Resources Inc.) has changed the company's focus to oil and gas exploration. Sintana's new web site no longer references precious metals. http://sintanaenergy.com/

Sirios Resources Corp. (PINK:SIREF) Sirios Resources Inc. is exploring for gold and base metals in the James Bay region of Eastern Canada. Exploration is heaviest at the company's Aquilon and Pontax properties. Drilling at Aquilon has graded as high as 834.4 g/t gold over 1.71m. Drilling at Pontax has graded as high as 821 g/t silver and 1.31 g/t gold over 4.4m. http://sirios.com/

Skeena Resources Ltd. (PINK:SKREF) Skeena Resources Limited is focused on the Tropico copper-platinum-palladium-gold project in Sinaloa State, Mexico. The low sulphidation system has shown historical assays of 0.50 to 1% copper and up to 1 g/t combined platinum, palladium and gold over widths of 15 to 160m. http://www.skeenaresources.com/

Sky Digital Stores Corp. (OTC:SKYC) Formerly Yellowcake Mining Inc., Sky Digital Stores Corporation appears to have moved away from mining. Very little is known about the company's operations since the name change on Dec. 13, 2010, but it appears precious metals are no longer on the agenda. Website n/a

Skyline Gold Corp. (PINK:SYGCF) Skyline Gold Corporation is focused on its flagship Bronson Slope property in northwestern British Columbia. The site contains a measured and indicated 2.2 million ounces of gold, as well as copper, magnetite, silver and moly. http://www.skylinegold.com/

Slam Exploration Ltd. (PINK:SLMXF) SLAM Exploration Ltd. has an NI 43-101 compliant resource estimate at its Nash Creek project in New Brunswick, Canada. The deposit contains an indicated resource of 468 million pounds zinc, 95 million pounds lead and 4.6 million ounces of silver plus an inferred resource of 71 million tonnes zinc, 14 million pounds lead and 700,000 ounces of silver. The company has also intercepted gold at its Reserve Creek project. Drill holes there have graded up to 274 g/t gold over 0.5m within a 16.85m interval grading 16.45 g/t. http://www.slamresources.com/

Solitario Exploration & Royalty Corp. (AMEX:XPL) Solitario's most advanced project is the Mt. Hamilton gold project in Nevada. The company has partnered with Ely Gold and Minerals, and they're targeting production early in 2014. Solitario could earn up to 80 percent interest in the project, which holds an estimated 1.8 million ounces of measured and indicated silver and 385,350 ounces of measured and indicated gold. http://www.solitarioresources.com/

Soltera Mining Corp. (PINK:SLTA) Soltera Mining Corp. is focused on its El Torno Gold Project in Argentina. Drilling at the site by Puma Minerals in 1997 concluded that one vein could contain more than 500,000 ounces of gold to a depth of 100m or 2 million ounces to a depth of 400m at an assumed grade of 10 g/t gold (not NI-43-101 compliant). http://www.solteramining.com/

EDITOR'S PICK: *Soltoro Ltd. (PINK:SLTOF)* Why we like it: More than 77 million ounces of silver and counting in Mexico. In December 2011, Soltoro Ltd. upped its measured and indicated resource estimate to 77.4 million ounces of silver on its 100% owned El Rayo silver project in the State of Jalisco, Mexico. Further exploration is ongoing as the company is working to expand its resource estimate at the site. http://www.soltoro.com/

Solvista Gold Corp. (PINK:SVVZF) Formed as a joint venture between Norvista Resources Corporation and Bullet Holdings Corp., Solvista Gold Corporation owns two exploration projects in northwest Colombia. Early stage drilling will kick off at both the Guadalupe Project and the Caramanta Project early in 2012. http://www.solvistagold.com/

Sono Resources Inc. (OTC:SRCI) Sono Resources has acquired three prospective mineral exploration licenses in Botswana totaling 1872.7 square kilometers known as the North Blocks. Located in the Kalahari Copper Belt, Sono's property abuts that owned by Discovery Metals. Discovery plans to start production in 2012 on a $560 million market cap copper-silver project. Sample grades from Sono's property were unknown at the time of this writing. http://www.sonoresourcesinc.com/

Sonora Gold and Silver (PINK:SOCJF) After initially exploring for precious metals in Sonora, Mexico, Sonora Gold and Silver Corp. has turned its focus to prospective gold properties in east Africa, namely in Tanzania. The company is currently appealing the cancellation of a mining license there. http://www.sonoragoldcorp.com/

Source Exploration (PINK:SRXLF) Source Exploration Corp. is focused on its Las Minas gold, silver and copper project in Veracruz, Mexico. Rock chip channel samples from the site have graded as high as 9.94 g/t gold and 6.8 g/t silver over 4m and 5.5 g/t gold and 87 g/t silver over 24m. http://www.sourceexploration.com/

Source Gold Corp. (OTC:SRGL) Source Gold Corp. recently acquired rights to a plot of land in Arizona that abuts the historic Vulture Mine. The Vulture Mine produced 380,000 ounces of gold and 280,000 ounces of silver between 1863 and 1942. An NI 43-101 report on the land is reportedly in the works. http://www.sourcegoldcorp.com/

EDITOR'S PICK: *South American Gold Corp. (OTC:SAGD)* Why we like it: New drilling in December 2011 doubled the company's resources. South American Gold Corp. is in the early stages of exploration at its Santacruz Gold Project in Colombia. Numerous gold veins were first recorded at the site by the Japanese and Colombian governments in the 1980s, and the company plans to start drilling at the site in the first half of 2012. Early-stage soil samples were unavailable at the time of this writing. http://www.sagoldcorp.com/

South American Silver Corp. (PINK:SOHAF) On Dec. 20, 2011, South American Silver Corp. announced its first NI 43-101 mineral resource estimate for its Escalones project in central Chile. At a 0.2% copper-equivalent cut-off grade, the Escalones project has inferred resources of 3.8 billion pounds copper, 56.9 million pounds molybdenum, 610,000 ounces gold and 16.8 million ounces silver. Those drill results doubled the company's resources in the ground (pushing them to 4.5 billion pounds of copper-equivalent metal). http://www.soamsilver.com/

Southern Silver Exploration Corp. (PINK:SSVFF) Southern Silver Exploration Corp. recently acquired the Cerro Las Minitas project, a silver-lead-zinc property in Durango State, Mexico. Drill holes there have intercepted 217 g/t silver over 1.6m and 38 g/t silver over 13.6m. http://www.southernsilverexploration.com/

EDITOR'S PICK: *Spanish Mountain Gold Ltd. (PINK:SPAZF)* Why we like it: A prefeasibility study is underway. Spanish Mountain Gold Ltd. is focused on its flagship Spanish Mountain Project in British Columbia. The project currently shows an NI 43-101 compliant resource of 2.1 million ounces gold and 2.8 million ounces silver (measured and indicated) and an inferred resource of 4 million ounces gold and 7.1 million ounces of silver. A prefeasibility study is underway. http://www.spmtngold.com/

St. Andrew Goldfields (PINK:STADF) St. Andrew Goldfields Ltd. is focused on bringing gold projects to production in Ontario. The company's Holt, Holloway and Hislop Mines were forecast to produce 65,000 to 75,000 ounces of gold in 2011. That number should grow to 100,000 ounces in 2012. All told, the company has mineral resources (including inferred) of 3.9 million ounces gold and mineral reserves of 700,000 ounces. http://www.sasgoldmines.com/

EDITOR'S PICK: *St. Elias Mines Ltd. (PINK:SELSF)* Why we like it: A good chart pattern with shares up 650% over the past five years. St. Elias Mines Ltd. is exploring for gold in Peru and British Columbia. The company's flagship Tesoro Gold Property in Peru has recovered 1,076 ounces of gold (at an average grade of 0.93 oz/t) from its underground bulk sampling program. More drilling and trenching will kick off in January 2012. http://steliasmines.com/

St. Eugene Mining Corp. Ltd. (PINK:STEUF) St. Eugene Mining Corporation Ltd. is developing gold properties in Manitoba and Saskatchewan. On Oct. 25, 2011, the company announced that it was being acquired by Claude Resources Inc. http://www.steugenemining.ca/

Starcore International Mines Ltd. (PINK:SHVLF) Starcore International Mines Ltd. owns a subsidiary called Compania Minera Pena de Bernal, which owns the San Martin mine in Queretaro, Mexico. Total proven and probable mineral reserves at the San Martin mine as of July 31, 2011 stand at 586,318 tonnes at a grade of 2.29 g/t gold and 39 g/t silver. The mine at the site is in production with a current output of 747 tpd. http://www.starcore.com/

Stealth Resources Inc. (OTC:SERS) There's been little news from Stealth Resources Inc. since the company acquired a 124.6 hectare mineral claim in British Columbia. As of May 31, 2010, exploration had not commenced at the so-called "Monkey" claim. Website n/a

Stikine Energy Corp. (PINK:SKNGF) Stikine Energy Corp.'s focus has shifted from metals to becoming a frac sand producer and supplier to British Columbia's shale gas industry. The company's basin projects should produce gas for more than 50 years. http://www.stikineenergy.com/

EDITOR'S PICK: *Stroud Resources Ltd. (PINK:SDURF)* Why we like it: More than 23 million ounces of silver in Mexico. Stroud Resources Ltd. is focused on the Santo Domingo epithermal silver-gold project in central Mexico. Recent drilling at the site intercepted 26m of 88.46 g/t silver and 0.11 g/t gold including 8m of 231.24 g/t silver and 0.19 g/t gold. The project contains an NI 43-101 compliant resource of 23.9 million silver equivalent ounces (measured, indicated and inferred) and 95,400 ounces of gold (measured, indicated and inferred). http://www.stroudresourcesltd.com/

Sunergy Inc. (PINK:SNEY) Sunergy, Inc. is focused on alluvial gold, silver and diamond projects in Ghana and Sierra Leone, West Africa. Historical reports from the company's Sierra Leone project indicate recoverable alluvial gold at over 500,000 ounces with average grades of 0.12 oz./t. "Substantial Rare Earth Elements (REE's) may equal or exceed gold values," the company writes. http://www.sunergygold.com/

EDITOR'S PICK: *Sunward Resources Ltd. (PINK:SNWRF)* Why we like it: More than 8 million ounces of gold in Colombia. Sunward Resources Ltd. has defined a large deposit at its Titiribi project in Colombia. An NI 43-101 compliant report shows an indicated mineral resource of 2.2 million ounces gold within 142.94 million tonnes grading 0.480 g/t gold and 0.148% copper, using a 0.3 g/t gold cut-off at Titiribi. The Titiribi project also hosts an inferred mineral resource of 6.08 million ounces gold within 372.7 million tonnes grading 0.507 g/t gold and 0.078% copper, using a 0.3 g/t gold cut-off. http://www.sunwardresources.com/

Superior Mining International (PINK:SUIFF) Superior Mining International Corporation is working to define a mineral resource at its Mangalisa gold and uranium project in South Africa. Phase I drilling returned intersections with grades as high as 45.8 g/t gold and 3.79 kg/t uranium over 0.45m and 91.8 g/t gold and 7.24 kg/t uranium over 0.21m. http://www.superiormining.com/

Sutter Gold Mining Inc. (PINK:SGMNF) Sutter Gold Mining, Inc. is focused on the Lincoln Project in California. Located in the California Mother Lode Gold Belt, the company's properties have yielded significant historical production (more than 3.5 million ounces). The Lincoln Project contains 681,958 total indicated and inferred ounces with production due to begin in 2012. http://www.suttergoldmining.com/

EDITOR'S PICK: *Tahoe Resources Inc. (PINK:THOEF)* Why we like it: More than 300 million ounces of silver in the ground. Tahoe Resources is a silver exploration company focused on its Escobal silver project in Southeast Guatemala. Escobal hosts an indicated silver resource of 245.2 million ounces at 500 g/t average grade, and an inferred silver resource of 71.7 million ounces at 271 g/t average grade. http://www.tahoeresourcesinc.com/

Takara Resources Inc. (PINK:TAKRF) Takara Resources Inc. is focused on gold properties in Guyana, South America, where the company holds 100 percent interest in the Tassawini Gold Project. Tassawini hosts an NI 43-101 compliant mineral resource of 437,000 ounces of gold (indicated) and 62,000 ounces of gold (inferred). http://www.takararesources.com/

Taku Gold Corp. (PINK:TAKUF) Taku Gold Corp. is exploring its Portland property in the Yukon. Drill results were released on Dec. 12, 2011 with the highest grade weighing in at 2.3 g/t gold over 1m and 0.5 g/t gold over 3m. "Although this zone is narrow and low-grade, it does provide direct evidence for the existence of gold-bearing zones parallel to the Gold Run structure," the company stated in a press release. http://www.takugold.com/

Tanzanian Royalty Exploration Corp. (AMEX:TRX) Exploring for gold properties in Tanzania, the company's flagship Buckreef Project has gold resources of 2.1 million ounces. Shares have gotten crushed recently, down 40 percent in a month, although the company claims underlying fundamentals haven't changed. http://www.tanzanianroyalty.com/

EDITOR'S PICK: *Tara Minerals Corp. (OTC:TARM)* Why we like it: On the cusp of production and a potential JV with Yamana. Tara Minerals appears on the cusp of production at its Tania (iron ore) and San Felipe (gold and silver) properties. The company has a 90 percent stake in Adit Resources Corp. That's exciting as Adit looks like it's planning a million-ounce+ joint venture with Yamana Gold. http://www.taraminerals.com/

Taranis Resources Inc. (PINK:TNREF) Taranis Resources Inc. is actively exploring gold and base metal properties in Finland. Drill results from the

Kettukuusikko gold property have yielded a range of results from 0.86 g/t over 21m to 5.7 g/t over 1.45m. http://www.taranis.us/

Temex Resources Corp. (PINK:TMXRF) Temex Resources Corp. is focused on its Juby joint venture property in northeastern Ontario. Individual grab samples at the site have graded between 0.59 g/t gold and 8.26 g/t gold. The Juby Main Zone has a resource of 14.1 million tonnes at a grade of 1.36 g/t gold for 614,000 ounces of gold in the indicated category and 18.3 million tonnes at a grade of 1.14 g/t gold for 602,000 ounces of gold in the inferred category. Temex also has an NI 43-101 compliant resource at its Gowganda Silver Project (with 2.96 million ounces of indicated silver). http://www.temexcorp.com/

Teras Resources Inc. (PINK:TRARF) Teras Resources Inc. is actively drilling at its Cahuilla gold-silver project in California. Recent assay results showed 1.5m of 104.3 g/t gold within 10.7m of 19.1 g/t gold and 9.2m of 8.7 g/t gold within 36.6m of 2.7 g/t gold. The company currently has interests in six projects in the U.S. and Canada. http://www.teras.ca/

EDITOR'S PICK: *Teuton Resources Corp. (PINK:TEUTF)* Why we like it: Holds land beside Pretium's Brucejack-Snowfield properties. Teuton Resources Corp. is focused on exploration in British Columbia's "Gold Triangle." The company controls prospective land along strike both to the north and south of the KSM and Brucejack-Snowfield properties of Seabridge Gold and Pretium Resources (which contain resources of over 70 million ounces of gold and 10 billion pounds of copper). Exploratory drilling is underway at both Treaty Creek and Tennyson. http://www.teuton.com/

Themac Resources Group (PINK:MACQF) THEMAC Resources Group Ltd. acquired 100 percent of the New Mexico Copper Flat Project in May 2011. The copper/moly deposit shows historic grades of 0.1 g/t gold and 2.36 g/t silver. A prefeasibility study at the site is expected in Q1 of 2012. http://www.themacresourcesgroup.com/

Threegold Resources (PINK:TRLDF) Threegold Resources Inc. kicked off Phase II drilling at its South Bay gold project in Quebec in December 2011. The drilling will follow up on grab samples and Phase I drilling that uncovered grades up to 27 g/t gold and a new silver discovery (which showed 135 g/t silver). http://www.threegold.ca/

Thundermin Resources Inc. (PINK:TUDMF) Thundermin Resources Inc.'s 2011 exploration efforts focused on the Little Deer Copper Deposit in Newfoundland. That culminated in a positive preliminary economic assessment for the deposit that was announced on Nov. 1. Little Deer shows indicated resources of 1,911,000 tonnes grading 2.37% copper (99.8 million pounds of copper) and inferred resources of 3,748,000 tonnes grading 2.13% copper (175.9 million pounds of copper). http://www.thundermin.com/

Tiger International Resources (PINK:TGILF) Tiger International Resources Inc. officially got the rights to explore the Esperanza Gold Project in the Philippines in 2011. "Our company (now) ... plans to apply separately to the local county for interim processing approval so we can conduct a 'run of mine production,'" company President Patric Barry writes on Tiger's Web site. Current resource estimates are unavailable, but the project is bounded on two sides by two other active drill sites (owned separately by Ivanhoe Canada and Indophil). http://www.tigerresources.com/

Timberline Resources Corp. (AMEX:TLR) Timberline has more than 1 million ounces of gold in the ground at its two largest projects: South Eureka, Nevada, and Butte Highlands, Montana (where the company has a 50 percent interest). The Butte project is slated to start production in Q1 2012 with estimates of producing up to 60,000 ounces of gold per year. http://www.timberline-resources.com/

Timmins Gold Corp. (AMEX:TGD) Timmins Gold Corp. is producing gold at its San Francisco Gold Property located in Sonora, Mexico. The past-producing open pit heap leach operation is estimating annual average production of 130,000 ounces of gold per year. http://www.timminsgold.com/

Tinka Resources Ltd. (PINK:TKRFF) Tinka Resources Limited is focused on two projects in Peru: the Colquipucro silver/base metal project and the Tibillos copper porphyry project. A recently completed independent NI 43-101 report at Colquipucro showed an inferred silver resource of 20.3 million ounces. More drilling is underway to expand the resource. http://www.tinkaresources.com/

TNR Gold Corp. (PINK:TRRXF) TNR Gold Corp. was busy in 2011. The company spun out International Lithium Corp., consolidated its holdings in the Shotgun gold project in Alaska (for a 100 percent interest) and confirmed the presence of rare earth elements at the Seabrook Lake project. Shotgun hosts a 1 million ounce historic gold deposit, according to the company. http://www.tnrgoldcorp.com/

EDITOR'S PICK: *Torex Gold Resources Inc. (PINK:TORXF)* Why we like it: 3.9 million ounces of gold in Mexico; Shares up 293% over past five years.

Torex Gold Resources Inc. is focused on the Morelos Gold Project in Mexico. The project's current NI 43-101 compliant resource estimate stands at 3 million ounces of gold in the measured and indicated category plus an additional 900,000 ounces of gold in the inferred category. http://www.torexgold.com/

EDITOR'S PICK: *Treasury Metals Inc. (PINK:TSRMF)* Why we like it: Shares are up more than 1,300% over the past five years. Treasury Metals Inc. is focused on two projects: the Goliath Gold Project and the Goldcliff Project. The Goliath project in northwestern Ontario contains 1.2 million ounces of indicated and inferred gold. The Goldcliff Property, also in Ontario, has returned grab samples grading as high as 106.4 g/t gold. http://www.treasurymetals.com/

Tri Origin Exploration Ltd. (PINK:TROIF) Tri Origin Exploration Ltd. is in the early stages of exploration at several gold and base metals projects in Ontario. Grab samples at the North Abitibi project have returned grades up to 23.4 g/t gold across 1.5m and 7.9 g/t gold across 4.5m. Tri Origin also holds indirect interest in Australia through its equity ownership in TriAusMin Limited. http://www.triorigin.com/

Tristar Gold Inc. (PINK:TSGZF) TriStar Gold, Inc. has three early-stage gold projects in Brazil. One - in the Tapajos Mineral Province - has been the site of small-scale artisanal mining for more than 50 years. The second, Castelo de Sonhos was previously owned by Barrick Gold and Osisko Mining Corp. The third, Bom Jardim, has returned one target with a range of base metals present. Sample grades were unknown at the time of this writing. http://www.tristarau.com/

Troon Ventures Ltd. (PINK:TVNLF) Troon Ventures Ltd. is focused on gold exploration in Ontario. The company's Fry Lake Project has returned grab samples with values as high as 448.5 g/t gold. The company's Troy Project is also in the early stages of exploration with grab and chip samples returning values ranging from 5.807 g/t to 0.337 g/t gold. http://www.troonventures.com/

Troymet Exploration Corp. (PINK:TRYXF) Troymet Exploration Corp. is exploring for gold and base metals in British Columbia and Manitoba. The company's Golden Eagle project in B.C. has returned intersections as high as 7.93 g/t gold and 23.8 g/t silver over 5.09m and 2.05 g/t gold and 43.8 g/t silver over 4.3m. Historic drilling at the company's McClarty Lake property intersected 4.17 g/t gold and 8.48 g/t silver over 4m. http://www.troymet.com/

EDITOR'S PICK: *Tyhee Gold Corp.* *(PINK:TYHJF)* Why we like it: Mine construction to start soon. Tyhee Gold Corp.'s current gold resource stands at 1.95 million ounces measured and indicated and 269,000 ounces inferred at the company's Yellowknife Gold Project in the Northwest Territories. Tyhee hopes to start mine construction at the site in 2012 or 2013. http://www.tyhee.com/

Typhoon Exploration (PINK:TYPFF) Typhoon Exploration Inc. is focused on its Fayolle Property. Drilling during 2011 returned promising intersections including 14.9 g/t gold over 30m and 1,480 g/t gold over 1m. Typhoon granted an option to Aurizon Mines Ltd. to acquire an interest of up to 65% in return for an investment in exploration of up to $25 million. http://www.typhoonexploration.com/

EDITOR'S PICK: *U.S. Precious Metals, Inc. (OTC:USPR)* Why we like it: Shares shot up 206% in 2011. With rights to 37,000 acres in the State of Michoacan, Mexico, U.S. Precious Metals, Inc. is focused on further exploring its Solidaridad Project. Drilling in 1997-98 not long after the deposit was discovered indicate a potential gold resource of 308,000 ounces as well as recoverable silver and copper. http://www.usprgold.com/

UC Resources Ltd. (PINK:UCRLF) UC Resources Ltd. repeatedly mentions working toward production at its La Yesca and Mar project, but it's unclear how much gold and silver are in the ground there. The company's also exploring for gold at its Copalquin project in Mexico. http://www.ucresources.net/

Unigold Inc. (PINK:UGDIF) Unigold Inc. is focused on gold exploration in the Dominican Republic. The company's Los Candelones target at its Neita project has shown promise with intersections of 2.1 g/t gold over 61m (including 6.9 g/t over 10m) and 1.1 g/t gold over 82m. http://www.unigoldinc.com/

United Mines, Inc. (OTC:UNMN) United Mines, Inc. holds rights to two silver projects, three gold projects and one copper project, all of which encompass 4,000 acres surrounding Tucson, Arizona. The company's La Colorada High Grade Mill and Heap Leach Facility show "estimated in-ground resources of 7 to 12 million tons with an average grade of 10 opt gold." http://unitedmines.com/

USCorp (PINK:USCS) USCorp has not published specific numbers regarding gold assays on the company's two prospective gold properties in the southwestern U.S.: the Twin Peaks project and the Picacho Salton project. During 2011, the company did however raise $2.1 million in funding for further exploration at Twin Peaks. http://uscorpgold.com/

Valencia Ventures (PINK:VVIVF) Valencia Ventures Inc. has focused on gold and silver projects in Chile in the past. The company has a 20 percent stake in Apogee's Chilean Cachinal Project, which could potentially produce one to two million ounces of silver a year. Valencia may be changing tack, though, as the company announced on Nov. 29, 2011, that it was in negotiations to acquire a phosphate project in Africa. http://www.valenciaventures.com/

ValGold Resources Ltd. (OTC:VALGF) ValGold Resources Ltd. has mining interests from the Ukraine to Venezuela and Ontario. Historical drill intersections at the company's MBK Project have returned up to 32.60m averaging 3.60 g/t gold, 31.60 g/t silver, 3.89% lead and 5.68% zinc. The company's Tower Mountain Gold Property in Ontario returned an intersection of 16.5m grading 1.136 g/t gold during Phase I drilling. http://www.valgold.com/

Vantex Resources Ltd. (PINK:VANTF) Vantex Resources Ltd. is exploring its Galloway property in Quebec. Historical drilling (non-NI 43-101 compliant) showed multiple drill intersections of 50 to 100+m over 1 g/t gold. An NI 43-101 compliant resource estimate is underway. http://www.vantexressources.com/

Vena Resources Inc. (PINK:VNARF) Vena Resources Inc. is exploring for gold and uranium in Peru. The company filed an NI 43-101 report on Dec. 19, 2011, which outlines a recommendation for $1.3 million in further exploration at the Pukara property. An earlier drill hole at Pukara intersected 14.92m of 0.23 g/t gold, 18.66 g/t silver and 8.3% lead. http://www.venaresources.com/

EDITOR'S PICK: *VHGI Holdings, Inc. (PINK:VHGI)* Why we like it: Shares up more than 500% in 2011. On Dec. 19, 2011, VHGI Holdings, Inc. announced that it was planning to spin out its holdings in Florida-based Medical Office Software, Inc. to focus entirely on the acquisition of an operating coal mine and future mineral exploration. The company has not identified any targets. http://www.vhgiholdings.com/

Victoria Gold Corp. (PINK:VITFF) Victoria Gold Corp. announced on Dec. 15, 2011, that it had inked a deal with the Na Cho Nyak Dun First Nation in Yukon to double the size of its holdings at the site of its Dublin

Gulch gold discovery. Already, the company boasts of a "current global mineral inventory of 7.7 million gold ounces." http://www.vitgoldcorp.com/

Victory Resources Corp. (PINK:VRCFF) Victory Resources Corporation is focused on its Reforma property in west central Mexico. The former mine (which was owned by Penoles) produced 2 million tonnes grading an average of 91.62 g/t gold, 1.90% lead, 7.44% zinc and 0.63% copper. Recent drilling at the site returned grades of 127.4 g/t silver, 3.125% lead and 0.88% copper over 9.6m. http://www.victoryresourcescorp.com/

Virginia Mines Inc. (PINK:VGMNF) Virginia Mines Inc. is sitting on a potential gold royalty at its Eleonore project in James Bay, Canada. The company is entitled to a 2-3.5% net smelter royalty at the opening of the mine, which was acquired by Goldcorp. That income (if and when it arrives) should help fund further exploration at the company's 19 other potential deposits. http://www.virginia.qc.ca/

Visible Gold Mines (PINK:VGMIF) Visible Gold Mines Inc. is exploring for gold in Quebec. The company's Lucky Break project has returned Phase I drill results grading up to 19.73 g/t gold over 1.5m. The company's Joutel gold project is exploring a historical mine that produced more than 1.1 million ounces of gold. The site also yielded 300,000 ounces of silver. http://www.visiblegoldmines.com/

EDITOR'S PICK: *Vista Gold Corp. (AMEX:VGZ)* Why we like it: $13 price target. Vista has five projects that contain a total of 11.6 million measured and indicated ounces of gold and 4.4 million inferred ounces. The stock's trading far below the average consensus analyst price target of $13.04 (per Fnno.com). http://www.vistagold.com/

Volta Resources Inc. (PINK:VLTAF) Volta Resources Inc. is exploring for gold in Burkina Faso, Ghana and Mali. A prefeasibility study at the company's Kiaka Gold Project in Burkina Faso is expected in Q1 2012. An NI 43-101 compliant resource at the site shows 3,018,000 ounces of gold (measured and indicated) and 1,260,000 ounces of gold inferred. The company also shows an NI 43-101 compliant resource of over 1,072,000 ounces of gold and 725 million pounds of copper at its Gaoua Copper-Gold Project. http://www.voltaresources.com/

VVC Exploration Corp. (PINK:VVCVF) VVC Exploration Corporation is exploring for gold in Canada and Mexico. The company's Beauce-Bellechasse Gold Property in Quebec has shown mineral occurrences with values of up to 12 g/t gold. The company also has four properties in Mexico, which could prove promising. The Cumeral Property has shown four grab samples ranging from 0.03 to 6.03 g/t gold. http://www.vvcexpl.com/

Wescan Goldfields Inc. (PINK:WEGOF) Wescan Goldfields Inc. is working on a potential preliminary economic assessment on its Jojay Gold Project in northern Saskatchewan. An NI 43-101 report on the property indicates 420,000 tonnes with an average grade of 3.7 g/t gold for 50,000 ounces. Inferred mineral resources amount to 630,000 tonnes with an average grade of 4.3 g/t gold for 87,000 ounces gold. Drilling at the company's Jasper gold project has also intersected grades of 74.4 g/t over 1m. http://wescangoldfields.com/

Wesdome Gold Mines Ltd. (PINK:WDOFF) Wesdome Gold Mines Ltd. announced on Nov. 1, 2011, that the company was lowering its production guidance to 45,000 to 50,000 ounces for fiscal 2011. The stock got hammered and has been struggling to recover ever since. Currently, the company has reserves of 319,000 ounces of gold and 839,000 ounces of gold resources (measured, indicated and inferred). http://www.wesdome.com/

Western Pacific Resources Corp. (PINK:WRPSF) Western Pacific Resources Corp. is exploring for gold and silver in Nevada and Idaho. The company's flagship project is at Mineral Gulch, the site of the historic Black Pine mine, which produced more than 500,000 ounces of gold. Recent drilling at the site returned grades up to 1.6 g/t gold over 24.4m. http://www.westernpacificresources.com/

White Pine Resources (PINK:WPRFF) White Pine Resources Inc. is exploring for precious and base metals in Ontario and the Yukon. Trenching at the company's Money Project in the Yukon has returned results of 1.6 g/t gold over 25m, including 11.1 g/t gold over 3m, and 1.0 g/t gold over 19m, including 8.5 g/t over 1.5m. http://www.whitepineresources.ca/

EDITOR'S PICK: *Wildcat Silver Corp. (PINK:WLDVF)* Why we like it: More than 120 million ounces of silver in the ground. Wildcat Silver Corporation is focused on its Hermosa property outside of Tucson, Arizona. Drill results announced on Dec. 21, 2011, returned grades as high as 9.1m of 395.2 g/t silver, 8.46% manganese, 0.15% zinc, 2.96% lead and 0.22% copper. The project currently has an indicated mineral resource of 6 million tonnes averaging 187.8 g/t silver for a total of 36 million ounces of silver in addition to an inferred mineral resource of 46.3 million tonnes averaging 58.6 g/t silver for a total of 85 million ounces of silver as announced on April 20, 2010. http://www.wildcatsilver.com/

Windarra Minerals Ltd. (PINK:WDRMF) Windarra Minerals Ltd. has several JV projects and net smelter royalties set up. These should, in theory, start generating positive cash flow for the company one day. At the moment, Windarra has a 1% net smelter royalty in the Magnacon Property, a 2% net smelter royalty on Messina Mineral Inc.'s share of production from the Tulks massive sulphide property in Newfoundland, and a Mishi Pit royalty of $1/tonne for ore from open pit mining and $2/tonne for underground mining in excess of 700,000 tonnes mined. http://www.windarra.com/

Wolverine Minerals Corp. (PINK:WLRMF) Wolverine Minerals Corp. is focused on gold exploration in the Yukon. The company's Dawson Range property has returned grades as high as 23.9 g/t gold over 3m, 1.67 g/t gold over 6.5m and a 36m wide zone of 1.173 g/t gold. http://www.wolverineminerals.ca/

Xmet Inc. (PINK:XMTTF) Xmet Inc. is exploring for gold in Quebec and Newfoundland. Phase 2 drilling at the company's Duquesne Ottoman project is focused on expanding the current inferred resource of 727,000 ounces of gold (853,000 ounces uncut). New results have returned grades as high as 5.18 g/t gold over 4.55m. http://xmet.ca/

Xtierra Ltd. (PINK:XRESF) Xtierra Inc.'s primary project is the Bilbao silver-zinc-lead-copper deposit in Zacatecas, Mexico. An NI 43-101 compliant report for the Bilbao deposit shows indicated resources of 10.62 million tonnes for a total of 688,258 tonnes zinc equivalent. http://www.xtierra.ca/

Yamana Gold Inc. (NYSE:AUY) Yamana has seven gold mines in operation, and it looks like the company is significantly under-valued compared to its peers. Despite rapidly increasing revenues, the stock's trading under analysts' price target of $18 a share (per SeekingAlpha). Yamana has 19,400,000 ounces gold in reserves. http://www.yamana.com/

Yinfu Gold Corp. (PINK:ELRE) Yinfu Gold Corp. owns 100% of Penglai Yinfu Mining Consulting Company Ltd., which owns gold mining and exploration concessions in Shandong Province, in China. The company applied to be listed on the NASDAQ on Sept. 16, 2010. Yinfu's Penglai Huwei Mine was in production in 2008, but production was suspended for further exploration. Historically, the mine has produced 77,000 tonnes of ore at a grade of 4.42 g/t gold. http://www.yinfucorp.com/

Yorbeau Resources Inc. (PINK:YRBAF) Yorbeau Resources Inc. is exploring for gold and base metals in Quebec. The company holds a 2005 NI 43-101 compliant resource estimate on the Astoria deposit showing a resource of 349,000 ounces measured and indicated gold and 61,000 ounces inferred. The company is currently exploring the Rouyn property on the Abitibi Greenstone Belt. 2010 drilling there returned grades as high as 27 g/t gold over 3m. http://www.yorbeauresources.com/

CHAPTER 4
SIXTY-THREE PROFITABLE GOLD AND SILVER MINING COMPANIES (LISTED BY EARNINGS PER SHARE)

Company	Ticker	Earnings Per Share
Silver Standard Resources Inc.	(NASD:SSRI)	6.28
Newmont Mining Corp.	(NYSE:NEM)	4.72
Barrick Gold Corp.	(NYSE:ABX)	4.36
Compania De Minas Buenaventura SA	(NYSE:BVN)	3.35
Randgold Resources Ltd.	(NASD:GOLD)	3.16
Anglogold Ashanti Ltd.	(NYSE:AU)	2.91
Pan American Silver Corp.	(NASD:PAAS)	2.34
Goldcorp Inc.	(NYSE:GG)	2.26
Handy And Harman Ltd.	(NASD:HNH)	1.57
Imperial Metals Corp.	(PINK:IPMLF)	1.56
Royal Gold, Inc.	(NASD:RGLD)	1.48
Silver Wheaton Corp.	(NYSE:SLW)	1.32
IAMGOLD Corp.	(NYSE:IAG)	1.07
Yamana Gold Inc.	(NYSE:AUY)	0.83
Kinross Gold Corp.	(NYSE:KGC)	0.81
Coeur D'Alene Mines Corp.	(NYSE:CDE)	0.80
Aurico Gold Inc.	(NYSE:AUQ)	0.76
Gold Fields Ltd.	(NYSE:GFI)	0.73

Company	Ticker	Earnings Per Share
Richmont Mines Inc.	(AMEX:RIC)	0.69
Agnico-Eagle Mines Ltd.	(NYSE:AEM)	0.67
Vista Gold Corp.	(AMEX:VGZ)	0.67
Eldorado Gold Corp.	(NYSE:EGO)	0.50
International Minerals Corp.	(PINK:IMZLF)	0.50
New Gold Inc.	(AMEX:NGD)	0.50
Nevsun Resources	(AMEX:NSU)	0.49
Silvercorp Metals Inc.	(NYSE:SVM)	0.48
Columbus Silver	(PINK:CSLVF)	0.45
Hecla Mining Company	(NYSE:HL)	0.40
Jinhao Motor Co., Ltd.	(PINK:GIMC)	0.37
China TMK Battery Systems Inc.	(OTC:DFEL)	0.36
Harmony Gold Mining Co.	(NYSE:HMY)	0.32
Minefinders Corp. Ltd.	(AMEX:MFN)	0.31
Allied Nevada Gold Corp.	(AMEX:ANV)	0.28
Argonaut Gold Inc.	(PINK:ARNGF)	0.26
Gold Resource Corp.	(AMEX:GORO)	0.22
Revett Minerals Inc.	(AMEX:RVM)	0.22
Orosur Mining Inc.	(PINK:OROXF)	0.19
Aurizon Mines Ltd.	(AMEX:AZK)	0.17
Scorpio Mining Corp.	(PINK:SMNPF)	0.15
Timmins Gold Corp.	(AMEX:TGD)	0.12
Alexco Resource Corp.	(AMEX:AXU)	0.11
Great Panther Silver Ltd.	(AMEX:GPL)	0.11
Valgold Resources Ltd.	(OTC:VALGF)	0.08
Dolly Varden Resources	(PINK:DVRRF)	0.07
Petaquilla Minerals Ltd.	(OTC:PTQMF)	0.06
Alhambra Resources Ltd.	(PINK:AHBRF)	0.05
Benton Resources Corp.	(PINK:BNRJF)	0.05
Eagle Plains Resources Ltd.	(PINK:EGPLF)	0.05
Riverside Resources Inc.	(PINK:RVSDF)	0.05
Claude Resources Inc.	(AMEX:CGR)	0.04
Corona Gold Corp.	(PINK:CRGAF)	0.04
Endeavour Silver Corp.	(NYSE:EXK)	0.04

Company	Ticker	Earnings Per Share
Fortune Minerals Ltd.	(PINK:FTMDF)	0.04
Minco Gold Corp.	(AMEX:MGH)	0.04
Atna Resources Ltd.	(OTC:ATNAF)	0.03
Avala Resources Ltd.	(PINK:AVLRF)	0.03
Tri Origin Exploration Ltd.	(PINK:TROIF)	0.03
Wesdome Gold Mines Ltd.	(PINK:WDOFF)	0.03
Aura Silver Resources Ltd.	(PINK:AUSVF)	0.02
Bellhaven Copper & Gold Inc.	(PINK:BHVCF)	0.02
Caledonia Mining Corp.	(OTC:CALVF)	0.02
Rockhaven Resources	(PINK:RKHNF)	0.02
Bullion Monarch Mining Inc.	(OTC:BULM)	0.01

CHAPTER 5
TWENTY-ONE GOLD AND SILVER MINING COMPANIES THAT PAY DIVIDENDS

Company	Ticker	Dividend Yield
Gold Resource Corp.	(AMEX:GORO)	2.47%
Newmont Mining Corp.	(NYSE:NEM)	2.21%
Agnico-Eagle Mines Ltd.	(NYSE:AEM)	1.69%
DRDGOLD Ltd.	(NASDAQ:DROOY)	1.69%
Hecla Mining Company	(NYSE:HL)	1.69%
Nevsun Resources	(AMEX:NSU)	1.63%
Gold Fields Ltd.	(NYSE:GFI)	1.54%
IAMGOLD Corp.	(NYSE:IAG)	1.48%
Compania De Minas Buenaventura SA	(NYSE:BVN)	1.45%
Silvercorp Metals Inc.	(NYSE:SVM)	1.38%
Yamana Gold Inc.	(NYSE:AUY)	1.28%
Barrick Gold Corp.	(NYSE:ABX)	1.26%
Goldcorp Inc.	(NYSE:GG)	1.19%
Silver Wheaton Corp.	(NYSE:SLW)	1.16%
Anglogold Ashanti Ltd.	(NYSE:AU)	1.00%
Kinross Gold Corp.	(NYSE:KGC)	0.95%
Royal Gold, Inc.	(NASDAQ:RGLD)	0.88%
Harmony Gold Mining Co.	(NYSE:HMY)	0.66%
Eldorado Gold Corp.	(NYSE:EGO)	0.42%
Pan American Silver Corp.	(NASDAQ:PAAS)	0.41%
Randgold Resources Ltd.	(NASDAQ:GOLD)	0.18%

CHAPTER 6
BEST AND WORST GOLD AND SILVER STOCK PERFORMANCES OF 2011

Company	Ticker	2011 Return
Liberty Gold Corp.	(OTC:LBGO)	1823333%
Roxgold Inc.	(PINK:ROGFF)	3528.97%
Stealth Resources Inc.	(OTC:SERS)	933.00%
Karmin Exploration Inc.	(PINK:KRMEF)	637.32%
VHGI Holdings, Inc.	(PINK:VHGI)	518.18%
Royal Standard Minerals Inc.	(OTC:RYSMF)	253.85%
U.S. Precious Metals, Inc.	(OTC:USPR)	206.31%
Newstrike Capital Inc.	(PINK:NWSKF)	193.40%
DNI Metals Inc.	(PINK:DMNKF)	193.12%
Kat Gold Holdings Corp.	(PINK:BVIG)	183.33%
Midway Gold Corp.	(AMEX:MDW)	151.28%
Pretium Resources Inc.	(NYSE:PVG)	138.31%
Alphamin Resources Corp.	(PINK:AFMJF)	115.02%
Richmont Mines Inc.	(AMEX:RIC)	110.57%
Bryn Resources Inc.	(PINK:BRYN)	107.69%
Wildcat Silver Corp.	(PINK:WLDVF)	106.88%
Pershimco Resources	(PINK:RSPRF)	106.75%
Red Metal Resources Ltd.	(OTC:RMES)	100.00%
Ruby Creek Resources Inc.	(OTC:RBYC)	91.18%
Canadian Orebodies	(PINK:CNOBF)	90.74%
Scorpio Mining Corp.	(PINK:SMNPF)	89.53%
Ascot Resources Ltd.	(PINK:ASOLF)	89.33%

Company	Ticker	2011 Return
NGEx Resources Inc.	(PINK:NGQRF)	87.97%
Redstar Gold Corp.	(PINK:RGCTF)	83.33%
Golden River Resources Corp.	(OTC:GORV)	80.00%
Starcore International Mines Ltd.	(PINK:SHVLF)	67.50%
Geo Minerals Ltd.	(PINK:GMNRF)	55.81%
Gold Reserve Inc.	(AMEX:GRZ)	54.70%
Stroud Resources Ltd.	(PINK:SDURF)	54.17%
Ireland Inc.	(OTC:IRLD)	53.85%
Argonaut Gold Inc.	(PINK:ARNGF)	51.67%
American Bonanza Gold Corp.	(PINK:ABGFF)	50.32%
Endeavour Silver Corp.	(NYSE:EXK)	48.47%
Sandstorm Gold Ltd.	(PINK:SNDXF)	48.27%
Reunion Gold Corp.	(PINK:RGDFF)	46.77%
VVC Exploration Corp.	(PINK:VVCVF)	43.81%
Astur Gold Corp.	(PINK:ATRGF)	43.50%
Golden Reign Resources Ltd.	(PINK:GRGNF)	41.39%
Canstar Resources Inc.	(PINK:CSRNF)	40.17%
Eastfield Resources Ltd.	(PINK:ETFLF)	38.77%
Soltoro Ltd.	(PINK:SLTOF)	37.86%
Galway Resources Ltd.	(PINK:GWYRF)	37.41%
Gogold Resources Inc.	(PINK:GLGDF)	36.48%
Freegold Ventures Ltd.	(PINK:FGOVF)	33.91%
Atna Resources Ltd.	(OTC:ATNAF)	33.87%
Alacer Gold Corp.	(PINK:ALIAF)	31.76%
Robex Resources	(PINK:RSRBF)	31.20%
Vista Gold Corp.	(AMEX:VGZ)	28.45%
Glen Eagle Resources Inc.	(PINK:GERFF)	28.01%
Probe Mines Ltd.	(PINK:PROBF)	27.86%
Merc International Minerals	(PINK:MIMZF)	26.23%
Spanish Mountain Gold Ltd.	(PINK:SPAZF)	25.82%
Sama Resources Inc.	(PINK:LNZCF)	25.60%
Taranis Resources Inc.	(PINK:TNREF)	25.00%
Randgold Resources Ltd.	(NASDAQ:GOLD)	24.01%
Royal Gold, Inc.	(NASDAQ:RGLD)	23.43%

Company	Ticker	2011 Return
Teuton Resources Corp.	(PINK:TEUTF)	22.15%
Scorpio Gold Corp.	(PINK:SRCRF)	21.08%
Buckingham Exploration Inc.	(OTC:BUKX)	20.00%
Sono Resources Inc.	(OTC:SRCI)	18.33%
Tahoe Resources Inc.	(PINK:THOEF)	18.00%
Tinka Resources Ltd.	(PINK:TKRFF)	17.81%
Calibre Mining Corp.	(PINK:CXBMF)	16.88%
Allied Nevada Gold Corp.	(AMEX:ANV)	15.09%
Sunward Resources Ltd.	(PINK:SNWRF)	14.86%
Yamana Gold Inc.	(NYSE:AUY)	14.77%
China Forest Energy Corp.	(OTC:CFEC)	13.04%
Auriga Gold Corp.	(PINK:AGRDF)	12.90%
Barker Minerals Ltd.	(PINK:BKMNF)	12.55%
DRDGOLD Ltd.	(NASDAQ:DROOY)	12.24%
Lucky Boy Silver Corp.	(PINK:LUCB)	10.00%
St. Elias Mines Ltd.	(PINK:SELSF)	9.24%
Saturn Minerals Inc.	(PINK:SAEUF)	9.12%
Sonora Gold And Silver	(PINK:SOCJF)	7.69%
Yorbeau Resources Inc.	(PINK:YRBAF)	6.62%
PMI Gold Corp.	(PINK:PMVGF)	6.37%
Columbus Gold Corp.	(PINK:CBGDF)	4.63%
Aurico Gold Inc.	(NYSE:AUQ)	4.56%
Athena Silver Corporation	(OTC:AHNR)	3.70%
New Gold Inc.	(AMEX:NGD)	3.28%
Victory Resources Corp.	(PINK:VRCFF)	2.94%
Artventive Medical Group, Inc.	(PINK:AVTD)	0.00%
BCGold Corp.	(PINK:BCGOF)	0.00%
Franklin Mining, Inc.	(PINK:FMNJ)	0.00%
Searchlight Minerals Corp.	(OTC:SRCH)	0.00%
Flm Minerals Inc.	(PINK:FLMS)	-0.99%
Huldra Silver Inc.	(PINK:HUSIF)	-1.11%
Oromin Explorations Ltd.	(OTC:OLEPF)	-1.11%
Virginia Mines Inc.	(PINK:VGMNF)	-2.26%
Newmont Mining Corp.	(NYSE:NEM)	-2.31%

Company	Ticker	2011 Return
Canadian Zinc Corp.	(OTC:CZICF)	-2.39%
RJK Exploration Ltd.	(PINK:RJKAF)	-2.69%
Shoshone Silver Mining Co.	(PINK:SHSH)	-3.23%
Tristar Gold Inc.	(PINK:TSGZF)	-3.50%
Goldcorp Inc.	(NYSE:GG)	-3.76%
Jasper Mining Corp.	(PINK:JAMGF)	-3.85%
Minefinders Corp. Ltd.	(AMEX:MFN)	-3.99%
Silver Bear Resources Inc.	(PINK:SVBRF)	-4.33%
Colibri Resource Corp.	(PINK:CRUCF)	-5.28%
Azimut Exploration	(PINK:AZMTF)	-6.43%
Puma Exploration	(PINK:PUXPF)	-6.55%
Torex Gold Resources Inc.	(PINK:TORXF)	-6.57%
Themac Resources Group	(PINK:MACQF)	-6.65%
Plato Gold	(PINK:PTOZF)	-7.17%
Harmony Gold Mining Co.	(NYSE:HMY)	-7.18%
Cream Minerals Ltd.	(OTC:CRMXF)	-7.50%
Silvercrest Mines	(OTC:STVZF)	-7.58%
Banro Corp.	(AMEX:BAA)	-7.96%
Gold Reach Resources	(PINK:GRVJF)	-8.00%
CB Gold Inc.	(PINK:CBHDF)	-8.54%
Revett Minerals Inc.	(AMEX:RVM)	-8.70%
Andes Gold Corp.	(PINK:AGCZ)	-8.82%
Columbus Silver	(PINK:CSLVF)	-9.13%
Adventure Gold Inc.	(PINK:AGONF)	-9.58%
Jaguar Mining Inc.	(NYSE:JAG)	-10.52%
IAMGOLD Corp.	(NYSE:IAG)	-10.96%
HuntMountain Resources Ltd.	(PINK:HNTM)	-11.29%
Coeur D'Alene Mines Corp.	(NYSE:CDE)	-11.64%
Glass Earth Gold Ltd.	(PINK:GELGF)	-12.36%
Bison Gold Resources Inc.	(PINK:BGEZF)	-12.39%
Cadillac Ventures Inc.	(PINK:CADIF)	-12.43%
Firesteel Resources Inc.	(PINK:FIEIF)	-12.50%
Maudore Minerals Ltd.	(PINK:MAOMF)	-13.05%
Sunergy Inc.	(PINK:SNEY)	-13.58%

Company	Ticker	2011 Return
GWR Resources Inc.	(PINK:GWRRF)	-13.71%
Anglogold Ashanti Ltd.	(NYSE:AU)	-13.77%
Habanero Resources	(PINK:HBNRF)	-13.80%
Barrick Gold Corp.	(NYSE:ABX)	-14.91%
Sutter Gold Mining Inc.	(PINK:SGMNF)	-14.99%
Global Minerals Ltd.	(PINK:GMLFF)	-15.55%
Odyssey Resources Ltd.	(PINK:ODXSF)	-15.57%
Samex Mining Corp.	(OTC:SMXMF)	-15.58%
Gold Fields Ltd.	(NYSE:GFI)	-15.89%
Dolly Varden Resources	(PINK:DVRRF)	-16.21%
Dia Bras Exploration Inc.	(PINK:DBEXF)	-16.54%
Alexco Resource Corp.	(AMEX:AXU)	-16.85%
Bowmore Exploration Ltd.	(PINK:BWMXF)	-17.58%
Manson Creek Resources	(PINK:MCKRF)	-18.12%
Tiger International Resources	(PINK:TGILF)	-18.12%
Thundermin Resources Inc.	(PINK:TUDMF)	-18.27%
Luna Gold Corp.	(PINK:LGCUF)	-18.55%
Midland Exploration Inc.	(PINK:MIDLF)	-18.94%
Troon Ventures Ltd.	(PINK:TVNLF)	-19.06%
New Jersey Mining Company	(PINK:NJMC)	-20.00%
Royal Mines And Minerals Corp.	(PINK:RYMM)	-20.00%
Manitou Gold Inc.	(PINK:MNTUF)	-20.14%
Gold Canyon Resources Inc.	(PINK:GDCRF)	-20.18%
Treasury Metals Inc.	(PINK:TSRMF)	-20.95%
Orosur Mining Inc.	(PINK:OROXF)	-20.99%
Global Gold Corp.	(PINK:GBGD)	-21.05%
Cassidy Gold Corp.	(PINK:CDXGF)	-21.52%
Compania De Minas Buenaventura SA	(NYSE:BVN)	-21.69%
Handy And Harman Ltd.	(NASDAQ:HNH)	-21.74%
Sienna Gold Inc.	(PINK:SNNGF)	-22.09%
Golden Goliath Resources Ltd.	(PINK:GGTHF)	-22.30%
Teras Resources Inc.	(PINK:TRARF)	-22.47%
New World Resource	(PINK:NWFFF)	-22.52%

Company	Ticker	2011 Return
Golden Predator Corp.	(PINK:GPRXF)	-22.85%
Moss Lake Gold Mine	(PINK:MLGXF)	-23.42%
Ginguro Exploration Inc.	(PINK:GNGXF)	-25.00%
Happy Creek Minerals	(PINK:HPYCF)	-25.00%
Jinhao Motor Co., Ltd.	(PINK:GIMC)	-25.00%
Santa Fe Gold Corp.	(OTC:SFEG)	-25.38%
Amerix Precious Metals Corp.	(PINK:APMFF)	-25.65%
International Minerals Corp.	(PINK:IMZLF)	-25.69%
Silver Wheaton Corp.	(NYSE:SLW)	-25.82%
Tara Minerals Corp.	(OTC:TARM)	-25.83%
Eldorado Gold Corp.	(NYSE:EGO)	-26.17%
Pan American Goldfields Ltd.	(OTC:MXOM)	-26.40%
Nevsun Resources	(AMEX:NSU)	-26.56%
Timmins Gold Corp.	(AMEX:TGD)	-27.06%
Gold Resource Corp.	(AMEX:GORO)	-27.99%
Typhoon Exploration	(PINK:TYPFF)	-28.43%
Fortress Minerals Co.	(PINK:FTMNF)	-28.57%
New Oroperu Resources	(PINK:NOPUF)	-28.90%
Riverside Resources Inc.	(PINK:RVSDF)	-28.98%
Colombia Crest Gold	(PINK:ECRTF)	-29.31%
Great Quest Metals Ltd.	(PINK:GQMLF)	-29.52%
Avala Resources Ltd.	(PINK:AVLRF)	-29.75%
Integra Gold Corp.	(PINK:KALRF)	-30.30%
Great Panther Silver Ltd.	(AMEX:GPL)	-30.36%
Gowest Gold Ltd.	(PINK:GWSAF)	-30.43%
Kaminak Gold Corp.	(PINK:KMKGF)	-30.92%
Guyana Goldfields Inc.	(PINK:GUYFF)	-31.59%
Orex Minerals Inc.	(PINK:ORXIF)	-31.71%
Dalradian Resources Inc.	(PINK:DRLDF)	-31.97%
Cornerstone Capital Resources Inc.	(PINK:CTNXF)	-32.16%
Sabina Gold And Silver Corp.	(PINK:SGSVF)	-32.60%
Aurizon Mines Ltd.	(AMEX:AZK)	-32.65%
Oroco Resource Corp.	(PINK:ORRCF)	-32.87%
CMQ Resources Inc.	(PINK:CMQRF)	-32.91%

Company	Ticker	2011 Return
Calais Resources Inc.	(PINK:CAAUF)	-33.00%
Metanor Resources Inc.	(PINK:MEAOF)	-33.20%
Mountain Lake Resources Inc.	(PINK:MLKRF)	-33.29%
Merrex Gold Inc.	(PINK:MXGIF)	-33.42%
Rubicon Minerals Corp.	(AMEX:RBY)	-33.80%
Monster Mining Corp.	(PINK:MMNGF)	-33.89%
Bralorne Gold Mines	(PINK:BPMSF)	-34.09%
Amerilithium Corp.	(OTC:AMEL)	-34.48%
Challenger Deep Resources	(PINK:CNDRF)	-34.53%
Carpathian Gold Inc.	(PINK:CPNFF)	-34.76%
Kobex Minerals Inc.	(AMEX:KXM)	-35.11%
Unigold Inc.	(PINK:UGDIF)	-35.40%
New Guinea Gold Corp.	(PINK:NGUGF)	-35.67%
USCorp	(PINK:USCS)	-35.71%
Eurasian Minerals Inc.	(PINK:ESMNF)	-35.79%
Wescan Goldfields Inc.	(PINK:WEGOF)	-35.97%
Orezone Gold Corp.	(PINK:ORZCF)	-36.78%
Pacific Rim Mining Corp.	(PINK:PFRMF)	-37.22%
Windarra Minerals Ltd.	(PINK:WDRMF)	-37.78%
Oroandes Resource Corp.	(PINK:OARFF)	-38.09%
Equitas Resources Corp.	(PINK:EQTRF)	-38.23%
Cogitore Resources Inc.	(PINK:CGORF)	-38.35%
Amarillo Gold Corp.	(PINK:AGCBF)	-38.50%
Kimber Resources, Inc.	(AMEX:KBX)	-38.57%
Commander Resources	(PINK:CMDRF)	-38.91%
Africo Resources Ltd.	(PINK:AFCRF)	-39.28%
Namibia Rare Earths Inc.	(PINK:NMREF)	-39.43%
Excel Gold Mining	(PINK:EGMXF)	-39.58%
Claude Resources Inc.	(AMEX:CGR)	-39.73%
Kinross Gold Corp.	(NYSE:KGC)	-39.87%
Ely Gold & Minerals Inc.	(PINK:ELYGF)	-40.01%
Maya Gold & Silver Inc.	(PINK:MYAGF)	-40.06%
Nevada Exploration Inc.	(PINK:NVDEF)	-40.07%
Skyline Gold Corp.	(PINK:SYGCF)	-40.31%

Company	Ticker	2011 Return
Premier Gold Mines	(PINK:PIRGF)	-40.46%
Novagold Resources Inc.	(AMEX:NG)	-40.57%
Bullion Monarch Mining Inc.	(OTC:BULM)	-40.87%
Crystallex International Corp.	(PINK:CRYXF)	-41.01%
White Pine Resources	(PINK:WPRFF)	-41.50%
Brazilian Gold Corp.	(PINK:BGOZF)	-41.52%
Foran Mining Corp.	(PINK:FMCXF)	-41.66%
Marifil Mines Ltd.	(PINK:MFMLF)	-41.77%
South American Silver Corp.	(PINK:SOHAF)	-41.78%
General Metals Corp.	(OTC:GNMT)	-41.87%
Balmoral Resources Ltd.	(PINK:BALMF)	-41.91%
Valencia Ventures	(PINK:VVIVF)	-42.60%
Western Pacific Resources Corp.	(PINK:WRPSF)	-42.74%
Clifton Star Resources	(PINK:CFMSF)	-42.85%
Tyhee Gold Corp.	(PINK:TYHJF)	-43.19%
Bayfield Ventures Corp.	(PINK:BYVVF)	-43.20%
Erin Ventures Inc.	(PINK:ERVFF)	-43.26%
El Capitan Precious Metals, Inc.	(OTC:ECPN)	-43.38%
Silver Bull Resources Inc.	(AMEX:SVBL)	-43.47%
Comstock Mining, Inc.	(AMEX:LODE)	-43.50%
Avino Silver & Gold Mines Ltd.	(AMEX:ASM)	-43.60%
St. Eugene Mining Corp. Ltd	(PINK:STEUF)	-43.64%
Mega Precious Metals Inc.	(PINK:MPRXF)	-44.37%
Eskay Mining Corp.	(PINK:ESKYF)	-44.67%
Kalimantan Gold Corp.	(PINK:KMGLF)	-45.02%
Barkerville Gold Mines Ltd.	(PINK:BGMZF)	-45.11%
Temex Resources Corp.	(PINK:TMXRF)	-45.15%
Caledonia Mining Corp.	(OTC:CALVF)	-45.16%
Northern Gold Mining Inc.	(PINK:NTGMF)	-45.20%
Petaquilla Minerals Ltd.	(OTC:PTQMF)	-45.23%
Dynacor Gold Mines	(PINK:DNGDF)	-45.34%
AKA Ventures Inc.	(PINK:AKAVF)	-45.43%
Rainy River Resource	(PINK:RRFFF)	-45.53%
North Country Gold	(PINK:NCGDF)	-45.88%

Company	Ticker	2011 Return
Orko Silver Corp.	(PINK:OKOFF)	-45.93%
Mag Silver Corp.	(AMEX:MVG)	-46.46%
Full Metal Minerals	(PINK:FLMTF)	-46.49%
Golden Arrow Resources Corp.	(PINK:GARWF)	-46.62%
Paramount Gold And Silver Corp.	(AMEX:PZG)	-46.62%
Almaden Minerals Ltd.	(AMEX:AAU)	-46.72%
Levon Resources Ltd.	(PINK:LVNVF)	-46.88%
Renaissance Gold Inc.	(PINK:RNSGF)	-46.99%
Sage Gold Inc.	(PINK:SGGDF)	-46.99%
Pan American Silver Corp.	(NASDAQ:PAAS)	-47.08%
Wesdome Gold Mines Ltd.	(PINK:WDOFF)	-47.22%
Malbex Resources Inc.	(PINK:MXRSF)	-47.36%
Seabridge Gold, Inc.	(AMEX:SA)	-47.49%
Lake Shore Gold Corp.	(AMEX:LSG)	-47.50%
Channel Resources Ltd.	(PINK:CHJRF)	-47.57%
Pacific Ridge Exploration	(PINK:PEXZF)	-48.06%
Valgold Resources Ltd.	(OTC:VALGF)	-48.11%
Anaconda Mining Inc.	(PINK:ANXGF)	-48.14%
LKA International Inc.	(PINK:LKAI)	-48.15%
Canasil Resources Inc.	(PINK:CNSUF)	-48.82%
Confederation Minerals Ltd.	(PINK:CNRMF)	-49.08%
American Consolidated Minerals	(PINK:AMERF)	-49.18%
Eagle Hill Exploration Corp.	(PINK:EHECF)	-49.46%
Beaufield Resources	(PINK:BFDRF)	-50.08%
Gold World Resources Inc.	(PINK:GLWDF)	-50.10%
Silvercorp Metals Inc.	(NYSE:SVM)	-50.12%
Rugby Mining Ltd.	(PINK:RBMNF)	-50.58%
China Ceetop.Com Inc.	(OTC:CTOP)	-50.98%
Silver Standard Resources Inc.	(NASDAQ:SSRI)	-50.99%
Silverado Gold Mines Ltd.	(OTC:SLGLF)	-51.52%
Andina Minerals Inc.	(PINK:ADMNF)	-51.71%
Rockhaven Resources	(PINK:RKHNF)	-51.84%
Timberline Resources Corp.	(AMEX:TLR)	-52.11%
Mines Management, Inc.	(AMEX:MGN)	-52.15%

Company	Ticker	2011 Return
Coral Gold Resources Ltd.	(OTC:CLHRF)	-52.16%
Giyani Gold Corp.	(PINK:CATPF)	-52.21%
Agnico-Eagle Mines Ltd.	(NYSE:AEM)	-52.65%
Bellhaven Copper & Gold Inc.	(PINK:BHVCF)	-52.70%
Imperial Metals Corp.	(PINK:IPMLF)	-52.85%
Olympus Pacific Minerals Inc.	(OTC:OLYMF)	-53.03%
Goldrich Mining Company	(OTC:GRMC)	-53.23%
Silvore Fox Minerals	(PINK:SVFMF)	-53.47%
Hecla Mining Company	(NYSE:HL)	-53.55%
Aurion Resources Ltd.	(PINK:AIRRF)	-53.59%
Caza Gold Corp.	(PINK:CZGDF)	-53.62%
Eastmain Resources Inc.	(PINK:EANRF)	-53.69%
International Silver Inc.	(PINK:ISLV)	-53.85%
Solvista Gold Corp.	(PINK:SVVZF)	-53.91%
Brigus Gold Corp.	(AMEX:BRD)	-54.05%
Golden Dawn Minerals Inc.	(PINK:GDMRF)	-54.37%
Armistice Resources Corp.	(PINK:AISCF)	-54.53%
Aldridge Minerals Inc.	(PINK:AGMIF)	-54.57%
Source Exploration	(PINK:SRXLF)	-54.83%
Sagebrush Gold Ltd.	(OTC:SAGE)	-54.91%
Sennen Resources Ltd.	(PINK:SNNJF)	-55.05%
Sirios Resources Corp	(PINK:SIREF)	-55.40%
China TMK Battery Systems Inc.	(OTC:DFEL)	-55.56%
La Quinta Resources Corp.	(PINK:LQRCF)	-55.65%
Arcus Development Group Inc.	(PINK:ARCUF)	-55.67%
First Point Minerals Corp.	(PINK:FPOCF)	-55.77%
Alhambra Resources Ltd.	(PINK:AHBRF)	-56.14%
Pacific Gold Corp.	(PINK:PCFG)	-56.25%
Romarco Minerals Inc.	(PINK:RTRAF)	-56.25%
Keegan Resources Inc.	(AMEX:KGN)	-56.43%
Cardero Resources Corp.	(AMEX:CDY)	-56.52%
Rochester Resources Ltd.	(PINK:RCTFF)	-56.56%
International Tower Hill Mines Ltd.	(AMEX:THM)	-56.70%

Company	Ticker	2011 Return
Rockridge Capital Corp.	(PINK:RRCPF)	-56.72%
XMET Inc.	(PINK:XMTTF)	-57.19%
Fortune Minerals Ltd.	(PINK:FTMDF)	-57.31%
Tri Origin Exploration Ltd.	(PINK:TROIF)	-57.47%
MDN Inc.	(PINK:MDNNF)	-57.65%
Silver Dragon Resources Inc.	(OTC:SDRG)	-57.69%
Northern Dynasty Minerals Ltd.	(AMEX:NAK)	-57.73%
Indigo Exploration Inc.	(PINK:IGXEF)	-57.94%
Exeter Resource Corp.	(AMEX:XRA)	-57.97%
Bravo Gold Corp.	(PINK:BVGIF)	-58.13%
Golden Valley Mines	(PINK:GLVMF)	-58.24%
Animas Resources Ltd.	(PINK:ANIMF)	-58.25%
Aldrin Resources Corp.	(PINK:AOUFF)	-58.31%
Hy Lake Gold Inc.	(PINK:HYLKF)	-58.67%
Mazorro Resources Inc.	(PINK:MZRRF)	-58.71%
United Mines, Inc.	(OTC:UNMN)	-58.75%
International PBX Ventures Ltd.	(PINK:IPBXF)	-58.87%
Golden Peaks Resources	(PINK:GDPEF)	-58.96%
Cantex Mine Development Corp.	(PINK:CTXDF)	-59.32%
Niblack Mineral Development, Inc.	(PINK:NIBMF)	-59.35%
Jayden Resources, Inc.	(PINK:PNMLF)	-59.57%
Caldera Resources Inc.	(PINK:CAEFF)	-59.60%
Crown Gold Corp.	(PINK:CWMZF)	-59.76%
Blue Note Mining Inc.	(PINK:BLNMF)	-59.98%
Endurance Gold Corp.	(PINK:ENDGF)	-60.00%
Golden Tag Resources Ltd.	(PINK:GTAGF)	-60.10%
Rogue Resources	(PINK:GCRIF)	-60.25%
Altai Resources Inc.	(PINK:ARSEF)	-60.26%
Canarc Resource Corp.	(OTC:CRCUF)	-60.71%
CMC Metals Ltd.	(PINK:CMCXF)	-60.80%
Rockcliff Resources Inc.	(PINK:RKLFF)	-60.91%
Colombian Mines Corp.	(PINK:CMBPF)	-60.98%
Solitario Exploration & Royalty Corp.	(AMEX:XPL)	-61.16%

Company	Ticker	2011 Return
Minaurum Gold Inc.	(PINK:MMRGF)	-61.21%
Volta Resources Inc.	(PINK:VLTAF)	-61.35%
Corona Gold Corp.	(PINK:CRGAF)	-61.79%
Serengeti Resources Inc.	(PINK:SGRNF)	-61.84%
Decade Resources	(PINK:DECXF)	-61.92%
Mansfield Minerals Inc.	(PINK:MFMNF)	-61.92%
Firestone Ventures	(PINK:FSVEF)	-62.32%
Northern Tiger Resources, Inc.	(PINK:NTGSF)	-62.41%
Alexandria Minerals Corp.	(PINK:ALXDF)	-62.49%
Miranda Gold Corp.	(OTC:MRDDF)	-62.57%
New Dimension Resources	(PINK:NWDMF)	-62.59%
Kilo Goldmines Ltd.	(PINK:KOGMF)	-62.70%
Golden Band Resources	(PINK:GBRIF)	-62.80%
Alder Resources Ltd.	(PINK:ARLSF)	-63.10%
Bonterra Resources Inc.	(PINK:BONXF)	-63.24%
North American Palladium Ltd.	(AMEX:PAL)	-63.26%
UC Resources Ltd.	(PINK:UCRLF)	-63.43%
Southern Silver Exploration Corp.	(PINK:SSVFF)	-63.45%
Victoria Gold Corp.	(PINK:VITFF)	-63.55%
Goldcliff Resource Corp.	(PINK:GCFFF)	-63.56%
Cline Mining Corp.	(PINK:CLNMF)	-63.77%
Argentex Mining Corp.	(OTC:AGXMF)	-63.93%
Tanzanian Royalty Exploration Corp.	(AMEX:TRX)	-63.96%
Golden Star Resources Ltd.	(AMEX:GSS)	-64.05%
Paget Minerals Corp.	(PINK:PGTMF)	-64.05%
Bear Creek Mining Corp.	(PINK:BCEKF)	-64.31%
Pelangio Exploration Inc.	(PINK:PGXPF)	-64.44%
Oro Mining Ltd.	(PINK:OMRGF)	-64.54%
King'S Bay Gold Corp	(PINK:KBGCF)	-64.56%
Magellan Minerals	(PINK:MAGNF)	-64.68%
African Gold Group Inc.	(PINK:AGGFF)	-64.80%
Champion Bear Resources	(PINK:CBRSF)	-64.95%
Entree Gold Inc.	(AMEX:EGI)	-65.32%

Company	Ticker	2011 Return
Search Minerals Inc.	(PINK:SHCMF)	-65.32%
Fjordland Exploration Inc.	(PINK:FEXXF)	-65.58%
St. Andrew Goldfields	(PINK:STADF)	-65.65%
Pilot Gold Inc.	(PINK:PLGTF)	-65.67%
Vena Resources Inc.	(PINK:VNARF)	-65.73%
Xtierra Ltd.	(PINK:XRESF)	-66.01%
Ryan Gold Corp.	(PINK:RYGZF)	-66.30%
Iron Creek Capital Corp.	(PINK:INCKF)	-66.82%
PC Gold Inc.	(PINK:PCGLF)	-67.74%
Kenai Resources Ltd.	(PINK:KAIFF)	-67.77%
Geologix Explorations Inc.	(PINK:GXEXF)	-67.84%
African Metals Corp.	(PINK:AFMCF)	-67.86%
Big Bear Mining Corp.	(OTC:BGBR)	-67.90%
Paragon Minerals Corp.	(PINK:PAONF)	-67.99%
Cedar Mountain Exploration	(PINK:CDRMF)	-68.03%
San Marco Resources Inc.	(PINK:SMREF)	-68.04%
Axmin Inc.	(PINK:AXMIF)	-68.06%
Heatherdale Resources Ltd.	(PINK:HTRRF)	-68.12%
Eagle Plains Resources Ltd.	(PINK:EGPLF)	-68.15%
Lincoln Mining Corp.	(PINK:LNCLF)	-68.15%
REBGold Corp.	(PINK:RBGCF)	-68.15%
Legend Gold Corp.	(OTC:NOATF)	-68.23%
Galore Resources Inc.	(PINK:GALOF)	-69.02%
Great Basin Gold Ltd.	(AMEX:GBG)	-69.22%
Northern Superior	(PINK:NSUPF)	-69.43%
Artha Resources Corp.	(PINK:ATHCF)	-69.48%
Conquest Resources	(PINK:CQRLF)	-70.54%
Sintana Energy Inc.	(PINK:DRFLF)	-70.58%
Hana Mining Ltd.	(PINK:HNMFF)	-70.59%
Murgor Resources Inc.	(PINK:MGRRF)	-70.64%
Rupert Resources Ltd	(PINK:RUPRF)	-70.64%
Vantex Resources Ltd.	(PINK:VANTF)	-70.70%
Corex Gold Corp.	(PINK:CGEKF)	-70.98%
TNR Gold Corp.	(PINK:TRRXF)	-71.01%

Company	Ticker	2011 Return
EMC Metals Corp.	(PINK:EMMCF)	-71.05%
Golden Phoenix Minerals, Inc.	(OTC:GPXM)	-71.10%
Newcastle Minerals Ltd.	(PINK:NCMBF)	-71.28%
Soltera Mining Corp.	(PINK:SLTA)	-71.43%
Harte Gold Corp.	(PINK:HRTFF)	-71.83%
Key Gold Holding Inc.	(PINK:KGHZF)	-71.85%
Slam Exploration Ltd.	(PINK:SLMXF)	-72.05%
Visible Gold Mines	(PINK:VGMIF)	-73.06%
Bear Lake Gold Ltd.	(PINK:BLGFF)	-73.46%
Guyana Frontier Mining Corp.	(OTC:SHESF)	-73.47%
Evolving Gold Corp.	(PINK:EVOGF)	-73.50%
Superior Mining International	(PINK:SUIFF)	-73.50%
Bravada Gold Corp.	(PINK:BGAVF)	-73.54%
Mexus Gold U.S.	(OTC:MXSG)	-74.00%
Silver Falcon Mining Inc.	(PINK:SFMI)	-74.45%
Benton Resources Corp.	(PINK:BNRJF)	-74.96%
Eloro Resources Ltd.	(PINK:ELRRD)	-75.00%
Orvana Minerals Corp.	(PINK:ORVMF)	-75.22%
Silver Predator Corp.	(PINK:SVROF)	-75.26%
Candente Copper Corp.	(PINK:CGDXF)	-75.42%
Seafield Resources Ltd.	(PINK:SRLTF)	-75.72%
Minco Gold Corp.	(AMEX:MGH)	-75.82%
Threegold Resources	(PINK:TRLDF)	-76.12%
Wolverine Minerals Corp.	(PINK:WLRMF)	-76.43%
Lake Victoria Mining Co., Inc.	(OTC:LVCA)	-77.14%
Microelectronics Technology Co.	(PINK:MELY)	-77.19%
Taku Gold Corp.	(PINK:TAKUF)	-77.94%
Golden Minerals Co.	(AMEX:AUMN)	-78.35%
First Mexican Gold Corp.	(PINK:FMGXF)	-78.43%
Global Security Agency Inc.	(OTC:GSAG)	-78.43%
Rusoro Mining Ltd.	(PINK:RMLFF)	-78.57%
Alto Ventures Ltd.	(PINK:ALVLD)	-78.85%
Siga Resources Inc.	(OTC:SGAE)	-79.17%
Source Gold Corp.	(OTC:SRGL)	-79.69%

Company	Ticker	2011 Return
Cadan Resources Corp.	(PINK:CADAF)	-79.76%
South American Gold Corp.	(OTC:SAGD)	-80.00%
INV Metals Inc.	(PINK:ILNLF)	-80.36%
Anglo Swiss Resources Inc.	(PINK:ASWRF)	-80.59%
Coro Mining Corp.	(PINK:CROJF)	-80.67%
Stikine Energy Corp.	(PINK:SKNGF)	-80.86%
Bolero Resources Corp.	(PINK:BRUZF)	-80.89%
Orofino Gold Corp.	(PINK:ORFG)	-81.25%
Polar Star Mining	(PINK:POSRF)	-81.78%
Rome Resources Ltd.	(PINK:RMRSF)	-81.96%
Reva Resources Corp.	(PINK:RVARF)	-82.00%
Northern Abitibi Mining Corp.	(PINK:NOMNF)	-82.06%
Plexmar Resources Inc.	(PINK:PLLGF)	-82.13%
Douglas Lake Minerals Inc.	(OTC:DLKM)	-82.43%
Dajin Resources Corp.	(PINK:DJIFF)	-82.61%
GMV Minerals Inc.	(PINK:GMVMF)	-83.85%
Goldsands Development Co.	(OTC:GSDC)	-84.05%
Aurora Gold Corporation	(PINK:ARXG)	-84.29%
Skeena Resources Ltd.	(PINK:SKREF)	-84.58%
Troymet Exploration Corp.	(PINK:TRYXF)	-85.35%
Aura Silver Resources Ltd.	(PINK:AUSVF)	-86.75%
Sacre-Couer Minerals	(PINK:SCRMF)	-87.91%
Gold American Mining Corp.	(OTC:SILA)	-88.48%
Goldbank Mining Corp.	(PINK:GLBKF)	-89.05%
Takara Resources Inc.	(PINK:TAKRF)	-89.74%
Geopulse Exploration Inc.	(OTC:GPLS)	-90.00%
Yinfu Gold Corp.	(PINK:ELRE)	-91.76%
Currie Rose Resource	(PINK:CUIRF)	-92.44%
Golden Touch Resources Corp.	(PINK:GNHRF)	-93.93%
East Asia Minerals Corp.	(PINK:EAIAF)	-94.34%
Coyote Resources, Inc.	(OTC:COYR)	-96.62%
Ardent Mines Ltd.	(PINK:ADNT)	-97.44%
Sky Digital Stores Corp.	(OTC:SKYC)	-97.80%
Dakota Gold Corp.	(OTC:DAKO)	-99.00%

Company	Ticker	2011 Return
Augen Gold Corp.	(PINK:AUGNF)	N/A
Century Mining Corp.	(PINK:CMNZF)	N/A
Northgate Minerals Corp.	(AMEX:NXG)	N/A
Peregrine Metals Ltd.	(PINK:PTTDF)	N/A
Loreto Resources Corp.	(OTC:LRTC)	-
Lounor Exploration Inc.	(PINK:LOUXF)	-

CHAPTER 7
BEST AND WORST GOLD AND SILVER STOCK PERFORMANCES OVER THE PAST 5 YEARS

Company	Ticker	Lifetime OR 5-Year Return
Ireland Inc.	(OTC:IRLD)	5233.00%
Golden Minerals Co.	(AMEX:AUMN)	4095.00%
Gold Resource Corp.	(AMEX:GORO)	1415.62%
Treasury Metals Inc.	(PINK:TSRMF)	1382.35%
Levon Resources Ltd.	(PINK:LVNVF)	1100.67%
Probe Mines Ltd.	(PINK:PROBF)	1075.98%
Ruby Creek Resources Inc.	(OTC:RBYC)	950.00%
Stealth Resources Inc.	(OTC:SERS)	933.00%
Orezone Gold Corp.	(PINK:ORZCF)	833.09%
Maudore Minerals Ltd.	(PINK:MAOMF)	821.42%
Bryn Resources Inc.	(PINK:BRYN)	716.66%
St. Elias Mines Ltd.	(PINK:SELSF)	652.35%
Allied Nevada Gold Corp.	(AMEX:ANV)	560.94%
Integra Gold Corp.	(PINK:KALRF)	425.24%
Clifton Star Resources	(PINK:CFMSF)	397.00%
Gold Canyon Resources Inc.	(PINK:GDCRF)	376.32%
Rubicon Minerals Corp.	(AMEX:RBY)	372.50%

Company	Ticker	Lifetime OR 5-Year Return
Foran Mining Corp.	(PINK:FMCXF)	366.00%
Richmont Mines Inc.	(AMEX:RIC)	355.93%
Bullion Monarch Mining Inc.	(OTC:BULM)	345.00%
Cline Mining Corp.	(PINK:CLNMF)	342.03%
Randgold Resources Ltd.	(NASDAQ:GOLD)	335.21%
Dynacor Gold Mines	(PINK:DNGDF)	326.92%
Romarco Minerals Inc.	(PINK:RTRAF)	312.08%
DNI Metals Inc.	(PINK:DMNKF)	303.84%
PMI Gold Corp.	(PINK:PMVGF)	299.78%
Torex Gold Resources Inc.	(PINK:TORXF)	293.14%
Themac Resources Group	(PINK:MACQF)	292.82%
Golden Reign Resources Ltd.	(PINK:GRGNF)	274.04%
Premier Gold Mines	(PINK:PIRGF)	273.87%
Pelangio Exploration Inc.	(PINK:PGXPF)	256.50%
Athena Silver Corporation	(OTC:AHNR)	250.00%
Sandstorm Gold Ltd.	(PINK:SNDXF)	224.66%
Barkerville Gold Mines Ltd.	(PINK:BGMZF)	215.33%
Alacer Gold Corp.	(PINK:ALIAF)	209.90%
Jinhao Motor Co., Ltd.	(PINK:GIMC)	207.00%
Redstar Gold Corp.	(PINK:RGCTF)	205.88%
Kaminak Gold Corp.	(PINK:KMKGF)	198.14%
Silver Falcon Mining Inc.	(PINK:SFMI)	192.00%
First Point Minerals Corp.	(PINK:FPOCF)	191.00%
Compania De Minas Buenaventura SA	(NYSE:BVN)	190.92%
Silver Bear Resources Inc.	(PINK:SVBRF)	182.67%
Silver Wheaton Corp.	(NYSE:SLW)	176.34%
Ascot Resources Ltd.	(PINK:ASOLF)	172.05%
South American Silver Corp.	(PINK:SOHAF)	167.30%
Teras Resources Inc.	(PINK:TRARF)	165.47%
Endeavour Silver Corp.	(NYSE:EXK)	157.75%
NGEx Resources Inc.	(PINK:NGQRF)	157.57%
Nevsun Resources	(AMEX:NSU)	154.84%

Company	Ticker	Lifetime OR 5-Year Return
Canadian Orebodies	(PINK:CNOBF)	151.22%
Typhoon Exploration	(PINK:TYPFF)	148.95%
Jayden Resources, Inc.	(PINK:PNMLF)	147.16%
Adventure Gold Inc.	(PINK:AGONF)	145.82%
Comstock Mining, Inc.	(AMEX:LODE)	144.18%
Pretium Resources Inc.	(NYSE:PVG)	138.31%
Great Quest Metals Ltd.	(PINK:GQMLF)	137.87%
New Oroperu Resources	(PINK:NOPUF)	137.71%
Dia Bras Exploration Inc.	(PINK:DBEXF)	136.72%
Glass Earth Gold Ltd.	(PINK:GELGF)	136.64%
Tahoe Resources Inc.	(PINK:THOEF)	134.26%
Midland Exploration Inc.	(PINK:MIDLF)	131.57%
Argonaut Gold Inc.	(PINK:ARNGF)	128.81%
Northern Tiger Resources, Inc.	(PINK:NTGSF)	121.37%
Eurasian Minerals Inc.	(PINK:ESMNF)	120.00%
Global Minerals Ltd.	(PINK:GMLFF)	119.66%
Soltoro Ltd.	(PINK:SLTOF)	118.10%
Pershimco Resources	(PINK:RSPRF)	114.24%
Galway Resources Ltd.	(PINK:GWYRF)	113.58%
St. Andrew Goldfields	(PINK:STADF)	111.06%
American Bonanza Gold Corp.	(PINK:ABGFF)	110.68%
Kat Gold Holdings Corp.	(PINK:BVIG)	104.00%
Virginia Mines Inc.	(PINK:VGMNF)	101.81%
Flm Minerals Inc.	(PINK:FLMS)	100.00%
South American Gold Corp.	(OTC:SAGD)	100.00%
Key Gold Holding Inc.	(PINK:KGHZF)	98.81%
Sono Resources Inc.	(OTC:SRCI)	96.26%
International Tower Hill Mines Ltd.	(AMEX:THM)	93.78%
Troymet Exploration Corp.	(PINK:TRYXF)	92.56%
Roxgold Inc.	(PINK:ROGFF)	89.87%
Royal Gold, Inc.	(NASDAQ:RGLD)	87.41%
Rainy River Resource	(PINK:RRFFF)	86.10%

Company	Ticker	Lifetime OR 5-Year Return
Keegan Resources Inc.	(AMEX:KGN)	82.85%
Aurizon Mines Ltd.	(AMEX:AZK)	82.41%
Sabina Gold And Silver Corp.	(PINK:SGSVF)	81.62%
IAMGOLD Corp.	(NYSE:IAG)	79.91%
Silvercrest Mines	(OTC:STVZF)	79.57%
Oroco Resource Corp.	(PINK:ORRCF)	77.69%
Amarillo Gold Corp.	(PINK:AGCBF)	74.59%
Tara Minerals Corp.	(OTC:TARM)	74.51%
Canstar Resources Inc.	(PINK:CSRNF)	67.14%
Victory Resources Corp.	(PINK:VRCFF)	66.67%
Sunward Resources Ltd.	(PINK:SNWRF)	62.37%
Barrick Gold Corp.	(NYSE:ABX)	61.15%
Newstrike Capital Inc.	(PINK:NWSKF)	56.14%
Goldcorp Inc.	(NYSE:GG)	55.59%
Glen Eagle Resources Inc.	(PINK:GERFF)	55.55%
Scorpio Gold Corp.	(PINK:SRCRF)	52.71%
Troon Ventures Ltd.	(PINK:TVNLF)	51.75%
Exeter Resource Corp.	(AMEX:XRA)	46.63%
Gowest Gold Ltd.	(PINK:GWSAF)	43.93%
Orvana Minerals Corp.	(PINK:ORVMF)	43.03%
Alexco Resource Corp.	(AMEX:AXU)	42.64%
Volta Resources Inc.	(PINK:VLTAF)	41.94%
Eastmain Resources Inc.	(PINK:EANRF)	41.06%
Tristar Gold Inc.	(PINK:TSGZF)	40.25%
Scorpio Mining Corp.	(PINK:SMNPF)	36.81%
Gogold Resources Inc.	(PINK:GLGDF)	36.48%
Corona Gold Corp.	(PINK:CRGAF)	35.46%
Columbus Silver	(PINK:CSLVF)	34.50%
Golden Predator Corp.	(PINK:GPRXF)	33.27%
Newmont Mining Corp.	(NYSE:NEM)	32.91%
New Gold Inc.	(AMEX:NGD)	32.46%
Evolving Gold Corp.	(PINK:EVOGF)	32.00%

Company	Ticker	Lifetime OR 5-Year Return
Endurance Gold Corp.	(PINK:ENDGF)	31.35%
Anglo Swiss Resources Inc.	(PINK:ASWRF)	30.89%
Xtierra Ltd.	(PINK:XRESF)	28.68%
Astur Gold Corp.	(PINK:ATRGF)	26.81%
Thundermin Resources Inc.	(PINK:TUDMF)	25.86%
Gold American Mining Corp.	(OTC:SILA)	25.00%
Imperial Metals Corp.	(PINK:IPMLF)	24.42%
Robex Resources	(PINK:RSRBF)	23.00%
Sonora Gold And Silver	(PINK:SOCJF)	21.79%
Karmin Exploration Inc.	(PINK:KRMEF)	20.37%
Eldorado Gold Corp.	(NYSE:EGO)	20.26%
Midway Gold Corp.	(AMEX:MDW)	20.07%
Dakota Gold Corp.	(OTC:DAKO)	20.00%
Minefinders Corp. Ltd.	(AMEX:MFN)	19.10%
International Minerals Corp.	(PINK:IMZLF)	18.20%
Caledonia Mining Corp.	(OTC:CALVF)	18.07%
Huldra Silver Inc.	(PINK:HUSIF)	17.53%
Gold Reach Resources	(PINK:GRVJF)	17.21%
Sama Resources Inc.	(PINK:LNZCF)	15.48%
Plato Gold	(PINK:PTOZF)	14.37%
Seabridge Gold, Inc.	(AMEX:SA)	14.09%
Alphamin Resources Corp.	(PINK:AFMJF)	13.40%
Avino Silver & Gold Mines Ltd.	(AMEX:ASM)	13.04%
China Forest Energy Corp.	(OTC:CFEC)	13.04%
Auriga Gold Corp.	(PINK:AGRDF)	12.90%
Claude Resources Inc.	(AMEX:CGR)	11.94%
Almaden Minerals Ltd.	(AMEX:AAU)	11.89%
Luna Gold Corp.	(PINK:LGCUF)	11.80%
Yamana Gold Inc.	(NYSE:AUY)	11.46%
Sage Gold Inc.	(PINK:SGGDF)	10.83%
Samex Mining Corp.	(OTC:SMXMF)	10.61%
Great Panther Silver Ltd.	(AMEX:GPL)	10.50%

Company	Ticker	Lifetime OR 5-Year Return
Geopulse Exploration Inc.	(OTC:GPLS)	10.13%
Lucky Boy Silver Corp.	(PINK:LUCB)	10.00%
VHGI Holdings, Inc.	(PINK:VHGI)	9.09%
Kenai Resources Ltd.	(PINK:KAIFF)	8.14%
Puma Exploration	(PINK:PUXPF)	7.24%
EMC Metals Corp.	(PINK:EMMCF)	5.77%
Channel Resources Ltd.	(PINK:CHJRF)	4.90%
Bayfield Ventures Corp.	(PINK:BYVVF)	4.41%
Paramount Gold And Silver Corp.	(AMEX:PZG)	1.43%
Stroud Resources Ltd.	(PINK:SDURF)	0.87%
Agnico-Eagle Mines Ltd.	(NYSE:AEM)	0.85%
Ardent Mines Ltd.	(PINK:ADNT)	0.00%
Artventive Medical Group, Inc.	(PINK:AVTD)	0.00%
Dolly Varden Resources	(PINK:DVRRF)	0.00%
Maya Gold & Silver Inc.	(PINK:MYAGF)	-0.19%
Bellhaven Copper & Gold Inc.	(PINK:BHVCF)	-0.59%
Sennen Resources Ltd.	(PINK:SNNJF)	-1.13%
Anglogold Ashanti Ltd.	(NYSE:AU)	-2.02%
Santa Fe Gold Corp.	(OTC:SFEG)	-2.02%
Jaguar Mining Inc.	(NYSE:JAG)	-2.60%
Excel Gold Mining	(PINK:EGMXF)	-3.25%
Lake Shore Gold Corp.	(AMEX:LSG)	-3.54%
Kinross Gold Corp.	(NYSE:KGC)	-4.04%
Cogitore Resources Inc.	(PINK:CGORF)	-5.30%
Skyline Gold Corp.	(PINK:SYGCF)	-5.90%
Teuton Resources Corp.	(PINK:TEUTF)	-6.16%
Bralorne Gold Mines	(PINK:BPMSF)	-6.89%
CB Gold Inc.	(PINK:CBHDF)	-6.89%
Source Exploration	(PINK:SRXLF)	-8.45%
Wesdome Gold Mines Ltd.	(PINK:WDOFF)	-8.65%
Tinka Resources Ltd.	(PINK:TKRFF)	-9.97%
Reva Resources Corp.	(PINK:RVARF)	-10.00%

Company	Ticker	Lifetime OR 5-Year Return
Wildcat Silver Corp.	(PINK:WLDVF)	-10.44%
Cantex Mine Development Corp.	(PINK:CTXDF)	-11.78%
Eastfield Resources Ltd.	(PINK:ETFLF)	-12.36%
Pan American Silver Corp.	(NASDAQ:PAAS)	-13.35%
Altai Resources Inc.	(PINK:ARSEF)	-13.89%
Revett Minerals Inc.	(AMEX:RVM)	-14.09%
Beaufield Resources	(PINK:BFDRF)	-15.19%
Balmoral Resources Ltd.	(PINK:BALMF)	-15.32%
Timmins Gold Corp.	(AMEX:TGD)	-16.91%
East Asia Minerals Corp.	(PINK:EAIAF)	-17.40%
Odyssey Resources Ltd.	(PINK:ODXSF)	-17.52%
Orex Minerals Inc.	(PINK:ORXIF)	-17.90%
Merc International Minerals	(PINK:MIMZF)	-18.12%
Northern Superior	(PINK:NSUPF)	-18.55%
Gold Fields Ltd.	(NYSE:GFI)	-19.23%
Manson Creek Resources	(PINK:MCKRF)	-19.63%
Pan American Goldfields Ltd.	(OTC:MXOM)	-20.00%
Windarra Minerals Ltd.	(PINK:WDRMF)	-20.00%
Manitou Gold Inc.	(PINK:MNTUF)	-20.14%
Northern Gold Mining Inc.	(PINK:NTGMF)	-20.60%
Harte Gold Corp.	(PINK:HRTFF)	-20.70%
Canadian Zinc Corp.	(OTC:CZICF)	-22.09%
Pacific Ridge Exploration	(PINK:PEXZF)	-22.38%
Entree Gold Inc.	(AMEX:EGI)	-23.08%
Yorbeau Resources Inc.	(PINK:YRBAF)	-23.60%
Riverside Resources Inc.	(PINK:RVSDF)	-23.82%
DRDGOLD Ltd.	(NASDAQ:DROOY)	-25.00%
Lake Victoria Mining Company, Inc.	(OTC:LVCA)	-25.00%
Northern Dynasty Minerals Ltd.	(AMEX:NAK)	-25.43%
Harmony Gold Mining Co.	(NYSE:HMY)	-26.10%
AKA Ventures Inc.	(PINK:AKAVF)	-26.47%
Atna Resources Ltd.	(OTC:ATNAF)	-26.50%

Company	Ticker	Lifetime OR 5-Year Return
Visible Gold Mines	(PINK:VGMIF)	-27.56%
Cardero Resources Corp.	(AMEX:CDY)	-27.70%
Pacific Rim Mining Corp.	(PINK:PFRMF)	-27.77%
Guyana Goldfields Inc.	(PINK:GUYFF)	-28.33%
Malbex Resources Inc.	(PINK:MXRSF)	-29.31%
Taranis Resources Inc.	(PINK:TNREF)	-29.51%
Renaissance Gold Inc.	(PINK:RNSGF)	-29.72%
Orosur Mining Inc.	(PINK:OROXF)	-30.75%
USCorp	(PINK:USCS)	-31.25%
CMQ Resources Inc.	(PINK:CMQRF)	-31.58%
Hecla Mining Company	(NYSE:HL)	-31.72%
Shoshone Silver Mining Co.	(PINK:SHSH)	-32.00%
CMC Metals Ltd.	(PINK:CMCXF)	-32.20%
Arcus Development Group Inc.	(PINK:ARCUF)	-32.70%
Avala Resources Ltd.	(PINK:AVLRF)	-32.71%
International Silver Inc.	(PINK:ISLV)	-33.30%
Dalradian Resources Inc.	(PINK:DRLDF)	-33.43%
Mountain Lake Resources Inc.	(PINK:MLKRF)	-33.67%
Monster Mining Corp.	(PINK:MMNGF)	-33.89%
Orko Silver Corp.	(PINK:OKOFF)	-34.01%
Western Pacific Resources Corp.	(PINK:WRPSF)	-34.21%
Magellan Minerals	(PINK:MAGNF)	-34.55%
Sagebrush Gold Ltd.	(OTC:SAGE)	-35.11%
Sutter Gold Mining Inc.	(PINK:SGMNF)	-35.18%
Tiger International Resources	(PINK:TGILF)	-35.26%
Carpathian Gold Inc.	(PINK:CPNFF)	-36.95%
Moss Lake Gold Mine	(PINK:MLGXF)	-36.96%
Cadillac Ventures Inc.	(PINK:CADIF)	-37.09%
Colibri Resource Corp.	(PINK:CRUCF)	-37.44%
Jasper Mining Corp.	(PINK:JAMGF)	-37.50%
Hy Lake Gold Inc.	(PINK:HYLKF)	-37.76%
Oroandes Resource Corp.	(PINK:OARFF)	-38.09%

Company	Ticker	Lifetime OR 5-Year Return
Valgold Resources Ltd.	(OTC:VALGF)	-38.23%
Olympus Pacific Minerals Inc.	(OTC:OLYMF)	-38.46%
Rockridge Capital Corp.	(PINK:RRCPF)	-38.47%
Oromin Explorations Ltd.	(OTC:OLEPF)	-38.86%
Namibia Rare Earths Inc.	(PINK:NMREF)	-39.43%
Challenger Deep Resources	(PINK:CNDRF)	-39.57%
Temex Resources Corp.	(PINK:TMXRF)	-39.70%
Erin Ventures Inc.	(PINK:ERVFF)	-40.00%
Gold Reserve Inc.	(AMEX:GRZ)	-40.68%
Mexus Gold U.S.	(OTC:MXSG)	-40.90%
North Country Gold	(PINK:NCGDF)	-41.56%
Ely Gold & Minerals Inc.	(PINK:ELYGF)	-41.86%
Iron Creek Capital Corp.	(PINK:INCKF)	-41.86%
PC Gold Inc.	(PINK:PCGLF)	-41.94%
Coeur D'Alene Mines Corp.	(NYSE:CDE)	-42.64%
Golden Goliath Resources Ltd.	(PINK:GGTHF)	-43.10%
Great Basin Gold Ltd.	(AMEX:GBG)	-43.33%
St. Eugene Mining Corp. Ltd	(PINK:STEUF)	-43.64%
Bison Gold Resources Inc.	(PINK:BGEZF)	-43.81%
Bowmore Exploration Ltd.	(PINK:BWMXF)	-43.88%
Cream Minerals Ltd.	(OTC:CRMXF)	-43.90%
RJK Exploration Ltd.	(PINK:RJKAF)	-44.00%
Golden Star Resources Ltd.	(AMEX:GSS)	-44.07%
Columbus Gold Corp.	(PINK:CBGDF)	-44.13%
Reunion Gold Corp.	(PINK:RGDFF)	-44.94%
Giyani Gold Corp.	(PINK:CATPF)	-44.96%
Saturn Minerals Inc.	(PINK:SAEUF)	-45.22%
Rockhaven Resources	(PINK:RKHNF)	-45.75%
Aurico Gold Inc.	(NYSE:AUQ)	-45.91%
Rochester Resources Ltd.	(PINK:RCTFF)	-46.00%
Firesteel Resources Inc.	(PINK:FIEIF)	-46.15%
International PBX Ventures Ltd.	(PINK:IPBXF)	-46.17%

Company	Ticker	Lifetime OR 5-Year Return
Golden Band Resources	(PINK:GBRIF)	-46.19%
VVC Exploration Corp.	(PINK:VVCVF)	-46.54%
Metanor Resources Inc.	(PINK:MEAOF)	-46.97%
Mansfield Minerals Inc.	(PINK:MFMNF)	-48.03%
Golden Valley Mines	(PINK:GLVMF)	-48.69%
Mag Silver Corp.	(AMEX:MVG)	-48.85%
Confederation Minerals Ltd.	(PINK:CNRMF)	-49.08%
Golden Tag Resources Ltd.	(PINK:GTAGF)	-49.38%
Silvercorp Metals Inc.	(NYSE:SVM)	-49.82%
Calais Resources Inc.	(PINK:CAAUF)	-50.00%
Happy Creek Minerals	(PINK:HPYCF)	-50.00%
U.S. Precious Metals, Inc.	(OTC:USPR)	-50.00%
Kobex Minerals Inc.	(AMEX:KXM)	-50.40%
Novagold Resources Inc.	(AMEX:NG)	-50.58%
Rugby Mining Ltd.	(PINK:RBMNF)	-50.58%
Conquest Resources	(PINK:CQRLF)	-50.95%
Royal Standard Minerals Inc.	(OTC:RYSMF)	-51.06%
Northern Abitibi Mining Corp.	(PINK:NOMNF)	-51.49%
Niblack Mineral Development, Inc.	(PINK:NIBMF)	-51.59%
Geologix Explorations Inc.	(PINK:GXEXF)	-51.82%
New World Resource	(PINK:NWFFF)	-52.03%
Minco Gold Corp.	(AMEX:MGH)	-52.52%
Tanzanian Royalty Exploration Corp.	(AMEX:TRX)	-52.58%
Colombian Mines Corp.	(PINK:CMBPF)	-53.33%
Silvore Fox Minerals	(PINK:SVFMF)	-53.47%
Ryan Gold Corp.	(PINK:RYGZF)	-53.52%
Aurion Resources Ltd.	(PINK:AIRRF)	-53.59%
Caza Gold Corp.	(PINK:CZGDF)	-53.77%
Solvista Gold Corp.	(PINK:SVVZF)	-53.91%
Victoria Gold Corp.	(PINK:VITFF)	-54.36%
Golden Dawn Minerals Inc.	(PINK:GDMRF)	-54.37%
Cedar Mountain Exploration	(PINK:CDRMF)	-54.52%

Company	Ticker	Lifetime OR 5-Year Return
El Capitan Precious Metals, Inc.	(OTC:ECPN)	-54.71%
XMET Inc.	(PINK:XMTTF)	-54.76%
Eagle Hill Exploration Corp.	(PINK:EHECF)	-54.97%
Silver Standard Resources Inc.	(NASDAQ:SSRI)	-55.01%
Spanish Mountain Gold Ltd.	(PINK:SPAZF)	-55.03%
Bear Creek Mining Corp.	(PINK:BCEKF)	-55.09%
Golden Arrow Resources Corp.	(PINK:GARWF)	-55.09%
Coral Gold Resources Ltd.	(OTC:CLHRF)	-55.18%
Southern Silver Exploration Corp.	(PINK:SSVFF)	-55.74%
Calibre Mining Corp.	(PINK:CXBMF)	-56.20%
TNR Gold Corp.	(PINK:TRRXF)	-56.21%
Seafield Resources Ltd.	(PINK:SRLTF)	-56.47%
Canasil Resources Inc.	(PINK:CNSUF)	-57.15%
Indigo Exploration Inc.	(PINK:IGXEF)	-57.94%
LKA International Inc.	(PINK:LKAI)	-58.41%
Armistice Resources Corp.	(PINK:AISCF)	-58.62%
Slam Exploration Ltd.	(PINK:SLMXF)	-58.68%
Mazorro Resources Inc.	(PINK:MZRRF)	-58.71%
Royal Mines And Minerals Corp.	(PINK:RYMM)	-58.82%
Crown Gold Corp.	(PINK:CWMZF)	-59.76%
Mines Management, Inc.	(AMEX:MGN)	-59.92%
Starcore International Mines Ltd.	(PINK:SHVLF)	-60.39%
Eagle Plains Resources Ltd.	(PINK:EGPLF)	-60.44%
Kimber Resources, Inc.	(AMEX:KBX)	-60.55%
Timberline Resources Corp.	(AMEX:TLR)	-60.70%
Orofino Gold Corp.	(PINK:ORFG)	-60.71%
Rockcliff Resources Inc.	(PINK:RKLFF)	-60.91%
Aldrin Resources Corp.	(PINK:AOUFF)	-61.06%
Yinfu Gold Corp.	(PINK:ELRE)	-61.11%
Minaurum Gold Inc.	(PINK:MMRGF)	-61.21%
Kilo Goldmines Ltd.	(PINK:KOGMF)	-61.97%
General Metals Corp.	(OTC:GNMT)	-62.04%

Company	Ticker	Lifetime OR 5-Year Return
Marifil Mines Ltd.	(PINK:MFMLF)	-62.26%
Sienna Gold Inc.	(PINK:SNNGF)	-63.17%
Fortune Minerals Ltd.	(PINK:FTMDF)	-63.50%
Lincoln Mining Corp.	(PINK:LNCLF)	-63.52%
Benton Resources Corp.	(PINK:BNRJF)	-63.57%
New Jersey Mining Company	(PINK:NJMC)	-63.63%
Vista Gold Corp.	(AMEX:VGZ)	-64.43%
Guyana Frontier Mining Corp.	(OTC:SHESF)	-64.63%
Bravada Gold Corp.	(PINK:BGAVF)	-65.09%
Alexandria Minerals Corp.	(PINK:ALXDF)	-65.19%
Search Minerals Inc.	(PINK:SHCMF)	-65.34%
Bolero Resources Corp.	(PINK:BRUZF)	-65.67%
Pilot Gold Inc.	(PINK:PLGTF)	-65.67%
Solitario Exploration & Royalty Corp.	(AMEX:XPL)	-65.68%
Banro Corp.	(AMEX:BAA)	-66.21%
REBGold Corp.	(PINK:RBGCF)	-66.32%
Wolverine Minerals Corp.	(PINK:WLRMF)	-66.39%
Bonterra Resources Inc.	(PINK:BONXF)	-66.43%
North American Palladium Ltd.	(AMEX:PAL)	-66.49%
Paget Minerals Corp.	(PINK:PGTMF)	-66.86%
Andina Minerals Inc.	(PINK:ADMNF)	-66.97%
Ginguro Exploration Inc.	(PINK:GNGXF)	-67.20%
Amerix Precious Metals Corp.	(PINK:APMFF)	-67.31%
Aldridge Minerals Inc.	(PINK:AGMIF)	-67.67%
Merrex Gold Inc.	(PINK:MXGIF)	-68.14%
New Dimension Resources	(PINK:NWDMF)	-68.24%
Fjordland Exploration Inc.	(PINK:FEXXF)	-68.46%
Oro Mining Ltd.	(PINK:OMRGF)	-69.01%
Alhambra Resources Ltd.	(PINK:AHBRF)	-69.11%
Hana Mining Ltd.	(PINK:HNMFF)	-69.16%
Petaquilla Minerals Ltd.	(OTC:PTQMF)	-69.27%
Candente Copper Corp.	(PINK:CGDXF)	-69.69%

Company	Ticker	Lifetime OR 5-Year Return
Serengeti Resources Inc.	(PINK:SGRNF)	-69.74%
Sintana Energy Inc.	(PINK:DRFLF)	-70.58%
Soltera Mining Corp.	(PINK:SLTA)	-70.58%
Valencia Ventures	(PINK:VVIVF)	-70.59%
Mega Precious Metals Inc.	(PINK:MPRXF)	-70.77%
Kalimantan Gold Corp.	(PINK:KMGLF)	-70.79%
GMV Minerals Inc.	(PINK:GMVMF)	-71.03%
Stikine Energy Corp.	(PINK:SKNGF)	-71.13%
Unigold Inc.	(PINK:UGDIF)	-71.20%
Murgor Resources Inc.	(PINK:MGRRF)	-71.25%
Alder Resources Ltd.	(PINK:ARLSF)	-71.63%
Heatherdale Resources Ltd.	(PINK:HTRRF)	-72.12%
San Marco Resources Inc.	(PINK:SMREF)	-72.23%
Champion Bear Resources	(PINK:CBRSF)	-72.35%
Rupert Resources Ltd	(PINK:RUPRF)	-72.50%
Argentex Mining Corp.	(OTC:AGXMF)	-72.53%
Brazilian Gold Corp.	(PINK:BGOZF)	-72.83%
Dajin Resources Corp.	(PINK:DJIFF)	-73.21%
Corex Gold Corp.	(PINK:CGEKF)	-73.88%
Africo Resources Ltd.	(PINK:AFCRF)	-74.34%
Barker Minerals Ltd.	(PINK:BKMNF)	-74.84%
China TMK Battery Systems Inc.	(OTC:DFEL)	-75.00%
Silver Predator Corp.	(PINK:SVROF)	-75.26%
INV Metals Inc.	(PINK:ILNLF)	-75.64%
Artha Resources Corp.	(PINK:ATHCF)	-75.69%
Newcastle Minerals Ltd.	(PINK:NCMBF)	-75.75%
Superior Mining International	(PINK:SUIFF)	-75.80%
African Gold Group Inc.	(PINK:AGGFF)	-76.68%
Siga Resources Inc.	(OTC:SGAE)	-77.27%
American Consolidated Minerals	(PINK:AMERF)	-77.33%
Fortress Minerals Co.	(PINK:FTMNF)	-77.77%
Cornerstone Capital Resources Inc.	(PINK:CTNXF)	-77.96%

Company	Ticker	Lifetime OR 5-Year Return
Azimut Exploration	(PINK:AZMTF)	-78.01%
Threegold Resources	(PINK:TRLDF)	-78.15%
Commander Resources	(PINK:CMDRF)	-78.33%
First Mexican Gold Corp.	(PINK:FMGXF)	-78.43%
Aura Silver Resources Ltd.	(PINK:AUSVF)	-78.46%
Freegold Ventures Ltd.	(PINK:FGOVF)	-79.00%
Vena Resources Inc.	(PINK:VNARF)	-79.34%
Global Gold Corp.	(PINK:GBGD)	-80.00%
United Mines, Inc.	(OTC:UNMN)	-80.12%
GWR Resources Inc.	(PINK:GWRRF)	-80.20%
La Quinta Resources Corp.	(PINK:LQRCF)	-80.46%
Galore Resources Inc.	(PINK:GALOF)	-80.52%
Big Bear Mining Corp.	(OTC:BGBR)	-82.00%
Coro Mining Corp.	(PINK:CROJF)	-82.29%
Goldcliff Resource Corp.	(PINK:GCFFF)	-82.66%
Tyhee Gold Corp.	(PINK:TYHJF)	-82.73%
Takara Resources Inc.	(PINK:TAKRF)	-82.99%
Bear Lake Gold Ltd.	(PINK:BLGFF)	-83.01%
Cassidy Gold Corp.	(PINK:CDXGF)	-83.50%
MDN Inc.	(PINK:MDNNF)	-83.75%
Legend Gold Corp.	(OTC:NOATF)	-83.88%
Golden Phoenix Minerals, Inc.	(OTC:GPXM)	-84.00%
Wescan Goldfields Inc.	(PINK:WEGOF)	-84.08%
Colombia Crest Gold	(PINK:ECRTF)	-84.18%
Animas Resources Ltd.	(PINK:ANIMF)	-84.29%
Silver Bull Resources Inc.	(AMEX:SVBL)	-84.44%
Vantex Resources Ltd.	(PINK:VANTF)	-84.50%
Gold World Resources Inc.	(PINK:GLWDF)	-84.75%
Miranda Gold Corp.	(OTC:MRDDF)	-84.86%
Alto Ventures Ltd.	(PINK:ALVLD)	-85.20%
New Guinea Gold Corp.	(PINK:NGUGF)	-85.23%
Equitas Resources Corp.	(PINK:EQTRF)	-85.29%

Company	Ticker	Lifetime OR 5-Year Return
Searchlight Minerals Corp.	(OTC:SRCH)	-85.56%
Canarc Resource Corp.	(OTC:CRCUF)	-85.67%
BCGold Corp.	(PINK:BCGOF)	-85.70%
Sunergy Inc.	(PINK:SNEY)	-86.00%
Cadan Resources Corp.	(PINK:CADAF)	-86.66%
Habanero Resources	(PINK:HBNRF)	-87.07%
Global Security Agency Inc.	(OTC:GSAG)	-87.27%
African Metals Corp.	(PINK:AFMCF)	-87.57%
Amerilithium Corp.	(OTC:AMEL)	-87.89%
Source Gold Corp.	(OTC:SRGL)	-88.18%
Anaconda Mining Inc.	(PINK:ANXGF)	-88.22%
Golden Peaks Resources	(PINK:GDPEF)	-88.54%
Paragon Minerals Corp.	(PINK:PAONF)	-88.78%
Polar Star Mining	(PINK:POSRF)	-88.88%
Taku Gold Corp.	(PINK:TAKUF)	-89.40%
Handy And Harman Ltd.	(NASDAQ:HNH)	-89.65%
Red Metal Resources Ltd.	(OTC:RMES)	-90.08%
Currie Rose Resource	(PINK:CUIRF)	-90.18%
Goldrich Mining Company	(OTC:GRMC)	-90.20%
King'S Bay Gold Corp	(PINK:KBGCF)	-90.20%
Full Metal Minerals	(PINK:FLMTF)	-90.59%
Firestone Ventures	(PINK:FSVEF)	-90.65%
Eskay Mining Corp.	(PINK:ESKYF)	-90.66%
Douglas Lake Minerals Inc.	(OTC:DLKM)	-91.03%
UC Resources Ltd.	(PINK:UCRLF)	-91.49%
Goldsands Development Co.	(OTC:GSDC)	-92.00%
Golden River Resources Corp.	(OTC:GORV)	-92.50%
Decade Resources	(PINK:DECXF)	-92.63%
Brigus Gold Corp.	(AMEX:BRD)	-92.72%
China Ceetop.Com Inc.	(OTC:CTOP)	-92.75%
Sacre-Couer Minerals	(PINK:SCRMF)	-92.77%
Sirios Resources Corp	(PINK:SIREF)	-92.77%

Company	Ticker	Lifetime OR 5-Year Return
Goldbank Mining Corp.	(PINK:GLBKF)	-92.94%
Caldera Resources Inc.	(PINK:CAEFF)	-93.01%
HuntMountain Resources Ltd.	(PINK:HNTM)	-93.13%
Rome Resources Ltd.	(PINK:RMRSF)	-93.26%
Eloro Resources Ltd.	(PINK:ELRRD)	-93.42%
Rogue Resources	(PINK:GCRIF)	-93.58%
Coyote Resources, Inc.	(OTC:COYR)	-93.69%
Skeena Resources Ltd.	(PINK:SKREF)	-93.71%
Aurora Gold Corporation	(PINK:ARXG)	-93.73%
Axmin Inc.	(PINK:AXMIF)	-94.40%
Tri Origin Exploration Ltd.	(PINK:TROIF)	-94.48%
Golden Touch Resources Corp.	(PINK:GNHRF)	-94.51%
Nevada Exploration Inc.	(PINK:NVDEF)	-94.89%
Andes Gold Corp.	(PINK:AGCZ)	-95.00%
Bravo Gold Corp.	(PINK:BVGIF)	-95.02%
Pacific Gold Corp.	(PINK:PCFG)	-95.25%
Plexmar Resources Inc.	(PINK:PLLGF)	-95.98%
White Pine Resources	(PINK:WPRFF)	-96.24%
Crystallex International Corp.	(PINK:CRYXF)	-97.30%
Rusoro Mining Ltd.	(PINK:RMLFF)	-97.34%
Silver Dragon Resources Inc.	(OTC:SDRG)	-97.38%
Sky Digital Stores Corp.	(OTC:SKYC)	-97.80%
Silverado Gold Mines Ltd.	(OTC:SLGLF)	-98.30%
Franklin Mining, Inc.	(PINK:FMNJ)	-99.26%
Blue Note Mining Inc.	(PINK:BLNMF)	-99.51%
Microelectronics Technology Co.	(PINK:MELY)	-99.90%
Buckingham Exploration Inc.	(OTC:BUKX)	-99.96%

CHAPTER 8
TOP 500 GOLD AND SILVER MINING COMPANIES
BY MARKET CAP

Company	Ticker	Market Cap ($)
Barrick Gold Corp.	(NYSE:ABX)	47,530,000,000
Goldcorp Inc.	(NYSE:GG)	36,780,000,000
Newmont Mining Corp.	(NYSE:NEM)	31,370,000,000
Anglogold Ashanti Ltd.	(NYSE:AU)	16,780,000,000
Kinross Gold Corp.	(NYSE:KGC)	14,390,000,000
Yamana Gold Inc.	(NYSE:AUY)	11,700,000,000
Gold Fields Ltd.	(NYSE:GFI)	11,200,000,000
Silver Wheaton Corp.	(NYSE:SLW)	10,960,000,000
Randgold Resources Ltd.	(NASD:GOLD)	9,960,000,000
Compania De Minas Buenaventura SA	(NYSE:BVN)	9,860,000,000
Eldorado Gold Corp.	(NYSE:EGO)	7,940,000,000
Agnico-Eagle Mines Ltd.	(NYSE:AEM)	6,400,000,000
IAMGOLD Corp.	(NYSE:IAG)	6,360,000,000
Harmony Gold Mining Co.	(NYSE:HMY)	5,060,000,000
New Gold Inc.	(AMEX:NGD)	4,740,000,000
Royal Gold, Inc.	(NASD:RGLD)	3,770,000,000
Alacer Gold Corp.	(PINK:ALIAF)	3,020,000,000
Allied Nevada Gold Corp.	(AMEX:ANV)	2,890,000,000

Company	Ticker	Market Cap ($)
Tahoe Resources Inc.	(PINK:THOEF)	2,700,000,000
Pan American Silver Corp.	(NASD:PAAS)	2,550,000,000
Aurico Gold Inc.	(NYSE:AUQ)	2,380,000,000
Coeur D'Alene Mines Corp.	(NYSE:CDE)	2,300,000,000
Novagold Resources Inc.	(AMEX:NG)	2,150,000,000
Hecla Mining Company	(NYSE:HL)	1,320,000,000
Pretium Resources Inc.	(NYSE:PVG)	1,300,000,000
Gold Resource Corp.	(AMEX:GORO)	1,280,000,000
Nevsun Resources	(AMEX:NSU)	1,220,000,000
Silvercorp Metals Inc.	(NYSE:SVM)	1,200,000,000
Silver Standard Resources Inc.	(NASDAQ:SSRI)	1,190,000,000
Minefinders Corp. Ltd.	(AMEX:MFN)	933,740,000
Imperial Metals Corp.	(PINK:IPMLF)	933,530,000
Rubicon Minerals Corp.	(AMEX:RBY)	912,830,000
Endeavour Silver Corp.	(NYSE:EXK)	900,250,000
Aurizon Mines Ltd.	(AMEX:AZK)	862,380,000
Banro Corp.	(AMEX:BAA)	821,550,000
Torex Gold Resources Inc.	(PINK:TORXF)	812,100,000
Seabridge Gold, Inc.	(AMEX:SA)	795,880,000
International Minerals Corp.	(PINK:IMZLF)	675,070,000
Romarco Minerals Inc.	(PINK:RTRAF)	672,600,000
Argonaut Gold Inc.	(PINK:ARNGF)	661,500,000
Premier Gold Mines	(PINK:PIRGF)	654,150,000
Sabina Gold And Silver Corp.	(PINK:SGSVF)	632,700,000
Rainy River Resource	(PINK:RRFFF)	629,400,000
Guyana Goldfields Inc.	(PINK:GUYFF)	609,150,000
Northern Dynasty Minerals Ltd.	(AMEX:NAK)	604,990,000
Jaguar Mining Inc.	(NYSE:JAG)	586,650,000
Lake Shore Gold Corp.	(AMEX:LSG)	544,200,000
North American Palladium Ltd.	(AMEX:PAL)	503,200,000
Great Basin Gold Ltd.	(AMEX:GBG)	485,520,000
Golden Star Resources Ltd.	(AMEX:GSS)	442,250,000
NGEx Resources Inc.	(PINK:NGQRF)	422,050,000
Sandstorm Gold Ltd.	(PINK:SNDXF)	416,600,000

Company	Ticker	Market Cap ($)
Alexco Resource Corp.	(AMEX:AXU)	395,700,000
Cline Mining Corp.	(PINK:CLNMF)	395,350,000
International Tower Hill Mines Ltd.	(AMEX:THM)	392,680,000
Mag Silver Corp.	(AMEX:MVG)	389,110,000
Scorpio Mining Corp.	(PINK:SMNPF)	388,100,000
Dia Bras Exploration Inc.	(PINK:DBEXF)	364,830,000
Richmont Mines Inc.	(AMEX:RIC)	357,460,000
Golden Minerals Co.	(AMEX:AUMN)	326,730,000
Paramount Gold And Silver Corp.	(AMEX:PZG)	325,550,000
Jinhao Motor Co., Ltd.	(PINK:GIMC)	308,700,000
Bear Creek Mining Corp.	(PINK:BCEKF)	305,980,000
Timmins Gold Corp.	(AMEX:TGD)	303,000,000
Great Panther Silver Ltd.	(AMEX:GPL)	302,750,000
Luna Gold Corp.	(PINK:LGCUF)	292,100,000
Keegan Resources Inc.	(AMEX:KGN)	289,920,000
Virginia Mines Inc.	(PINK:VGMNF)	283,700,000
Newstrike Capital Inc.	(PINK:NWSKF)	282,420,000
Tanzanian Royalty Exploration Corp.	(AMEX:TRX)	275,000,000
Sunward Resources Ltd.	(PINK:SNWRF)	268,900,000
Exeter Resource Corp.	(AMEX:XRA)	259,270,000
Carpathian Gold Inc.	(PINK:CPNFF)	252,390,000
Claude Resources Inc.	(AMEX:CGR)	246,530,000
Vista Gold Corp.	(AMEX:VGZ)	241,700,000
Levon Resources Ltd.	(PINK:LVNVF)	234,410,000
PMI Gold Corp.	(PINK:PMVGF)	232,880,000
Midway Gold Corp.	(AMEX:MDW)	231,100,000
Orezone Gold Corp.	(PINK:ORZCF)	222,660,000
DRDGOLD Ltd.	(NASD:DROOY)	211,960,000
Orko Silver Corp.	(PINK:OKOFF)	208,700,000
Brigus Gold Corp.	(AMEX:BRD)	200,420,000
Wildcat Silver Corp.	(PINK:WLDVF)	197,500,000
Silvercrest Mines	(OTC:STVZF)	191,100,000
Avala Resources Ltd.	(PINK:AVLRF)	186,260,000

Company	Ticker	Market Cap ($)
Gold Canyon Resources Inc.	(PINK:GDCRF)	186,160,000
Galway Resources Ltd.	(PINK:GWYRF)	182,680,000
St. Andrew Goldfields	(PINK:STADF)	169,000,000
Kalimantan Gold Corp.	(PINK:KMGLF)	165,400,000
Gold Reserve Inc.	(AMEX:GRZ)	159,530,000
Kaminak Gold Corp.	(PINK:KMKGF)	159,400,000
Revett Minerals Inc.	(AMEX:RVM)	155,610,000
Wesdome Gold Mines Ltd.	(PINK:WDOFF)	154,600,000
Volta Resources Inc.	(PINK:VLTAF)	153,700,000
Reunion Gold Corp.	(PINK:RGDFF)	152,860,000
Probe Mines Ltd.	(PINK:PROBF)	152,010,000
Oromin Explorations Ltd.	(OTC:OLEPF)	147,790,000
Orvana Minerals Corp.	(PINK:ORVMF)	147,500,000
Almaden Minerals Ltd.	(AMEX:AAU)	147,170,000
South American Silver Corp.	(PINK:SOHAF)	144,800,000
St. Elias Mines Ltd.	(PINK:SELSF)	140,700,000
Entree Gold Inc.	(AMEX:EGI)	138,640,000
Maudore Minerals Ltd.	(PINK:MAOMF)	137,400,000
Petaquilla Minerals Ltd.	(OTC:PTQMF)	134,790,000
Victoria Gold Corp.	(PINK:VITFF)	134,700,000
CB Gold Inc.	(PINK:CBHDF)	132,840,000
Handy And Harman Ltd.	(NASD:HNH)	130,890,000
Searchlight Minerals Corp.	(OTC:SRCH)	123,900,000
Olympus Pacific Minerals Inc.	(OTC:OLYMF)	121,900,000
Pershimco Resources	(PINK:RSPRF)	116,700,000
Hana Mining Ltd.	(PINK:HNMFF)	114,500,000
Eurasian Minerals Inc.	(PINK:ESMNF)	114,200,000
Spanish Mountain Gold Ltd.	(PINK:SPAZF)	109,000,000
Dalradian Resources Inc.	(PINK:DRLDF)	105,500,000
Scorpio Gold Corp.	(PINK:SRCRF)	103,000,000
Roxgold Inc.	(PINK:ROGFF)	101,900,000
Rockcliff Resources Inc.	(PINK:RKLFF)	100,000,000
Atna Resources Ltd.	(OTC:ATNAF)	99,560,000
El Capitan Precious Metals, Inc.	(OTC:ECPN)	98,740,000

Company	Ticker	Market Cap ($)
Eastmain Resources Inc.	(PINK:EANRF)	97,700,000
Liberty Gold Corp.	(OTC:LBGO)	95,030,000
Samex Mining Corp.	(OTC:SMXMF)	92,500,000
American Bonanza Gold Corp.	(PINK:ABGFF)	92,450,000
Clifton Star Resources	(PINK:CFMSF)	91,200,000
Kimber Resources, Inc.	(AMEX:KBX)	90,680,000
Santa Fe Gold Corp.	(OTC:SFEG)	89,800,000
Cardero Resources Corp.	(AMEX:CDY)	89,700,000
Andina Minerals Inc.	(PINK:ADMNF)	88,750,000
Kat Gold Holdings Corp.	(PINK:BVIG)	83,500,000
Fortune Minerals Ltd.	(PINK:FTMDF)	82,100,000
Barkerville Gold Mines Ltd.	(PINK:BGMZF)	79,900,000
Canadian Zinc Corp.	(OTC:CZICF)	79,800,000
Golden Band Resources	(PINK:GBRIF)	79,720,000
Ascot Resources Ltd.	(PINK:ASOLF)	78,220,000
Golden Predator Corp.	(PINK:GPRXF)	77,700,000
Gogold Resources Inc.	(PINK:GLGDF)	77,000,000
Silver Bull Resources Inc.	(AMEX:SVBL)	73,500,000
Pilot Gold Inc.	(PINK:PLGTF)	72,700,000
Columbus Gold Corp.	(PINK:CBGDF)	71,350,000
Orosur Mining Inc.	(PINK:OROXF)	71,300,000
Amarillo Gold Corp.	(PINK:AGCBF)	71,150,000
Sagebrush Gold Ltd.	(OTC:SAGE)	70,700,000
Loreto Resources Corp.	(OTC:LRTC)	70,300,000
North Country Gold	(PINK:NCGDF)	69,610,000
Great Quest Metals Ltd.	(PINK:GQMLF)	68,660,000
Ryan Gold Corp.	(PINK:RYGZF)	67,800,000
Northern Superior	(PINK:NSUPF)	66,600,000
Ireland Inc.	(OTC:IRLD)	63,730,000
Magellan Minerals	(PINK:MAGNF)	63,700,000
Metanor Resources Inc.	(PINK:MEAOF)	62,810,000
Solitario Exploration & Royalty Corp.	(AMEX:XPL)	59,800,000
East Asia Minerals Corp.	(PINK:EAIAF)	59,630,000

Company	Ticker	Market Cap ($)
Pelangio Exploration Inc.	(PINK:PGXPF)	58,300,000
Mines Management, Inc.	(AMEX:MGN)	57,480,000
Decade Resources	(PINK:DECXF)	56,900,000
Giyani Gold Corp.	(PINK:CATPF)	56,200,000
Malbex Resources Inc.	(PINK:MXRSF)	56,100,000
Mansfield Minerals Inc.	(PINK:MFMNF)	54,500,000
Astur Gold Corp.	(PINK:ATRGF)	54,200,000
VHGI Holdings, Inc.	(PINK:VHGI)	53,400,000
Soltoro Ltd.	(PINK:SLTOF)	52,600,000
Treasury Metals Inc.	(PINK:TSRMF)	51,900,000
Themac Resources Group	(PINK:MACQF)	51,500,000
Mountain Lake Resources Inc.	(PINK:MLKRF)	50,400,000
Comstock Mining, Inc.	(AMEX:LODE)	50,200,000
Mega Precious Metals Inc.	(PINK:MPRXF)	49,400,000
Caledonia Mining Corp.	(OTC:CALVF)	49,050,000
Tara Minerals Corp.	(OTC:TARM)	48,600,000
Balmoral Resources Ltd.	(PINK:BALMF)	47,290,000
Africo Resources Ltd.	(PINK:AFCRF)	46,700,000
Evolving Gold Corp.	(PINK:EVOGF)	46,600,000
Alhambra Resources Ltd.	(PINK:AHBRF)	46,130,000
Bellhaven Copper & Gold Inc.	(PINK:BHVCF)	45,000,000
Foran Mining Corp.	(PINK:FMCXF)	44,600,000
Harte Gold Corp.	(PINK:HRTFF)	44,300,000
Avino Silver & Gold Mines Ltd.	(AMEX:ASM)	44,100,000
Ruby Creek Resources Inc.	(OTC:RBYC)	43,880,000
Robex Resources	(PINK:RSRBF)	43,500,000
Rusoro Mining Ltd.	(PINK:RMLFF)	42,980,000
Armistice Resources Corp.	(PINK:AISCF)	41,350,000
Lucky Boy Silver Corp.	(PINK:LUCB)	40,800,000
Minco Gold Corp.	(AMEX:MGH)	40,330,000
Merrex Gold Inc.	(PINK:MXGIF)	39,710,000
African Gold Group Inc.	(PINK:AGGFF)	39,410,000
Global Minerals Ltd.	(PINK:GMLFF)	39,070,000
Brazilian Gold Corp.	(PINK:BGOZF)	38,300,000

Company	Ticker	Market Cap ($)
Teras Resources Inc.	(PINK:TRARF)	37,500,000
Freegold Ventures Ltd.	(PINK:FGOVF)	36,120,000
Midland Exploration Inc.	(PINK:MIDLF)	35,300,000
Redstar Gold Corp.	(PINK:RGCTF)	35,100,000
Cream Minerals Ltd.	(OTC:CRMXF)	35,000,000
First Point Minerals Corp.	(PINK:FPOCF)	34,250,000
Yorbeau Resources Inc.	(PINK:YRBAF)	33,200,000
PC Gold Inc.	(PINK:PCGLF)	32,800,000
Microelectronics Technology Co.	(PINK:MELY)	32,270,000
Coro Mining Corp.	(PINK:CROJF)	32,100,000
Renaissance Gold Inc.	(PINK:RNSGF)	31,970,000
Namibia Rare Earths Inc.	(PINK:NMREF)	31,500,000
Huldra Silver Inc.	(PINK:HUSIF)	31,030,000
Timberline Resources Corp.	(AMEX:TLR)	30,900,000
Geologix Explorations Inc.	(PINK:GXEXF)	30,550,000
Golden Reign Resources Ltd.	(PINK:GRGNF)	30,510,000
Solvista Gold Corp.	(PINK:SVVZF)	30,500,000
Bayfield Ventures Corp.	(PINK:BYVVF)	30,450,000
Tyhee Gold Corp.	(PINK:TYHJF)	30,250,000
Heatherdale Resources Ltd.	(PINK:HTRRF)	29,800,000
Argentex Mining Corp.	(OTC:AGXMF)	29,650,000
Axmin Inc.	(PINK:AXMIF)	29,530,000
Bullion Monarch Mining Inc.	(OTC:BULM)	29,450,000
Azimut Exploration	(PINK:AZMTF)	29,430,000
Crystallex International Corp.	(PINK:CRYXF)	29,200,000
Northern Gold Mining Inc.	(PINK:NTGMF)	29,020,000
Alphamin Resources Corp.	(PINK:AFMJF)	28,900,000
GWR Resources Inc.	(PINK:GWRRF)	28,830,000
Golden Peaks Resources	(PINK:GDPEF)	28,650,000
Benton Resources Corp.	(PINK:BNRJF)	28,600,000
Kobex Minerals Inc.	(AMEX:KXM)	28,560,000
Kilo Goldmines Ltd.	(PINK:KOGMF)	28,200,000
Sama Resources Inc.	(PINK:LNZCF)	28,200,000
Skyline Gold Corp.	(PINK:SYGCF)	28,000,000

Company	Ticker	Market Cap ($)
Jayden Resources, Inc.	(PINK:PNMLF)	27,400,000
Tristar Gold Inc.	(PINK:TSGZF)	27,200,000
Riverside Resources Inc.	(PINK:RVSDF)	27,100,000
Dynacor Gold Mines	(PINK:DNGDF)	27,000,000
Douglas Lake Minerals Inc.	(OTC:DLKM)	26,900,000
Tinka Resources Ltd.	(PINK:TKRFF)	26,900,000
Silver Bear Resources Inc.	(PINK:SVBRF)	26,170,000
Beaufield Resources	(PINK:BFDRF)	26,060,000
Temex Resources Corp.	(PINK:TMXRF)	25,900,000
Polar Star Mining	(PINK:POSRF)	25,700,000
Karmin Exploration Inc.	(PINK:KRMEF)	25,600,000
Calibre Mining Corp.	(PINK:CXBMF)	25,550,000
Unigold Inc.	(PINK:UGDIF)	25,400,000
Seafield Resources Ltd.	(PINK:SRLTF)	25,000,000
International PBX Ventures Ltd.	(PINK:IPBXF)	24,950,000
Manitou Gold Inc.	(PINK:MNTUF)	24,900,000
Gowest Gold Ltd.	(PINK:GWSAF)	24,700,000
Rugby Mining Ltd.	(PINK:RBMNF)	23,600,000
Sutter Gold Mining Inc.	(PINK:SGMNF)	23,590,000
China Forest Energy Corp.	(OTC:CFEC)	23,510,000
Golden Phoenix Minerals, Inc.	(OTC:GPXM)	23,440,000
Rockridge Capital Corp.	(PINK:RRCPF)	23,400,000
Orex Minerals Inc.	(PINK:ORXIF)	23,100,000
Aldridge Minerals Inc.	(PINK:AGMIF)	22,900,000
Royal Standard Minerals Inc.	(OTC:RYSMF)	22,640,000
Bralorne Gold Mines	(PINK:BPMSF)	22,610,000
Merc International Minerals	(PINK:MIMZF)	22,500,000
Vena Resources Inc.	(PINK:VNARF)	22,300,000
Adventure Gold Inc.	(PINK:AGONF)	22,060,000
Canadian Orebodies	(PINK:CNOBF)	21,900,000
Pacific Rim Mining Corp.	(PINK:PFRMF)	21,900,000
Sienna Gold Inc.	(PINK:SNNGF)	21,700,000
Starcore International Mines Ltd.	(PINK:SHVLF)	21,600,000
Channel Resources Ltd.	(PINK:CHJRF)	21,400,000

Company	Ticker	Market Cap ($)
Integra Gold Corp.	(PINK:KALRF)	21,400,000
MDN Inc.	(PINK:MDNNF)	21,260,000
Cornerstone Capital Resources Inc.	(PINK:CTNXF)	21,240,000
DNI Metals Inc.	(PINK:DMNKF)	21,220,000
Colombia Crest Gold	(PINK:ECRTF)	21,200,000
Sintana Energy Inc.	(PINK:DRFLF)	20,800,000
Cadillac Ventures Inc.	(PINK:CADIF)	20,700,000
Glass Earth Gold Ltd.	(PINK:GELGF)	20,500,000
Silver Falcon Mining Inc.	(PINK:SFMI)	20,400,000
Victory Resources Corp.	(PINK:VRCFF)	20,300,000
Puma Exploration	(PINK:PUXPF)	20,200,000
Cantex Mine Development Corp.	(PINK:CTXDF)	20,100,000
Teuton Resources Corp.	(PINK:TEUTF)	19,500,000
U.S. Precious Metals, Inc.	(OTC:USPR)	19,300,000
Jasper Mining Corp.	(PINK:JAMGF)	18,200,000
EMC Metals Corp.	(PINK:EMMCF)	18,080,000
Eagle Plains Resources Ltd.	(PINK:EGPLF)	18,060,000
Rockhaven Resources	(PINK:RKHNF)	18,000,000
Sono Resources Inc.	(OTC:SRCI)	17,500,000
Bowmore Exploration Ltd.	(PINK:BWMXF)	17,300,000
Canstar Resources Inc.	(PINK:CSRNF)	17,300,000
Golden Valley Mines	(PINK:GLVMF)	17,300,000
Xtierra Ltd.	(PINK:XRESF)	17,300,000
Golden Tag Resources Ltd.	(PINK:GTAGF)	17,260,000
Maya Gold & Silver Inc.	(PINK:MYAGF)	17,100,000
Troon Ventures Ltd.	(PINK:TVNLF)	17,000,000
Gold Reach Resources	(PINK:GRVJF)	16,900,000
Oro Mining Ltd.	(PINK:OMRGF)	16,400,000
Confederation Minerals Ltd.	(PINK:CNRMF)	16,250,000
Miranda Gold Corp.	(OTC:MRDDF)	16,220,000
Northern Tiger Resources, Inc.	(PINK:NTGSF)	16,220,000
United Mines, Inc.	(OTC:UNMN)	16,200,000
Eagle Hill Exploration Corp.	(PINK:EHECF)	16,020,000
INV Metals Inc.	(PINK:ILNLF)	16,000,000

Company	Ticker	Market Cap ($)
Bison Gold Resources Inc.	(PINK:BGEZF)	15,940,000
South American Gold Corp.	(OTC:SAGD)	15,800,000
Calais Resources Inc.	(PINK:CAAUF)	15,780,000
Golden Goliath Resources Ltd.	(PINK:GGTHF)	15,740,000
Auriga Gold Corp.	(PINK:AGRDF)	15,400,000
Stroud Resources Ltd.	(PINK:SDURF)	15,400,000
St. Eugene Mining Corp. Ltd	(PINK:STEUF)	15,060,000
Global Gold Corp.	(PINK:GBGD)	15,040,000
Challenger Deep Resources	(PINK:CNDRF)	15,000,000
Bryn Resources Inc.	(PINK:BRYN)	14,800,000
China TMK Battery Systems Inc.	(OTC:DFEL)	14,800,000
Fortress Minerals Co.	(PINK:FTMNF)	14,800,000
International Silver Inc.	(PINK:ISLV)	14,710,000
Minaurum Gold Inc.	(PINK:MMRGF)	14,600,000
Moss Lake Gold Mine	(PINK:MLGXF)	14,600,000
Silvore Fox Minerals	(PINK:SVFMF)	14,400,000
Golden Arrow Resources Corp.	(PINK:GARWF)	14,370,000
Oroco Resource Corp.	(PINK:ORRCF)	14,210,000
Anaconda Mining Inc.	(PINK:ANXGF)	14,200,000
Legend Gold Corp.	(OTC:NOATF)	14,200,000
Candente Copper Corp.	(PINK:CGDXF)	14,020,000
Alexandria Minerals Corp.	(PINK:ALXDF)	14,000,000
Caza Gold Corp.	(PINK:CZGDF)	13,750,000
Erin Ventures Inc.	(PINK:ERVFF)	13,700,000
Southern Silver Exploration Corp.	(PINK:SSVFF)	13,600,000
Andes Gold Corp.	(PINK:AGCZ)	13,500,000
Commander Resources	(PINK:CMDRF)	13,490,000
Slam Exploration Ltd.	(PINK:SLMXF)	13,300,000
Bravo Gold Corp.	(PINK:BVGIF)	13,200,000
Threegold Resources	(PINK:TRLDF)	13,200,000
Coral Gold Resources Ltd.	(OTC:CLHRF)	13,090,000
Bonterra Resources Inc.	(PINK:BONXF)	13,060,000
Goldrich Mining Company	(OTC:GRMC)	12,670,000
African Metals Corp.	(PINK:AFMCF)	12,600,000

Company	Ticker	Market Cap ($)
Saturn Minerals Inc.	(PINK:SAEUF)	12,300,000
TNR Gold Corp.	(PINK:TRRXF)	12,300,000
Iron Creek Capital Corp.	(PINK:INCKF)	12,230,000
Glen Eagle Resources Inc.	(PINK:GERFF)	12,200,000
Pacific Gold Corp.	(PINK:PCFG)	12,080,000
Source Exploration	(PINK:SRXLF)	12,000,000
Red Metal Resources Ltd.	(OTC:RMES)	11,900,000
VVC Exploration Corp.	(PINK:VVCVF)	11,800,000
Search Minerals Inc.	(PINK:SHCMF)	11,700,000
Happy Creek Minerals	(PINK:HPYCF)	11,600,000
New Guinea Gold Corp.	(PINK:NGUGF)	11,500,000
Canasil Resources Inc.	(PINK:CNSUF)	11,490,000
Cadan Resources Corp.	(PINK:CADAF)	11,440,000
Paget Minerals Corp.	(PINK:PGTMF)	11,400,000
Typhoon Exploration	(PINK:TYPFF)	11,400,000
Marifil Mines Ltd.	(PINK:MFMLF)	11,260,000
Ely Gold & Minerals Inc.	(PINK:ELYGF)	11,140,000
Corona Gold Corp.	(PINK:CRGAF)	10,810,000
Mexus Gold U.S.	(OTC:MXSG)	10,700,000
Sunergy Inc.	(PINK:SNEY)	10,500,000
Full Metal Minerals	(PINK:FLMTF)	10,390,000
Thundermin Resources Inc.	(PINK:TUDMF)	10,300,000
Visible Gold Mines	(PINK:VGMIF)	10,300,000
Bear Lake Gold Ltd.	(PINK:BLGFF)	10,230,000
Silver Predator Corp.	(PINK:SVROF)	10,200,000
USCorp	(PINK:USCS)	10,200,000
Anglo Swiss Resources Inc.	(PINK:ASWRF)	10,170,000
Sonora Gold And Silver	(PINK:SOCJF)	10,100,000
Monster Mining Corp.	(PINK:MMNGF)	10,000,000
Serengeti Resources Inc.	(PINK:SGRNF)	10,000,000
Cassidy Gold Corp.	(PINK:CDXGF)	9,900,000
Pan American Goldfields Ltd.	(OTC:MXOM)	9,800,000
CMC Metals Ltd.	(PINK:CMCXF)	9,770,000
Silver Dragon Resources Inc.	(OTC:SDRG)	9,400,000

Company	Ticker	Market Cap ($)
Dolly Varden Resources	(PINK:DVRRF)	9,300,000
Excel Gold Mining	(PINK:EGMXF)	9,200,000
BCGold Corp.	(PINK:BCGOF)	9,130,000
Pacific Ridge Exploration	(PINK:PEXZF)	9,100,000
Athena Silver Corporation	(OTC:AHNR)	9,070,000
Hy Lake Gold Inc.	(PINK:HYLKF)	9,000,000
New Jersey Mining Company	(PINK:NJMC)	9,000,000
Shoshone Silver Mining Co.	(PINK:SHSH)	9,000,000
Western Pacific Resources Corp.	(PINK:WRPSF)	9,000,000
Lake Victoria Mining Company, Inc.	(OTC:LVCA)	8,800,000
UC Resources Ltd.	(PINK:UCRLF)	8,800,000
Colombian Mines Corp.	(PINK:CMBPF)	8,690,000
Ginguro Exploration Inc.	(PINK:GNGXF)	8,600,000
Oroandes Resource Corp.	(PINK:OARFF)	8,600,000
Habanero Resources	(PINK:HBNRF)	8,590,000
Cogitore Resources Inc.	(PINK:CGORF)	8,500,000
RJK Exploration Ltd.	(PINK:RJKAF)	8,500,000
Sennen Resources Ltd.	(PINK:SNNJF)	8,500,000
Superior Mining International	(PINK:SUIFF)	8,500,000
Canarc Resource Corp.	(OTC:CRCUF)	8,470,000
Wolverine Minerals Corp.	(PINK:WLRMF)	8,400,000
Bravada Gold Corp.	(PINK:BGAVF)	8,230,000
Niblack Mineral Development, Inc.	(PINK:NIBMF)	8,200,000
Amerilithium Corp.	(OTC:AMEL)	8,130,000
Galore Resources Inc.	(PINK:GALOF)	8,130,000
Guyana Frontier Mining Corp.	(OTC:SHESF)	8,090,000
China Ceetop.Com Inc.	(OTC:CTOP)	8,070,000
Plato Gold	(PINK:PTOZF)	8,000,000
Aurion Resources Ltd.	(PINK:AIRRF)	7,990,000
Sacre-Couer Minerals	(PINK:SCRMF)	7,800,000
General Metals Corp.	(OTC:GNMT)	7,730,000
Taranis Resources Inc.	(PINK:TNREF)	7,700,000
Valencia Ventures	(PINK:VVIVF)	7,700,000

Company	Ticker	Market Cap ($)
Barker Minerals Ltd.	(PINK:BKMNF)	7,630,000
Corex Gold Corp.	(PINK:CGEKF)	7,630,000
Goldsands Development Co.	(OTC:GSDC)	7,610,000
Blue Note Mining Inc.	(PINK:BLNMF)	7,600,000
Murgor Resources Inc.	(PINK:MGRRF)	7,600,000
AKA Ventures Inc.	(PINK:AKAVF)	7,580,000
Rochester Resources Ltd.	(PINK:RCTFF)	7,400,000
Vantex Resources Ltd.	(PINK:VANTF)	7,400,000
Animas Resources Ltd.	(PINK:ANIMF)	7,340,000
Siga Resources Inc.	(OTC:SGAE)	7,200,000
Nevada Exploration Inc.	(PINK:NVDEF)	7,100,000
Dakota Gold Corp.	(OTC:DAKO)	7,000,000
Eskay Mining Corp.	(PINK:ESKYF)	6,900,000
Flm Minerals Inc.	(PINK:FLMS)	6,900,000
LKA International Inc.	(PINK:LKAI)	6,900,000
Lincoln Mining Corp.	(PINK:LNCLF)	6,850,000
New Oroperu Resources	(PINK:NOPUF)	6,820,000
Buckingham Exploration Inc.	(OTC:BUKX)	6,810,000
Sage Gold Inc.	(PINK:SGGDF)	6,800,000
Aldrin Resources Corp.	(PINK:AOUFF)	6,700,000
Altai Resources Inc.	(PINK:ARSEF)	6,700,000
GMV Minerals Inc.	(PINK:GMVMF)	6,620,000
Eastfield Resources Ltd.	(PINK:ETFLF)	6,500,000
Kenai Resources Ltd.	(PINK:KAIFF)	6,400,000
White Pine Resources	(PINK:WPRFF)	6,400,000
Franklin Mining, Inc.	(PINK:FMNJ)	6,290,000
Aura Silver Resources Ltd.	(PINK:AUSVF)	6,250,000
Fjordland Exploration Inc.	(PINK:FEXXF)	6,220,000
Stealth Resources Inc.	(OTC:SERS)	6,200,000
Yinfu Gold Corp.	(PINK:ELRE)	6,200,000
Colibri Resource Corp.	(PINK:CRUCF)	6,130,000
Mazorro Resources Inc.	(PINK:MZRRF)	6,100,000
Stikine Energy Corp.	(PINK:SKNGF)	6,100,000
Wescan Goldfields Inc.	(PINK:WEGOF)	6,100,000

Company	Ticker	Market Cap ($)
Royal Mines And Minerals Corp.	(PINK:RYMM)	6,000,000
Source Gold Corp.	(OTC:SRGL)	6,000,000
Tiger International Resources	(PINK:TGILF)	6,000,000
Columbus Silver	(PINK:CSLVF)	5,950,000
CMQ Resources Inc.	(PINK:CMQRF)	5,900,000
Lounor Exploration Inc.	(PINK:LOUXF)	5,900,000
Rogue Resources	(PINK:GCRIF)	5,900,000
REBGold Corp.	(PINK:RBGCF)	5,800,000
Reva Resources Corp.	(PINK:RVARF)	5,800,000
XMET Inc.	(PINK:XMTTF)	5,800,000
Odyssey Resources Ltd.	(PINK:ODXSF)	5,700,000
Eloro Resources Ltd.	(PINK:ELRRD)	5,600,000
Troymet Exploration Corp.	(PINK:TRYXF)	5,600,000
Indigo Exploration Inc.	(PINK:IGXEF)	5,500,000
Taku Gold Corp.	(PINK:TAKUF)	5,500,000
Valgold Resources Ltd.	(OTC:VALGF)	5,500,000
Sky Digital Stores Corp.	(OTC:SKYC)	5,400,000
Endurance Gold Corp.	(PINK:ENDGF)	5,320,000
Firestone Ventures	(PINK:FSVEF)	5,300,000
Golden River Resources Corp.	(OTC:GORV)	5,110,000
Cedar Mountain Exploration	(PINK:CDRMF)	5,100,000
Champion Bear Resources	(PINK:CBRSF)	5,030,000
Manson Creek Resources	(PINK:MCKRF)	4,970,000
Conquest Resources	(PINK:CQRLF)	4,960,000
Alder Resources Ltd.	(PINK:ARLSF)	4,900,000
Caldera Resources Inc.	(PINK:CAEFF)	4,900,000
Takara Resources Inc.	(PINK:TAKRF)	4,900,000
First Mexican Gold Corp.	(PINK:FMGXF)	4,800,000
Gold American Mining Corp.	(OTC:SILA)	4,710,000
Artha Resources Corp.	(PINK:ATHCF)	4,700,000
Equitas Resources Corp.	(PINK:EQTRF)	4,700,000
Silverado Gold Mines Ltd.	(OTC:SLGLF)	4,700,000
Golden Dawn Minerals Inc.	(PINK:GDMRF)	4,670,000
Paragon Minerals Corp.	(PINK:PAONF)	4,560,000

Company	Ticker	Market Cap ($)
Amerix Precious Metals Corp.	(PINK:APMFF)	4,500,000
Plexmar Resources Inc.	(PINK:PLLGF)	4,400,000
Arcus Development Group Inc.	(PINK:ARCUF)	4,390,000
Global Security Agency Inc.	(OTC:GSAG)	4,360,000
La Quinta Resources Corp.	(PINK:LQRCF)	4,300,000
Northern Abitibi Mining Corp.	(PINK:NOMNF)	4,300,000
New Dimension Resources	(PINK:NWDMF)	4,220,000
HuntMountain Resources Ltd.	(PINK:HNTM)	4,190,000
Windarra Minerals Ltd.	(PINK:WDRMF)	4,100,000
Geopulse Exploration Inc.	(OTC:GPLS)	4,090,000
Rome Resources Ltd.	(PINK:RMRSF)	4,000,000
Orofino Gold Corp.	(PINK:ORFG)	3,900,000
Firesteel Resources Inc.	(PINK:FIEIF)	3,800,000
King'S Bay Gold Corp	(PINK:KBGCF)	3,800,000
Rupert Resources Ltd	(PINK:RUPRF)	3,800,000
Tri Origin Exploration Ltd.	(PINK:TROIF)	3,800,000
Aurora Gold Corporation	(PINK:ARXG)	3,740,000
San Marco Resources Inc.	(PINK:SMREF)	3,700,000
Bolero Resources Corp.	(PINK:BRUZF)	3,590,000
Sirios Resources Corp	(PINK:SIREF)	3,500,000
American Consolidated Minerals	(PINK:AMERF)	3,400,000
Dajin Resources Corp.	(PINK:DJIFF)	3,340,000
Soltera Mining Corp.	(PINK:SLTA)	3,340,000
Alto Ventures Ltd.	(PINK:ALVLD)	3,300,000
Crown Gold Corp.	(PINK:CWMZF)	3,100,000
Golden Touch Resources Corp.	(PINK:GNHRF)	2,900,000
Gold World Resources Inc.	(PINK:GLWDF)	2,700,000
Newcastle Minerals Ltd.	(PINK:NCMBF)	2,700,000
Big Bear Mining Corp.	(OTC:BGBR)	2,690,000
New World Resource	(PINK:NWFFF)	2,510,000
Goldbank Mining Corp.	(PINK:GLBKF)	2,400,000
Coyote Resources, Inc.	(OTC:COYR)	2,350,000
Goldcliff Resource Corp.	(PINK:GCFFF)	2,300,000
Currie Rose Resource	(PINK:CUIRF)	1,960,000

Company	Ticker	Market Cap ($)
Skeena Resources Ltd.	(PINK:SKREF)	1,800,000
Key Gold Holding Inc.	(PINK:KGHZF)	1,700,000
Ardent Mines Ltd.	(PINK:ADNT)	1,470,000
Artventive Medical Group, Inc.	(PINK:AVTD)	0
Augen Gold Corp.	(PINK:AUGNF)	N/A
Century Mining Corp.	(PINK:CMNZF)	N/A
Geo Minerals Ltd.	(PINK:GMNRF)	N/A
Northgate Minerals Corp.	(AMEX:NXG)	N/A
Peregrine Metals Ltd.	(PINK:PTTDF)	N/A

CHAPTER 9
TOP 400 GOLD AND SILVER MINING STOCKS
BY TRADING VOLUME

Company	Ticker	Trading Volume
Hecla Mining Company	(NYSE:HL)	9,130,000
Barrick Gold Corp.	(NYSE:ABX)	6,690,000
Kinross Gold Corp.	(NYSE:KGC)	6,530,000
Yamana Gold Inc.	(NYSE:AUY)	5,600,000
Newmont Mining Corp.	(NYSE:NEM)	5,200,000
Goldcorp Inc.	(NYSE:GG)	4,530,000
Eldorado Gold Corp.	(NYSE:EGO)	3,600,000
Silver Wheaton Corp.	(NYSE:SLW)	3,600,000
Aurico Gold Inc.	(NYSE:AUQ)	3,370,000
New Gold Inc.	(AMEX:NGD)	2,880,000
Gold Fields Ltd.	(NYSE:GFI)	2,840,000
Golden Star Resources Ltd.	(AMEX:GSS)	2,550,000
Novagold Resources Inc.	(AMEX:NG)	2,420,000
Great Basin Gold Ltd.	(AMEX:GBG)	2,260,000
IAMGOLD Corp.	(NYSE:IAG)	2,150,000
Jaguar Mining Inc.	(NYSE:JAG)	1,930,000
Harmony Gold Mining Co.	(NYSE:HMY)	1,900,000
Franklin Mining, Inc.	(PINK:FMNJ)	1,850,000
Sunergy Inc.	(PINK:SNEY)	1,800,000

Company	Ticker	Trading Volume
Agnico-Eagle Mines Ltd.	(NYSE:AEM)	1,730,000
Pacific Gold Corp.	(PINK:PCFG)	1,700,000
Anglogold Ashanti Ltd.	(NYSE:AU)	1,500,000
Silvercorp Metals Inc.	(NYSE:SVM)	1,500,000
Coeur D'Alene Mines Corp.	(NYSE:CDE)	1,440,000
Endeavour Silver Corp.	(NYSE:EXK)	1,300,000
Silver Falcon Mining Inc.	(PINK:SFMI)	1,300,000
Silver Standard Resources Inc.	(NASDAQ:SSRI)	1,100,000
Compania De Minas Buenaventura SA	(NYSE:BVN)	1,040,000
Allied Nevada Gold Corp.	(AMEX:ANV)	1,020,000
Great Panther Silver Ltd.	(AMEX:GPL)	994,045
Silverado Gold Mines Ltd.	(OTC:SLGLF)	973,100
Silver Dragon Resources Inc.	(OTC:SDRG)	972,400
North American Palladium Ltd.	(AMEX:PAL)	921,200
Paramount Gold And Silver Corp.	(AMEX:PZG)	883,400
Pan American Silver Corp.	(NASDAQ:PAAS)	854,200
U.S. Precious Metals, Inc.	(OTC:USPR)	812,100
Royal Gold, Inc.	(NASDAQ:RGLD)	806,000
Brigus Gold Corp.	(AMEX:BRD)	780,597
Rubicon Minerals Corp.	(AMEX:RBY)	700,700
Crystallex International Corp.	(PINK:CRYXF)	637,000
Aurizon Mines Ltd.	(AMEX:AZK)	589,072
Minefinders Corp. Ltd.	(AMEX:MFN)	571,402
Golden Phoenix Minerals, Inc.	(OTC:GPXM)	507,421
Alexco Resource Corp.	(AMEX:AXU)	496,931
Nevsun Resources	(AMEX:NSU)	458,328
Midway Gold Corp.	(AMEX:MDW)	445,000
Searchlight Minerals Corp.	(OTC:SRCH)	416,000
International Tower Hill Mines Ltd.	(AMEX:THM)	408,400
Randgold Resources Ltd.	(NASDAQ:GOLD)	405,100
Vista Gold Corp.	(AMEX:VGZ)	405,100
Amerilithium Corp.	(OTC:AMEL)	395,500

Company	Ticker	Trading Volume
El Capitan Precious Metals, Inc.	(OTC:ECPN)	362,686
Tanzanian Royalty Exploration Corp.	(AMEX:TRX)	352,900
Exeter Resource Corp.	(AMEX:XRA)	320,747
Claude Resources Inc.	(AMEX:CGR)	297,699
Keegan Resources Inc.	(AMEX:KGN)	295,752
Golden Minerals Co.	(AMEX:AUMN)	283,605
Banro Corp.	(AMEX:BAA)	275,560
Mines Management, Inc.	(AMEX:MGN)	271,126
Caledonia Mining Corp.	(OTC:CALVF)	257,520
Seabridge Gold, Inc.	(AMEX:SA)	242,100
Gold Resource Corp.	(AMEX:GORO)	238,500
Goldsands Development Co.	(OTC:GSDC)	237,028
Richmont Mines Inc.	(AMEX:RIC)	217,800
Timberline Resources Corp.	(AMEX:TLR)	195,500
Douglas Lake Minerals Inc.	(OTC:DLKM)	182,975
Royal Standard Minerals Inc.	(OTC:RYSMF)	177,300
Sagebrush Gold Ltd.	(OTC:SAGE)	173,900
Northern Dynasty Minerals Ltd.	(AMEX:NAK)	165,400
Sandstorm Gold Ltd.	(PINK:SNDXF)	153,700
Canadian Zinc Corp.	(OTC:CZICF)	152,356
Almaden Minerals Ltd.	(AMEX:AAU)	151,302
Lake Shore Gold Corp.	(AMEX:LSG)	147,900
Timmins Gold Corp.	(AMEX:TGD)	140,800
Alexandria Minerals Corp.	(PINK:ALXDF)	140,500
Aura Silver Resources Ltd.	(PINK:AUSVF)	139,184
Source Gold Corp.	(OTC:SRGL)	136,700
AKA Ventures Inc.	(PINK:AKAVF)	136,500
Kimber Resources, Inc.	(AMEX:KBX)	133,125
General Metals Corp.	(OTC:GNMT)	128,018
USCorp	(PINK:USCS)	119,500
Gold American Mining Corp.	(OTC:SILA)	117,697
Minco Gold Corp.	(AMEX:MGH)	116,744
Mag Silver Corp.	(AMEX:MVG)	115,907

Company	Ticker	Trading Volume
Entree Gold Inc.	(AMEX:EGI)	113,446
Cardero Resources Corp.	(AMEX:CDY)	113,346
Alder Resources Ltd.	(PINK:ARLSF)	109,000
Northern Gold Mining Inc.	(PINK:NTGMF)	106,200
Comstock Mining, Inc.	(AMEX:LODE)	101,763
Ardent Mines Ltd.	(PINK:ADNT)	99,227
Andes Gold Corp.	(PINK:AGCZ)	95,600
VHGI Holdings, Inc.	(PINK:VHGI)	86,300
DRDGOLD Ltd.	(NASD:DROOY)	83,099
Oromin Explorations Ltd.	(OTC:OLEPF)	79,900
Silver Bull Resources Inc.	(AMEX:SVBL)	77,000
Seafield Resources Ltd.	(PINK:SRLTF)	76,900
Goldrich Mining Company	(OTC:GRMC)	75,843
DNI Metals Inc.	(PINK:DMNKF)	74,969
Solitario Exploration & Royalty Corp.	(AMEX:XPL)	73,200
Cream Minerals Ltd.	(OTC:CRMXF)	72,866
Samex Mining Corp.	(OTC:SMXMF)	69,800
Pilot Gold Inc.	(PINK:PLGTF)	69,600
Revett Minerals Inc.	(AMEX:RVM)	68,100
Pan American Goldfields Ltd.	(OTC:MXOM)	67,700
Argentex Mining Corp.	(OTC:AGXMF)	64,561
American Bonanza Gold Corp.	(PINK:ABGFF)	64,500
Buckingham Exploration Inc.	(OTC:BUKX)	61,534
Evolving Gold Corp.	(PINK:EVOGF)	56,875
Levon Resources Ltd.	(PINK:LVNVF)	56,350
Kaminak Gold Corp.	(PINK:KMKGF)	52,900
Petaquilla Minerals Ltd.	(OTC:PTQMF)	48,900
Pretium Resources Inc.	(NYSE:PVG)	48,800
Mexus Gold U.S.	(OTC:MXSG)	48,600
Spanish Mountain Gold Ltd.	(PINK:SPAZF)	47,500
Shoshone Silver Mining Co.	(PINK:SHSH)	47,100
Merc International Minerals	(PINK:MIMZF)	47,000
Bravo Gold Corp.	(PINK:BVGIF)	46,400

Company	Ticker	Trading Volume
Barkerville Gold Mines Ltd.	(PINK:BGMZF)	46,225
Andina Minerals Inc.	(PINK:ADMNF)	44,840
Mega Precious Metals Inc.	(PINK:MPRXF)	44,300
Silvercrest Mines	(OTC:STVZF)	44,200
Luna Gold Corp.	(PINK:LGCUF)	44,000
Golden Dawn Minerals Inc.	(PINK:GDMRF)	42,793
Carpathian Gold Inc.	(PINK:CPNFF)	42,378
China TMK Battery Systems Inc.	(OTC:DFEL)	41,500
Gold Reserve Inc.	(AMEX:GRZ)	40,248
Bowmore Exploration Ltd.	(PINK:BWMXF)	40,000
St. Elias Mines Ltd.	(PINK:SELSF)	39,600
Bullion Monarch Mining Inc.	(OTC:BULM)	39,372
Tinka Resources Ltd.	(PINK:TKRFF)	39,300
Big Bear Mining Corp.	(OTC:BGBR)	39,133
Bayfield Ventures Corp.	(PINK:BYVVF)	38,943
Solvista Gold Corp.	(PINK:SVVZF)	38,400
Murgor Resources Inc.	(PINK:MGRRF)	37,800
Sono Resources Inc.	(OTC:SRCI)	36,800
CB Gold Inc.	(PINK:CBHDF)	35,882
Currie Rose Resource	(PINK:CUIRF)	35,562
Golden Band Resources	(PINK:GBRIF)	35,377
Tristar Gold Inc.	(PINK:TSGZF)	35,000
Heatherdale Resources Ltd.	(PINK:HTRRF)	34,800
Bellhaven Copper & Gold Inc.	(PINK:BHVCF)	34,585
Orofino Gold Corp.	(PINK:ORFG)	34,500
Santa Fe Gold Corp.	(OTC:SFEG)	34,300
Takara Resources Inc.	(PINK:TAKRF)	34,000
Northern Tiger Resources, Inc.	(PINK:NTGSF)	33,600
Atna Resources Ltd.	(OTC:ATNAF)	33,120
East Asia Minerals Corp.	(PINK:EAIAF)	32,714
Wesdome Gold Mines Ltd.	(PINK:WDOFF)	32,400
PC Gold Inc.	(PINK:PCGLF)	31,400
Gold Canyon Resources Inc.	(PINK:GDCRF)	30,812
Eskay Mining Corp.	(PINK:ESKYF)	30,700

Company	Ticker	Trading Volume
GWR Resources Inc.	(PINK:GWRRF)	30,100
Alhambra Resources Ltd.	(PINK:AHBRF)	29,800
Glen Eagle Resources Inc.	(PINK:GERFF)	29,200
Tyhee Gold Corp.	(PINK:TYHJF)	28,900
Victoria Gold Corp.	(PINK:VITFF)	28,500
Newcastle Minerals Ltd.	(PINK:NCMBF)	27,500
Sintana Energy Inc.	(PINK:DRFLF)	27,500
Taku Gold Corp.	(PINK:TAKUF)	26,600
Global Minerals Ltd.	(PINK:GMLFF)	26,036
Orvana Minerals Corp.	(PINK:ORVMF)	25,900
Cedar Mountain Exploration	(PINK:CDRMF)	25,000
Ruby Creek Resources Inc.	(OTC:RBYC)	25,000
Tri Origin Exploration Ltd.	(PINK:TROIF)	25,000
Bryn Resources Inc.	(PINK:BRYN)	24,792
Conquest Resources	(PINK:CQRLF)	24,788
Avino Silver & Gold Mines Ltd.	(AMEX:ASM)	24,525
Ireland Inc.	(OTC:IRLD)	24,336
Orex Minerals Inc.	(PINK:ORXIF)	24,200
Geologix Explorations Inc.	(PINK:GXEXF)	24,000
Tara Minerals Corp.	(OTC:TARM)	24,000
Handy And Harman Ltd.	(NASDAQ:HNH)	23,717
Global Gold Corp.	(PINK:GBGD)	23,486
Columbus Gold Corp.	(PINK:CBGDF)	23,170
Troymet Exploration Corp.	(PINK:TRYXF)	22,500
Golden Predator Corp.	(PINK:GPRXF)	21,800
Soltoro Ltd.	(PINK:SLTOF)	21,600
American Consolidated Minerals	(PINK:AMERF)	21,500
TNR Gold Corp.	(PINK:TRRXF)	21,500
Gowest Gold Ltd.	(PINK:GWSAF)	21,100
Soltera Mining Corp.	(PINK:SLTA)	21,000
Golden Goliath Resources Ltd.	(PINK:GGTHF)	20,673
Guyana Frontier Mining Corp.	(OTC:SHESF)	20,036
Orko Silver Corp.	(PINK:OKOFF)	19,700
Global Security Agency Inc.	(OTC:GSAG)	19,395

Company	Ticker	Trading Volume
Eagle Hill Exploration Corp.	(PINK:EHECF)	19,283
Romarco Minerals Inc.	(PINK:RTRAF)	18,700
Canarc Resource Corp.	(OTC:CRCUF)	18,636
Thundermin Resources Inc.	(PINK:TUDMF)	18,300
Alacer Gold Corp.	(PINK:ALIAF)	17,211
Pelangio Exploration Inc.	(PINK:PGXPF)	17,200
Sunward Resources Ltd.	(PINK:SNWRF)	17,200
EMC Metals Corp.	(PINK:EMMCF)	17,109
New Guinea Gold Corp.	(PINK:NGUGF)	17,000
Canstar Resources Inc.	(PINK:CSRNF)	16,700
Scorpio Gold Corp.	(PINK:SRCRF)	16,700
Skyline Gold Corp.	(PINK:SYGCF)	16,700
Benton Resources Corp.	(PINK:BNRJF)	16,594
Anglo Swiss Resources Inc.	(PINK:ASWRF)	16,560
Northern Abitibi Mining Corp.	(PINK:NOMNF)	16,500
Colombia Crest Gold	(PINK:ECRTF)	16,300
Cline Mining Corp.	(PINK:CLNMF)	15,908
Rusoro Mining Ltd.	(PINK:RMLFF)	15,800
Athena Silver Corporation	(OTC:AHNR)	15,500
Puma Exploration	(PINK:PUXPF)	15,500
First Point Minerals Corp.	(PINK:FPOCF)	15,370
Bravada Gold Corp.	(PINK:BGAVF)	15,000
Pacific Rim Mining Corp.	(PINK:PFRMF)	15,000
Rockhaven Resources	(PINK:RKHNF)	15,000
Scorpio Mining Corp.	(PINK:SMNPF)	15,000
Source Exploration	(PINK:SRXLF)	15,000
Teuton Resources Corp.	(PINK:TEUTF)	14,600
Premier Gold Mines	(PINK:PIRGF)	14,400
Pacific Ridge Exploration	(PINK:PEXZF)	14,100
King'S Bay Gold Corp	(PINK:KBGCF)	14,000
South American Silver Corp.	(PINK:SOHAF)	14,000
Bear Creek Mining Corp.	(PINK:BCEKF)	13,968
Confederation Minerals Ltd.	(PINK:CNRMF)	13,900
Cornerstone Capital Resources	(PINK:CTNXF)	13,803

Company	Ticker	Trading Volume
Inc.		
Torex Gold Resources Inc.	(PINK:TORXF)	13,700
Metanor Resources Inc.	(PINK:MEAOF)	13,600
Argonaut Gold Inc.	(PINK:ARNGF)	13,500
PMI Gold Corp.	(PINK:PMVGF)	13,477
Ely Gold & Minerals Inc.	(PINK:ELYGF)	13,360
Serengeti Resources Inc.	(PINK:SGRNF)	13,300
Volta Resources Inc.	(PINK:VLTAF)	13,000
Olympus Pacific Minerals Inc.	(OTC:OLYMF)	12,900
Stroud Resources Ltd.	(PINK:SDURF)	12,800
REBGold Corp.	(PINK:RBGCF)	12,600
Miranda Gold Corp.	(OTC:MRDDF)	12,500
Wildcat Silver Corp.	(PINK:WLDVF)	12,500
Xtierra Ltd.	(PINK:XRESF)	12,400
Geopulse Exploration Inc.	(OTC:GPLS)	12,222
Eurasian Minerals Inc.	(PINK:ESMNF)	12,200
Glass Earth Gold Ltd.	(PINK:GELGF)	12,200
Lake Victoria Mining Company, Inc.	(OTC:LVCA)	12,200
Columbus Silver	(PINK:CSLVF)	12,000
Orosur Mining Inc.	(PINK:OROXF)	12,000
Mansfield Minerals Inc.	(PINK:MFMNF)	11,900
Marifil Mines Ltd.	(PINK:MFMLF)	11,600
Sabina Gold And Silver Corp.	(PINK:SGSVF)	11,500
Royal Mines And Minerals Corp.	(PINK:RYMM)	11,400
Vena Resources Inc.	(PINK:VNARF)	11,300
Full Metal Minerals	(PINK:FLMTF)	11,100
Northern Superior	(PINK:NSUPF)	11,000
Sutter Gold Mining Inc.	(PINK:SGMNF)	10,800
CMC Metals Ltd.	(PINK:CMCXF)	10,709
Roxgold Inc.	(PINK:ROGFF)	10,700
Southern Silver Exploration Corp.	(PINK:SSVFF)	10,700
Galway Resources Ltd.	(PINK:GWYRF)	10,450
Silver Bear Resources Inc.	(PINK:SVBRF)	10,300

Company	Ticker	Trading Volume
Barker Minerals Ltd.	(PINK:BKMNF)	10,267
Blue Note Mining Inc.	(PINK:BLNMF)	10,200
BCGold Corp.	(PINK:BCGOF)	10,193
Brazilian Gold Corp.	(PINK:BGOZF)	10,000
Calibre Mining Corp.	(PINK:CXBMF)	10,000
Crown Gold Corp.	(PINK:CWMZF)	10,000
Kalimantan Gold Corp.	(PINK:KMGLF)	10,000
Lucky Boy Silver Corp.	(PINK:LUCB)	10,000
Balmoral Resources Ltd.	(PINK:BALMF)	9,750
Champion Bear Resources	(PINK:CBRSF)	9,500
Erin Ventures Inc.	(PINK:ERVFF)	9,500
Oro Mining Ltd.	(PINK:OMRGF)	9,400
Eagle Plains Resources Ltd.	(PINK:EGPLF)	9,073
Guyana Goldfields Inc.	(PINK:GUYFF)	9,059
Animas Resources Ltd.	(PINK:ANIMF)	8,805
Mountain Lake Resources Inc.	(PINK:MLKRF)	8,800
Western Pacific Resources Corp.	(PINK:WRPSF)	8,700
Fortune Minerals Ltd.	(PINK:FTMDF)	8,500
UC Resources Ltd.	(PINK:UCRLF)	8,500
Adventure Gold Inc.	(PINK:AGONF)	8,259
African Gold Group Inc.	(PINK:AGGFF)	8,023
Probe Mines Ltd.	(PINK:PROBF)	8,000
Calais Resources Inc.	(PINK:CAAUF)	7,787
Colombian Mines Corp.	(PINK:CMBPF)	7,784
Aurion Resources Ltd.	(PINK:AIRRF)	7,680
Commander Resources	(PINK:CMDRF)	7,549
Magellan Minerals	(PINK:MAGNF)	7,500
Malbex Resources Inc.	(PINK:MXRSF)	7,500
Redstar Gold Corp.	(PINK:RGCTF)	7,500
Giyani Gold Corp.	(PINK:CATPF)	7,452
Candente Copper Corp.	(PINK:CGDXF)	7,445
Silver Predator Corp.	(PINK:SVROF)	7,400
Coyote Resources, Inc.	(OTC:COYR)	7,318
Kobex Minerals Inc.	(AMEX:KXM)	7,300

Company	Ticker	Trading Volume
Polar Star Mining	(PINK:POSRF)	7,300
Fjordland Exploration Inc.	(PINK:FEXXF)	7,188
African Metals Corp.	(PINK:AFMCF)	7,000
International Silver Inc.	(PINK:ISLV)	6,949
Tahoe Resources Inc.	(PINK:THOEF)	6,800
Nevada Exploration Inc.	(PINK:NVDEF)	6,700
Sienna Gold Inc.	(PINK:SNNGF)	6,700
Starcore International Mines Ltd.	(PINK:SHVLF)	6,600
Alphamin Resources Corp.	(PINK:AFMJF)	6,500
Ascot Resources Ltd.	(PINK:ASOLF)	6,377
Canasil Resources Inc.	(PINK:CNSUF)	6,276
NGEx Resources Inc.	(PINK:NGQRF)	6,200
Merrex Gold Inc.	(PINK:MXGIF)	6,100
Huldra Silver Inc.	(PINK:HUSIF)	5,900
Coral Gold Resources Ltd.	(OTC:CLHRF)	5,740
Aldrin Resources Corp.	(PINK:AOUFF)	5,600
Niblack Mineral Development, Inc.	(PINK:NIBMF)	5,600
Ryan Gold Corp.	(PINK:RYGZF)	5,600
Channel Resources Ltd.	(PINK:CHJRF)	5,300
Eastmain Resources Inc.	(PINK:EANRF)	5,300
Renaissance Gold Inc.	(PINK:RNSGF)	5,100
Riverside Resources Inc.	(PINK:RVSDF)	5,100
Altai Resources Inc.	(PINK:ARSEF)	5,000
La Quinta Resources Corp.	(PINK:LQRCF)	5,000
Siga Resources Inc.	(OTC:SGAE)	4,800
Endurance Gold Corp.	(PINK:ENDGF)	4,793
Golden Peaks Resources	(PINK:GDPEF)	4,611
Maudore Minerals Ltd.	(PINK:MAOMF)	4,500
Lincoln Mining Corp.	(PINK:LNCLF)	4,422
International PBX Ventures Ltd.	(PINK:IPBXF)	4,274
Freegold Ventures Ltd.	(PINK:FGOVF)	4,200
Bonterra Resources Inc.	(PINK:BONXF)	4,198
Armistice Resources Corp.	(PINK:AISCF)	4,000

Company	Ticker	Trading Volume
Minaurum Gold Inc.	(PINK:MMRGF)	4,000
Monster Mining Corp.	(PINK:MMNGF)	4,000
Jayden Resources, Inc.	(PINK:PNMLF)	3,900
Unigold Inc.	(PINK:UGDIF)	3,800
Golden Valley Mines	(PINK:GLVMF)	3,725
Virginia Mines Inc.	(PINK:VGMNF)	3,700
Search Minerals Inc.	(PINK:SHCMF)	3,500
St. Andrew Goldfields	(PINK:STADF)	3,500
Imperial Metals Corp.	(PINK:IPMLF)	3,470
Beaufield Resources	(PINK:BFDRF)	3,446
Golden Arrow Resources Corp.	(PINK:GARWF)	3,410
Bralorne Gold Mines	(PINK:BPMSF)	3,347
Cassidy Gold Corp.	(PINK:CDXGF)	3,300
Colibri Resource Corp.	(PINK:CRUCF)	3,300
Rainy River Resource	(PINK:RRFFF)	3,200
GMV Minerals Inc.	(PINK:GMVMF)	3,163
Aurora Gold Corporation	(PINK:ARXG)	3,150
Happy Creek Minerals	(PINK:HPYCF)	3,000
Legend Gold Corp.	(OTC:NOATF)	3,000
Newstrike Capital Inc.	(PINK:NWSKF)	3,000
Reunion Gold Corp.	(PINK:RGDFF)	3,000
Yorbeau Resources Inc.	(PINK:YRBAF)	3,000
New Jersey Mining Company	(PINK:NJMC)	2,900
Superior Mining International	(PINK:SUIFF)	2,800
Azimut Exploration	(PINK:AZMTF)	2,776
Kenai Resources Ltd.	(PINK:KAIFF)	2,700
Alto Ventures Ltd.	(PINK:ALVLD)	2,600
Dynacor Gold Mines	(PINK:DNGDF)	2,588
Manson Creek Resources	(PINK:MCKRF)	2,550
Indigo Exploration Inc.	(PINK:IGXEF)	2,500
Maya Gold & Silver Inc.	(PINK:MYAGF)	2,500
Red Metal Resources Ltd.	(OTC:RMES)	2,500
Rome Resources Ltd.	(PINK:RMRSF)	2,500
HuntMountain Resources Ltd.	(PINK:HNTM)	2,434

Company	Ticker	Trading Volume
Golden Tag Resources Ltd.	(PINK:GTAGF)	2,350
Bolero Resources Corp.	(PINK:BRUZF)	2,320
United Mines, Inc.	(OTC:UNMN)	2,300
North Country Gold	(PINK:NCGDF)	2,200
Pershimco Resources	(PINK:RSPRF)	2,200
Arcus Development Group Inc.	(PINK:ARCUF)	2,175
Oroco Resource Corp.	(PINK:ORRCF)	2,100
Challenger Deep Resources	(PINK:CNDRF)	2,000
Eloro Resources Ltd.	(PINK:ELRRD)	2,000
Robex Resources	(PINK:RSRBF)	2,000
Wescan Goldfields Inc.	(PINK:WEGOF)	2,000
Corex Gold Corp.	(PINK:CGEKF)	1,900
Orezone Gold Corp.	(PINK:ORZCF)	1,900
Paget Minerals Corp.	(PINK:PGTMF)	1,800
Galore Resources Inc.	(PINK:GALOF)	1,715
Avala Resources Ltd.	(PINK:AVLRF)	1,700
Amerix Precious Metals Corp.	(PINK:APMFF)	1,600
Dajin Resources Corp.	(PINK:DJIFF)	1,587
Golden Reign Resources Ltd.	(PINK:GRGNF)	1,472
LKA International Inc.	(PINK:LKAI)	1,400
Caza Gold Corp.	(PINK:CZGDF)	1,346
Equitas Resources Corp.	(PINK:EQTRF)	1,300
Rochester Resources Ltd.	(PINK:RCTFF)	1,300
Sage Gold Inc.	(PINK:SGGDF)	1,300
Harte Gold Corp.	(PINK:HRTFF)	1,200
Treasury Metals Inc.	(PINK:TSRMF)	1,200
Great Quest Metals Ltd.	(PINK:GQMLF)	1,143
Cadan Resources Corp.	(PINK:CADAF)	1,125
Anaconda Mining Inc.	(PINK:ANXGF)	1,100
Corona Gold Corp.	(PINK:CRGAF)	1,071
Coro Mining Corp.	(PINK:CROJF)	1,000
Decade Resources	(PINK:DECXF)	1,000
First Mexican Gold Corp.	(PINK:FMGXF)	1,000
Gogold Resources Inc.	(PINK:GLGDF)	1,000

Company	Ticker	Trading Volume
Goldbank Mining Corp.	(PINK:GLBKF)	1,000
Bear Lake Gold Ltd.	(PINK:BLGFF)	881
Integra Gold Corp.	(PINK:KALRF)	779
Temex Resources Corp.	(PINK:TMXRF)	775
Iron Creek Capital Corp.	(PINK:INCKF)	767
Paragon Minerals Corp.	(PINK:PAONF)	767
Habanero Resources	(PINK:HBNRF)	765
Hy Lake Gold Inc.	(PINK:HYLKF)	643
Aldridge Minerals Inc.	(PINK:AGMIF)	500
Liberty Gold Corp.	(OTC:LBGO)	500
Midland Exploration Inc.	(PINK:MIDLF)	500
Dia Bras Exploration Inc.	(PINK:DBEXF)	490
International Minerals Corp.	(PINK:IMZLF)	463
New Dimension Resources	(PINK:NWDMF)	375

CHAPTER 10
TWO-HUNDRED+ GOLD AND SILVER COMPANIES RANKED BY GOLD AND SILVER IN THE GROUND

Note: The point of the chart that follows is to direct readers toward companies that have actual gold and silver in the ground. This is not a scientific and exhaustive list. Gold and silver mining companies have different ways of reporting their mineral resources. In some cases, the numbers below refer to gold or silver resources. In others they refer to gold or silver reserves, and in some cases, a combination of both. Some numbers may be historical or inferred resources only. Please use the chart as a jumping off point for further research on the featured companies.

Company	Metals in the Ground
Silver Standard Resources Inc.	993,000,000 oz./silver
Bear Creek Mining Corp.	500,000,000 oz./silver
Levon Resources Ltd.	450,000,000 oz./silver
Allied Nevada Gold Corp.	400,000,000 oz./silver
Tahoe Resources Inc.	316,900,000 oz./silver
Revett Minerals Inc.	300,000,000 oz./silver
Coeur D'Alene Mines Corp.	278,000,000 oz./silver
Gold Fields Ltd.	270,280,000 oz./gold (total resource)
Anglogold Ashanti Ltd.	264,300,000 oz./gold (total resource)
Harmony Gold Mining Co.	237,300,000 oz./gold

Company	Metals in the Ground
Barrick Gold Corp.	226,920,000 oz./gold (total resource)
Golden Tag Resources Ltd.	218,550,000 oz./silver equivalent
Orko Silver Corp.	159,000,000 oz./silver
Newmont Mining Corp.	142,670,000 oz./gold (total resource)
Wildcat Silver Corp.	121,000,000 oz./silver
Kinross Gold Corp.	92,060,000 oz./gold (total resource)
Mag Silver Corp.	90,000,000 oz./silver
Goldcorp Inc.	81,590,000 oz./gold (total resource), 1,300,000,000 oz./silver
Soltoro Ltd.	77,400,000 oz./silver
Northern Dynasty Minerals Ltd.	66,900,000 oz./gold
Mines Management, Inc.	63,000,000 oz./silver
DRDGOLD Ltd.	60,000,000 oz./gold
Cream Minerals Ltd.	54,600,000 oz./silver equivalent
Novagold Resources Inc.	51,000,000 oz./gold
Silver Bear Resources Inc.	49,000,000 oz./silver
Yamana Gold Inc.	46,350,000 oz./gold (total resource)
Silver Bull Resources Inc.	46,313,000 oz./silver
Silver Dragon Resources Inc.	45,000,000 oz./silver equivalent
Coyote Resources, Inc.	40,000,000 oz./silver (non-NI 43-101 compliant)
Seabridge Gold, Inc.	38,500,000 oz./gold
Agnico-Eagle Mines Ltd.	38,320,000 oz./gold (total resource)
Great Basin Gold Ltd.	30,700,000 oz./gold
Pelangio Exploration Inc.	29,530,000 oz./gold
Exeter Resource Corp.	26,400,000 oz./gold
Global Minerals Ltd.	23,000,000 oz./silver
Andina Minerals Inc.	20,600,000 oz./gold
Tinka Resources Ltd.	20,300,000 oz./silver
International Tower Hill Mines Ltd.	20,000,000 oz./gold
Silver Predator Corp.	16,800,000 oz./silver
Crystallex International Corp.	16,800,000 oz./gold
Hana Mining Ltd.	16,100,000 oz./silver

Company	Metals in the Ground
Vista Gold Corp.	16,000,000 oz./gold
Liberty Gold Corp.	13,900,000 oz./gold equivalent
Ireland Inc.	13,756,000 oz./gold equivalent
International Minerals Corp.	12,300,000 oz./gold equivalent
Foran Mining Corp.	11,400,000 oz./silver
Randgold Resources Ltd.	10,000,000 oz./gold
Columbus Silver	8,657,641 oz./silver
Pretium Resources Inc.	8,360,000 oz./gold, 34,300,000 oz./silver
Great Panther Silver Ltd.	8,230,000 oz./silver
Jaguar Mining Inc.	7,700,000 oz./gold
Victoria Gold Corp.	7,700,000 oz./gold
Global Gold Corp.	7,400,000 oz./gold
Rainy River Resource	6,730,000 oz./gold
RJK Exploration Ltd.	6,520,000 oz./gold, 36,300,000 oz./silver
Aurico Gold Inc.	6,500,000 oz./gold
INV Metals Inc.	6,386,350 oz./silver
Sunward Resources Ltd.	6,280,000 oz./gold
Spanish Mountain Gold Ltd.	6,100,000 oz./gold, 9,900,000 oz./silver
Sabina Gold And Silver Corp.	6,050,000 oz./gold
Guyana Goldfields Inc.	5,710,000 oz./gold (measured and indicated)
Alacer Gold Corp.	5,500,000 oz./gold
Volta Resources Inc.	5,350,000 oz./gold
Slam Exploration Ltd.	5,300,000 oz./silver
Keegan Resources Inc.	5,190,000 oz./gold
St. Andrew Goldfields	4,600,000 oz./gold
PMI Gold Corp.	4,510,000 oz./gold
Orezone Gold Corp.	4,500,000 oz./gold
NGEx Resources Inc.	4,400,000 oz./gold
Huldra Silver Inc.	4,380,000 oz./silver
Probe Mines Ltd.	4,100,000 oz./gold
Torex Gold Resources Inc.	3,900,000 oz./gold
Olympus Pacific Minerals Inc.	3,870,506 oz./gold

Company	Metals in the Ground
Paramount Gold And Silver Corp.	3,700,000 oz./gold, 33,500,000 oz./silver
Oromin Explorations Ltd.	3,700,000 oz./gold
Premier Gold Mines	3,600,000 oz./gold
Coral Gold Resources Ltd.	3,400,000 oz./gold
Aura Silver Resources Ltd.	3,300,000 oz./silver
Century Mining Corp.	3,275,125 oz./gold
Atna Resources Ltd.	3,240,000 oz./gold
Romarco Minerals Inc.	3,100,000 oz./gold
Mansfield Minerals Inc.	2,950,000 oz./gold
Argonaut Gold Inc.	2,930,000 oz./gold
International Silver Inc.	2,880,000 oz./silver
Northgate Minerals Corp.	2,726,000 oz./gold (proven and probable)
Serengeti Resources Inc.	2,500,000 oz./gold, 17,600,000 oz./silver
Peregrine Metals Ltd.	2,410,000 oz./gold
Tyhee Gold Corp.	2,219,000 oz./gold
Skyline Gold Corp.	2,200,000 oz./gold
Tanzanian Royalty Exploration Corp.	2,100,000 oz./gold
Freegold Ventures Ltd.	2,030,000 oz./gold
Astur Gold Corp.	2,021,000 oz./gold
Kilo Goldmines Ltd.	2,000,000 oz./gold
Richmont Mines Inc.	1,987,984 oz./gold
Robex Resources	1,921,455 oz./gold
Columbus Gold Corp.	1,900,000 oz./gold
Golden Minerals Co.	1,800,000 oz./gold, 212,000,000 oz./silver
Mega Precious Metals Inc.	1,800,000 oz./gold
Candente Copper Corp.	1,700,000 oz./gold, 45,200,000 oz./silver
Pacific Rim Mining Corp.	1,700,000 oz./gold equivalent
New Oroperu Resources	1,700,000 oz./gold (historical)
Magellan Minerals	1,700,000 oz./gold
Bellhaven Copper & Gold Inc.	1,600,000 oz./gold equivalent

Company	Metals in the Ground
Geologix Explorations Inc.	1,600,000 oz./gold
Dalradian Resources Inc.	1,560,000 oz./gold
Moss Lake Gold Mine	1,510,000 oz./gold
Comstock Mining, Inc.	1,500,000 oz./gold, 14,300,000 oz./silver
Alhambra Resources Ltd.	1,397,200 oz./gold
Amarillo Gold Corp.	1,331,300 oz./gold
Luna Gold Corp.	1,312,000 oz./gold
PC Gold Inc.	1,260,000 oz./gold
Eastmain Resources Inc.	1,240,000 oz./gold
Claude Resources Inc.	1,230,000 oz./gold
Temex Resources Corp.	1,216,000 oz./gold, 2,960,000 oz./silver
Gowest Gold Ltd.	1,200,000 oz./gold
Maudore Minerals Ltd.	1,200,000 oz./gold
Treasury Metals Inc.	1,200,000 oz./gold
Wesdome Gold Mines Ltd.	1,158,000 oz./gold
Nevsun Resources	1,140,000 oz./gold, 11,900,000 oz./silver
Midway Gold Corp.	1,130,000 oz./gold
Canarc Resource Corp.	1,100,000 oz./gold
Caldera Resources Inc.	1,052,299 oz./gold, 51,300,000 oz./silver
Cassidy Gold Corp.	1,043,000 oz./gold
Orex Minerals Inc.	1,030,000 oz./gold
Puma Exploration	1,000,000 oz./silver
Banro Corp.	1,000,000 + oz./gold
TNR Gold Corp.	1,000,000 oz./gold (historical)
Ardent Mines Ltd.	1,000,000 oz./gold (estimated)
Minco Gold Corp.	1,000,000 oz./gold
Malbex Resources Inc.	1,000,000 + oz./gold
Timberline Resources Corp.	1,000,000 + oz./gold
Northern Gold Mining Inc.	983,500 oz./gold
Firestone Ventures	978,000 oz./of silver
Bear Lake Gold Ltd.	960,800 oz./gold
Brazilian Gold Corp.	937,000 oz./gold
Seafield Resources Ltd.	920,000 oz./gold

Company	Metals in the Ground
Fortune Minerals Ltd.	907,000 oz./gold
Alexandria Minerals Corp.	899,760 oz./gold
Golden Star Resources Ltd.	830,000 oz./gold (proven and probable)
Pershimco Resources	823,900 oz./gold
Mountain Lake Resources Inc.	812,000 oz./gold
Metanor Resources Inc.	771,000 oz./gold
Paragon Minerals Corp.	765,753 oz./gold
Petaquilla Minerals Ltd.	756,586 oz./gold
North Country Gold	750,000 oz./gold
African Gold Group Inc.	740,000 oz./gold
Auriga Gold Corp.	732,000 oz./gold
XMET Inc.	727,000 oz./gold
Bravo Gold Corp.	721,000 oz./gold, 14,820,000 oz./silver
Animas Resources Ltd.	720,000 oz./gold (non-NI 43 101)
Erin Ventures Inc.	708,000 oz./gold (inferred)
Eagle Hill Exploration Corp.	708,000 oz./gold
Reva Resources Corp.	705,831 oz./silver (non-NI 43-101 compliant)
Andes Gold Corp.	695,000 oz./gold
Sutter Gold Mining Inc.	681,958 oz./gold
Integra Gold Corp.	681,605 oz./gold
South American Silver Corp.	610,000 oz./gold, 16,800,000 oz./silver
Alto Ventures Ltd.	609,000 oz./gold
Legend Gold Corp.	600,000 oz./gold
Royal Standard Minerals Inc.	600,000 oz./gold
Axmin Inc.	588,969 oz./gold
American Bonanza Gold Corp.	569,000 oz./gold
Lincoln Mining Corp.	518,800 oz./gold
Kimber Resources, Inc.	510,000 oz./gold, 30,000,000 oz./silver
Sunergy Inc.	500,000 oz./gold
Takara Resources Inc.	499,000 oz./gold
Bravada Gold Corp.	498,000 oz./gold
Niblack Mineral Development, Inc.	494,122 oz./gold

Company	Metals in the Ground
Pan American Goldfields Ltd.	474,000 oz./gold, 33,400,000 oz./silver
Sacre-Couer Minerals	451,397 oz./gold
Heatherdale Resources Ltd.	450,000 oz./gold
Oro Mining Ltd.	433,000 oz./gold
Crown Gold Corp.	410,000 oz./gold
Harte Gold Corp.	397,000 oz./gold
Glass Earth Gold Ltd.	390,000 + oz./gold
Oroco Resource Corp.	389,733 oz./gold, 6,193,000 oz./silver
Imperial Metals Corp.	386,000 oz./gold
Solitario Exploration & Royalty Corp.	385,350 oz./gold, 1,800,000 oz./silver
Merrex Gold Inc.	377,700 oz./gold
Cadan Resources Corp.	360,000 oz./gold, 1,600,000 oz./silver
Scorpio Gold Corp.	357,000 oz./gold
Maya Gold & Silver Inc.	342,094 oz./gold, 7,500,000 oz./silver
Silverado Gold Mines Ltd.	340,700 oz./gold
U.S. Precious Metals, Inc.	308,000 oz./gold (historical)
Orvana Minerals Corp.	282,000 oz./gold
Golden Dawn Minerals Inc.	279,300 oz./gold (inferred)
General Metals Corp.	272,500 oz./gold, 3,868,000 oz./silver
Kenai Resources Ltd.	265,260 oz./gold
Orosur Mining Inc.	249,000 oz./gold
Redstar Gold Corp.	225,000 oz./gold, 1,000,000 oz./silver (non-NI 43-101 compliant)
Golden Band Resources	200,000 + oz./gold (measured and indicated)
Blue Note Mining Inc.	185,260 oz./gold
New Guinea Gold Corp.	180,000 oz./gold
Plato Gold	176,527 oz./gold
Anaconda Mining Inc.	175,000 oz./gold (probable)
American Consolidated Minerals	173,562 oz./gold (indicated)
Africo Resources Ltd.	164,296 tonnes copper, 38,485 tonnes of cobalt
Golden River Resources Corp.	160,000 oz./gold (measured and

Company	Metals in the Ground indicated)
Sagebrush Gold Ltd.	155,000 oz./gold
Sage Gold Inc.	147,400 oz./gold
Wescan Goldfields Inc.	137,000 oz./gold
Northern Abitibi Mining Corp.	131,511 oz./gold
Aurora Gold Corporation	130,000 oz./gold
La Quinta Resources Corp.	119,225 oz./gold
Glen Eagle Resources Inc.	110,000 oz./gold
Altai Resources Inc.	107,920 oz./gold
Colombia Crest Gold	96,145 oz./gold
Stroud Resources Ltd.	95,400 oz./gold, 23,900,000 oz./silver
Golden Peaks Resources	91,000 oz./gold
Starcore International Mines Ltd.	47,361 oz./gold, 806,588 oz./silver
New Jersey Mining Company	27,885 oz./gold
Red Metal Resources Ltd.	25,510 oz./silver
BCGold Corp.	25,000 oz./gold
Mazorro Resources Inc.	22,197 oz./gold
Rockcliff Resources Inc.	17,397 oz./gold, 268,205 oz./silver
Calais Resources Inc.	11,824 oz./gold, 175,170 oz./silver
Karmin Exploration Inc.	5,500 oz./gold

CHAPTER 11
TOP 48 SILVER STOCKS AS MEASURED BY SILVER IN THE GROUND

Note: The point of the chart that follows is to direct readers toward companies that have actual silver in the ground. This is not a scientific and exhaustive list. Silver mining companies have different ways of reporting their mineral resources. In some cases, the numbers below refer to silver resources. In others they refer to silver reserves (or silver equivalent ounces), and in some cases, a combination of all three. Some numbers may be historical or inferred resources only. Please use the chart as a jumping off point for further research on the featured companies.

Company	Silver in the Ground
Goldcorp Inc.	1,300,000,000 oz./silver
Silver Standard Resources Inc.	993,000,000 oz./silver
Bear Creek Mining Corp.	500,000,000 oz./silver
Levon Resources Ltd.	450,000,000 oz./silver
Allied Nevada Gold Corp.	400,000,000 oz./silver
Tahoe Resources Inc.	316,900,000 oz./silver
Revett Minerals Inc.	300,000,000 oz./silver
Coeur D'Alene Mines Corp.	278,000,000 oz./silver
Golden Tag Resources Ltd.	218,550,000 oz./silver equivalent
Golden Minerals Co.	212,000,000 oz./silver

Company	Silver in the Ground
Orko Silver Corp.	159,000,000 oz./silver
Wildcat Silver Corp.	121,000,000 oz./silver
Mag Silver Corp.	90,000,000 oz./silver
Soltoro Ltd.	77,400,000 oz./silver
Mines Management, Inc.	63,000,000 oz./silver
Cream Minerals Ltd.	54,600,000 oz./silver equivalent
Caldera Resources Inc.	51,300,000 oz./silver
Silver Bear Resources Inc.	49,000,000 oz./silver
Silver Bull Resources Inc.	46,313,000 oz./silver
Silver Dragon Resources Inc.	45,000,000 oz./silver equivalent
RJK Exploration Ltd.	36,300,000 oz./silver
Paramount Gold And Silver Corp.	33,500,000 oz./silver
Pan American Goldfields Ltd.	33,400,000 oz./silver
Pretium Resources Inc.	34,300,000 oz./silver
Kimber Resources, Inc.	30,000,000 oz./silver
Stroud Resources Ltd.	23,900,000 oz./silver
Global Minerals Ltd.	23,000,000 oz./silver
Tinka Resources Ltd.	20,300,000 oz./silver
Serengeti Resources Inc.	17,600,000 oz./silver
Silver Predator Corp.	16,800,000 oz./silver
South American Silver Corp.	16,800,000 oz./silver
Hana Mining Ltd.	16,100,000 oz./silver
Bravo Gold Corp.	14,820,000 oz./silver
Nevsun Resources	11,900,000 oz./silver
Spanish Mountain Gold Ltd.	9,900,000 oz./silver
Columbus Silver	8,657,641 oz./silver
Great Panther Silver Ltd.	8,230,000 oz./silver
Maya Gold & Silver Inc.	7,500,000 oz./silver
Oroco Resource Corp.	6,193,000 oz./silver
Slam Exploration Ltd.	5,300,000 oz./silver
Huldra Silver Inc.	4,380,000 oz./silver
Aura Silver Resources Ltd.	3,300,000 oz./silver
Cadan Resources Corp.	1,600,000 oz./silver
Puma Exploration	1,000,000 oz./silver

Company	**Silver in the Ground**
Redstar Gold Corp.	1,000,000 oz./silver (non-NI 43-101 compliant)
Starcore International Mines Ltd.	806,588 oz./silver
Red Metal Resources Ltd.	25,510 oz./silver

CHAPTER 12
TOP 100 GOLD AND SILVER STOCK PICKS
FOR 2012 AND BEYOND

Below, we've summed up why we like each of these companies in one sentence. See Chapter 3 for more detailed information on each of these companies.

Company	Why We Like It
Agnico-Eagle Mines Ltd.	1.69% dividend; More than 21 million ounces of gold reserves
Alacer Gold Corp.	Looking to produce 800,000 ounces of gold a year by 2015; Shares up 31% in 2011
Alexco Resource Corp.	1,000 g/t silver at Bellekeno in the Yukon
Allied Nevada Gold Corp.	$190 cash cost per ounce of gold; Shares up 15% in 2011
Alphamin Resources Corp.	Good chart pattern with shares up 100%+ in 2011
Andina Minerals Inc.	Nearing 20 million ounces of gold in Chile
Argonaut Gold Inc.	A small-cap producer with nearly 3 million ounces of gold in the ground; Shares were up 51% in

Company	Why We Like It 2011
Ascot Resources Ltd.	Actively exploring a past-producing mine; Shares up 89% in 2011
Athena Silver Corporation	Exploring the historic Langtry Mine, which produced 52 million ounces of silver
Atna Resources Ltd.	Early-stage gold producer; Expects to mine 50,000 ounces a year by 2015
Aurizon Mines Ltd.	A major producer with a bonanza-grade deposit
Bear Creek Mining Corp.	More than 500 million ounces of silver in Peru
Calibre Mining Corp.	Yamana holds a 7% interest in Calibre
Coeur D'Alene Mines Corp.	The largest primary silver producer in the US
Colibri Resource Corp.	Sprott and Agnico-Eagle hold 30% of Colibri
Compania De Minas Buenaventura SA	Yielding 1.45%; Shares have returned 190% over past five years
DRDGOLD Ltd.	No more strikes in South Africa
Dynacor Gold Mines	Production rose 34% in 2011
Endeavour Silver Corp.	Surging revenue; Shares were up 48% in 2011
Exeter Resource Corp.	Sitting on a huge deposit in Chile
Global Minerals Ltd.	Sitting on 23 million ounces of silver and 78 million pounds of copper
Gold Canyon Resources Inc.	An initial resource estimate is on its way
Gold Fields Ltd.	Suring earnings
Gold Resource Corp.	Aggressively buying back shares
Goldcorp Inc.	Stability from a major; Monthly dividends
Golden Minerals Co.	More than 200 million ounces of silver
Golden Predator Corp.	Moving toward a production

Company	Why We Like It
	decision
Golden Star Resources Ltd.	Growing revenue in Ghana
Great Basin Gold Ltd.	30 million ounces of gold and a COO from Gold Fields Limited
Great Panther Silver Ltd.	An early-stage silver producer
Harmony Gold Mining Co.	Expanding reserves, more than 200 million ounces of gold in the ground
Hecla Mining Company	Negative cash costs; High-volume stock
Huldra Silver Inc.	Coeur d'Alene holds a 7% interest in Huldra
IAMGOLD Corp.	Looking to spend $1 billion on new gold assets
International PBX Ventures Ltd.	An NI 43-101 Technical Report is in the works
International Tower Hill Mines Ltd.	A potential takeover target?
Ireland Inc.	Shares up more than 5,000% over the past five years
Jaguar Mining Inc.	Nearing production in Brazil
Jayden Resources, Inc.	Expect a prefeasibility study in 2012
Kaminak Gold Corp.	Analyst approved
Keegan Resources Inc.	More than 5 million ounces in West Africa
Kinross Gold Corp.	A once-in-a-generation gold discovery
Levon Resources Ltd.	More than 450 million ounces of silver
Mag Silver Corp.	More than 90 million ounces of silver in Mexico
Maudore Minerals Ltd.	Potential for a high-grade deposit in Quebec
Midway Gold Corp.	Momentum on their side with shares up more than 150% in 2011
Minco Gold Corp.	Sprott-approved mining in the PRC
Nevsun Resources	Recent stock upgrade
New Gold Inc.	New mine online soon

Company	Why We Like It
Newmont Mining Corp.	Rapidly-growing dividends
Newstrike Capital Inc.	Experienced management
NGEx Resources Inc.	More than 4 million ounces of gold in the ground
North Country Gold	Rated outperform
Novagold Resources Inc.	More than 50 million ounces of gold
Olympus Pacific Minerals Inc.	Up and coming gold producer
Orezone Gold Corp.	A growing deposit in Burkina Faso
Orko Silver Corp.	More than 150 million ounces of silver
Pan American Silver Corp.	Investor overreaction?
Pelangio Exploration Inc.	Approaching 30 million ounces of gold
Pershimco Resources	Good chart pattern with shares up more than 100% in 2011
PMI Gold Corp.	A ballooning gold deposit in Ghana
Premier Gold Mines	$8.50 price target
Pretium Resources Inc.	A world class deposit
Probe Mines Ltd.	Royalties and a growing resource
Rainy River Resource	Lots of cash and lots of drilling
Randgold Resources Ltd.	Ahead of schedule on a very large mine
Red Metal Resources Ltd.	Promising gold and copper deposits in Chile
Redstar Gold Corp.	A good chart pattern with shares up more than 80% in 2011
Richmont Mines Inc.	An early-stage gold producer
Romarco Minerals Inc.	Looking to pour their first gold in 2014
Roxgold Inc.	A growing deposit in Burkina Faso; Shares up 3,500% in 2011
Royal Gold, Inc.	A gold-streaming company
Royal Standard Minerals Inc.	Moving toward feasibility
Rubicon Minerals Corp.	Agnico-Eagle owns a 9% stake in Rubicon
Ruby Creek Resources Inc.	Recently acquired a mining license

Company	Why We Like It
Sabina Gold And Silver Corp.	Sitting on more than 6 million ounces of gold
Sandstorm Gold Ltd.	A gold-streaming company
Scorpio Mining Corp.	An early-stage silver producer with a nice chart pattern
Silver Bear Resources Inc.	A large silver deposit in Russia
Silver Dragon Resources Inc.	Silver mines behind the Great Wall
Silver Falcon Mining Inc.	On the cusp of production
Silver Standard Resources Inc.	A potential takeover target?
Silver Wheaton Corp.	A silver-streaming dream
Silvercorp Metals Inc.	Negative cash costs
Soltoro Ltd.	More than 77 million ounces of silver and counting in Mexico
South American Silver Corp.	New drilling in December 2011 doubled the company's resources
Spanish Mountain Gold Ltd.	A prefeasibility study is underway
St. Elias Mines Ltd.	A good chart pattern with shares up 650% over the past five years
Stroud Resources Ltd.	More than 23 million ounces of silver in Mexico
Sunward Resources Ltd.	More than 8 million ounces of gold in Colombia
Tahoe Resources Inc.	More than 300 million ounces of silver in the ground
Tara Minerals Corp.	On the cusp of production and a potential JV with Yamana
Teuton Resources Corp.	Holds land beside Pretium's Brucejack-Snowfield properties
Torex Gold Resources Inc.	3.9 million ounces of gold in Mexico; Shares up 293% over past five years
Treasury Metals Inc.	Shares are up more than 1,300% over the past five years
Tyhee Gold Corp.	Mine construction to start soon
U.S. Precious Metals, Inc.	Shares shot up 206% in 2011
VHGI Holdings, Inc.	Shares up more than 500% in 2011

Company	Why We Like It
Vista Gold Corp.	$13 price target
Wildcat Silver Corp.	More than 120 million ounces of silver in the ground

ABOUT THE AUTHOR

Fred Marion is the co-founder of the investing Web site www.tradingstocks.me (along with Fred Mason). He's been covering gold, silver and technology stocks for three years.

www.ingramcontent.com/pod-product-compliance
Lightning Source LLC
Chambersburg PA
CBHW051504170526
45166CB00001B/376